EDEXCEL AS/A-LEVEL RELIGIOUS STUD

PAPER 3 NEW TESTAMENT STUDIE

COMPLETE AS / A-LEVEL YEAR 1 STUDY GUIDE

Published independently by Tinderspark Press
© Jonathan Rowe 2018
www.philosophydungeon.weebly.com

CONTENTS

ABOUT THIS BOOK

This book offers advice for teachers and students approaching Edexcel AS or A-Level Religious Studies, Paper 3 (New Testament Studies). It brings together material from three study guides covering these Topics:

1 **Social, historical and religious context of the New Testament**

2 **Texts and interpretation of the Person of Jesus**

3 **Interpreting the text and issues of relationship, purpose and authorship**

This material is also summarised in note format in **Revision Guide 1**, which also includes revision exercises, quizzes and exam-style questions for AS and A-Level but doesn't have the sort of detailed explanations that are in this study guide.

The remaining books cover the topics in Year 2 of the A-Level and can be purchased separately.

4 **Ways of interpreting the scripture**

5 **Texts and interpretation: the Kingdom of God, conflict, the death and resurrection of Jesus**

6 **Scientific and historical-critical challenges, ethical living and the works of scholars**

The **New Testament Year 2 Study Guide** brings all 3 of these books together in one volume similar to this book. This material is summarised in note format in **Revision Guide 2**, but there is also **Revision Guide 3** which covers all 6 study guides in note format and has exam questions for the entire A-Level (but not AS).

Text that is indented and shaded like this is a quotation from a scholar or from the Bible. Candidates should use some of these quotations in their exam responses.

Text in this typeface and boxed represents the author's comments, observations and reflections. Such texts are not intended to guide candidates in writing exam answers.

TOPIC 1: CONTEXT OF THE NEW TESTAMENT

Prophecy regarding the Messiah
- The Suffering Servant of Isaiah, the importance of the line of David, the idea of the messianic secret.
- The significance of these expectations and their impact on New Testament texts, including Matthew's proof texts in the birth narratives and for understanding the Gospel texts.
- With reference to the ideas of Raymond E. Brown and Morna Hooker.

The world of the first century and the significance of this context for the life and work of Jesus
- Religious groups in Palestine.
- Hellenism.
- Roman occupation.
- The role and impact of these influences on legal and ethical dimensions of life in first-century Palestine and the relationship of Jesus' life and work to these influences.

TOPIC 1: CONTEXT OF THE NEW TESTAMENT

What's this topic about?

What is the setting for the New Testament? Where does it take place, geographically and historically? This unit looks at the background to the New Testament in the Jewish religion, the politics of the land of Palestine and the religious conflicts of Jesus' day.

1.1 PROPHECY REGARDING THE MESSIAH

This topic looks at the history of the **line of King David** and the **Suffering Servant** in the Book of Isaiah; it links these to the New Testament, especially **Matthew's 'proof texts'** which show Jesus to be the Messiah and the concept of the **"Messianic Secret" in Mark's Gospel**. **Raymond Brown** and **Morna Hooker** are the key scholars here.

1.2 THE WORLD OF THE FIRST CENTURY

This topic looks at the importance of **Hellenism** (Greek culture) and the **Roman occupation** for the Jews of Palestine as well as the different **Jewish sect**s formed in response to these influences. There are no key scholars for this section but the ancient historian Flavius Josephus is the main source.

Before you go any further...

... there are some things you need to know.

"WHO WROTE THE BIBLE?"

The Bible isn't one book: it's a collection of books by different authors, living in different places and different centuries. It's divided into two collections:

- The **OLD TESTAMENT** was written by Jewish authors, stored on scrolls and brought together as a complete collection some time around 500 BCE. The Jewish religion doesn't have a single authority to decide what counts as Scripture and what doesn't, so the collection is based on tradition. There are some books (scrolls) of the Old Testament that aren't accepted as Scripture by everyone.

- The **NEW TESTAMENT** was written by Christian authors (most of whom – perhaps ALL of whom – were Jewish before they converted to Christianity) over the period of about 100 years after the lifetime of Jesus – certainly all were written by 120 CE and some as early as 50 CE. For reference, Jesus was crucified in 30 CE (although some historians argue for 33 CE). Not all of the New Testament authors knew each other personally and we can only identify a few by name.

The earliest Christian writings are the **epistles** (letters) that the missionary **Paul** wrote to his Christian converts in Turkey and Greece and later to Christians in Rome. These letters were written in the 50s CE and early 60s, within living memory of Jesus.

The four Gospels that describe Jesus' life, death and resurrection come later. **Mark**'s Gospel is believed to be the earliest, probably in the late 60s CE; **Matthew** and **Luke** were written later, in the 80s CE; **John**'s Gospel is widely believed to be the latest, in the 90s or early 100s CE.

> *As you can see, the people who knew Jesus personally were already old or dying when the first New Testament texts were written; most were dead by the time the later Gospels were written. You should reflect on how much you think this matters.*

The first Christians were Jews who believed Jesus to be the Messiah their prophets had predicted. Gradually, more and more **Gentiles** (non-Jews) joined the Christian community. These converts often had little understanding of Judaism. The biggest event for the early church was the **Great Jewish Revolt** of 66-73 CE. This ended when the Romans destroyed Jerusalem and the Jewish Temple. After this point, the Jewish Christians seem to have been rejected by their Jewish friends and relatives and the Gentile Christians broke off their connection with Judaism. Christianity and Judaism went their separate ways as distinct religions.

> *Most of the New Testament texts come from the period when Christians were figuring out their identity as a religion separate from Judaism. These writers were looking at Jesus' life, death and Resurrection with 'the wisdom of hindsight' and it coloured the way they describe Jesus and his dealings with the Jewish religion.*

"WHAT'S ALL THIS BCE AND CE DATING STUFF?"

For centuries, Westerners have followed the Christian dating system that makes the (supposed) birth of Jesus "Year Zero". All dates before that are **B.C.** ("Before Christ") and after it are **A.D.** ("*Anno Domini*" or "In the Year of the Lord"). This dating system is based on the Christian belief that the arrival of Jesus was the most important event in word history and a 'turning point' for the human race.

Other religions have their own dating systems. In the Jewish dating system, all dates are calculated from the Creation of the world in the Bible and are known as **A.M.** ("*Anno Mundi*" or "In the Year of the Word"). Islamic calendars are calculated from Muhammad's flight to Medina (the *Hijra*), which took place in AD 622 in the Christian calendar.

The fact that the world uses the Christian calendar is largely due to the spread of European empires and colonialism. However, scholars writing for a modern, multicultural world are moving away from a dating system based on such religious values. In its place, the terms **B.C.E.** ("Before the Common Era") and **C.E.** ("Common Era") are used. This is a sort of compromise that keeps the same starting point for the calendar but removes explicit links to the Christian religion.

> *Before you start grumbling about "political correctness gone mad", reflect that the BC/AD system wasn't invented until the 6th century and was only used by monks for the first 500 years – and that the BCE/CE system dates from the 17th century and has been used by Bible scholars pretty consistently - which is why I'll be using it and so should you.*

TOPIC 1.1 PROPHECIES CONCERNING THE MESSIAH

The idea of Jesus as the long-awaited **Messiah** is central to Christianity, but it's a complicated concept with some controversial views. Most Jews rejected the claim that Jesus was the Messiah they were expecting and Jews continue to reject it to this day; Christians have argued that Jesus was a different TYPE of Messiah from the one that was expected.

What is Prophecy?

A **PROPHECY** is a message inspired by God. This means it is a form of **revelation**. A person who passes on prophecies is a **PROPHET**.

> *We're used to thinking of a "prophecy" as a prediction about the future - but as New Testament students you need to get over this misconception. Some prophecies predict the future, but many (perhaps most) are messages about the present. A big debate in New Testament studies is whether certain prophecies should be understood as referring to the future (**futurist**) or the present (**preterist**).*

Prophecies come in different forms:

- **Writing.** The Bible describes God giving Moses the Ten Commandments in written form
- **Through angels.** God uses an angel to tell Moses the message he must deliver to Pharaoh of Egypt (**Exodus 3:2-4**) and an angel tells Mary about the birth of Jesus (**Luke 1: 26-48**).
- **Visions.** Visions sometimes happen while the prophet is awake (**Isaiah 1:1**) but others happen while the prophet is in a trance (**Acts 10:10**) or asleep (**Daniel 7:1**); an angel tells Joseph about the birth of Jesus in a dream (**Matthew 1: 20**, see p33)
- **Mental guidance.** God guides the thoughts of his prophets to convey his message, influencing how they write things down; this is the meaning of the Bible's statement: *"All Scripture is inspired by God."* (**2 Timothy 3:16**).

When Jesus speaks to a Samaritan woman (**John 4: 1-26**), he reveals things about her past that he could know only by divine revelation. She recognizes him as a prophet even though he had makes no predictions about the future (**John 4:17-19**). At Jesus' trial, his enemies blindfold him, hit him, and then said: *"Prophesy! Who is it that struck you?"* They are not asking Jesus to foretell the future but to use his supernatural power to identify who had hit him (**Luke 22:63-64**).

Because of this, Biblical prophecies are difficult to interpret. A prophet might be saying things about his own time – about kings and empires and moral problems for the society he is living in. However, readers years later find that the words of the prophecy seem to apply to them too. This is certainly true for the Old Testament prophets.

From a **PRETERIST** viewpoint, the Old Testament prophets are talking about:

- God's anger with the people *of their own time* for their sinful ways
- A criticism of the kings *of their own time* for failing to follow God's laws
- A warning that the rival empires of Assyria and Babylonia are plotting to overthrow the Jewish Kingdom (which eventually took place in 597 BCE, see p16)
- A hope that a better king would come along to save the Jewish Kingdom from its enemies, rule justly and restore good religion (which in fact never happened)

For example, Martin Luther King was often described as "prophetic" for his speeches about racism in America. He wasn't predicting the future, but he WAS telling the American public a deep truth about themselves and their society that they didn't want to here. This is what made him "prophetic".

From a **FUTURIST or HISTORICIST** viewpoint, the prophets are talking about:

- God's *future* destruction of sinners on Judgment Day
- *Future empires* that will persecute God's people (such as the Roman Empire or the Nazis)
- Predictions of Jesus as the Saviour and Messiah who succeeds where previous kings and warlords failed

Believers don't agree on how to interpret prophecy. LIBERAL believers tend to take a preterist view and treat the prophets as describing their own time and only accidentally describing future events; CONSERVATIVE and FUNDAMENTALIST believers tend to take a futurist/historicist view in which the prophets (whether they realised it or not) were describing events centuries in the future. Of course, prophecies can do both: they can describe the present and the future.

A good example comes from one of the greatest Old Testament prophets, **Isaiah**:

For to us a child is born, to us a son is given, and the government will be on his shoulders. And he will be called Wonderful Counselor, Mighty God, Everlasting Father, Prince of Peace – **Isaiah 9: 6**

Sounds familiar? You probably recognise it from carol services - it's often read out at Christmas in churches

From a **preterist perspective**, Isaiah is describing the birth of a royal baby and hoping that the young prince will grow up to be a wise and successful king. From a **futurist/historicist perspective**, Isaiah is describing the birth of Jesus (700 years later) and predicting the arrival of the Son of God in a stable in Bethlehem.

Critics who don't believe in supernatural powers prefer the preterist interpretation of prophecy; religious believers often prefer the futurist/historicist interpretation. Of course, not all futurist prophecy has to be strictly supernatural: wisdom and insight can enable a person to predict the future too.

*You could link this to propositional vs non-propositional revelation in **Philosophy of Religion**.*

Introducing the Messiah

The Messiah is referred to throughout the Bible as a chosen one of God who will come in the future to set the world to right and save God's people.

MESSIAH comes from the Hebrew word, **Mashiach**, meaning *"the anointed one,"* or *"the chosen one."* In Old Testament times, prophets, priests, and kings were anointed when they were given their positions of responsibility. This ceremony involved pouring oil into the hair and beard to make it shine. The anointing was a sign that God had chosen them.

> *In Europe, crowns were placed on the heads of kings and popes. In the British coronation ceremony, the monarch is crowned <u>and</u> anointed with oil, showing they have political and religious power.*

Over time, "messiah" stopped meaning *anyone* who had been anointed to be God's chosen leader – it started to mean a *particular* person who was chosen by God for a very special destiny.

Christos (Christ) is the Greek equivalent of the Hebrew term, **Messiah**. When Andrew met Jesus, the meeting was a sort of **religious experience** for him. He went to his brother, Simon Peter, and told him, *"We have found the Messiah*" (**John 1: 41**).

> *So 'Christ' isn't Jesus' surname. 'Jesus Christ' means 'Jesus the Messiah'.*

The Messiah is referred to directly or indirectly throughout the Bible. For example, **in Genesis 3: 15**, God describes how a descendant of Eve's will crush the Serpent who tempted humans to Fall. Many believe this to be the first reference to a Messiah. Later on, Moses tells the Israelites:

> *The LORD will raise up for you a prophet like me from among yourselves, from your own kinsmen* – **Deuteronomy 18: 15**

This is also interpreted as predicting the future Messiah.

Isaiah has many prophecies about the birth of a prince interpreted as predicting the Messiah (p33); **Micah** describes the Messiah as being born in Bethlehem (p35). Many of the **Psalms** (religious songs in the Old Testament) are interpreted as describing the Messiah.

Despite (or because of) all these references to the Messiah, Jews in the 1st Century had arrived at differing expectations about what the Messiah would be like.

THE KINGLY MESSIAH

Most of the time, the word "messiah" is used in the Old Testament to refer to a king and many Jews expected the future messiah to be a great king. In the 1st century, the Jews were occupied by the Romans and their supposed-kings were the sons of the hated **King Herod the Great**. In contrast to these pagan emperors and tyrants, the Jews looked forward to a true king of the **line of David** (p15) who would rule fairly and wisely.

Some looked forward to more than that. They hoped for the **occupying Romans** (p54) to be driven out of the land and the **publicans** (collaborators) who had worked with them to be punished – in other words, a settling of scores. These Jews hoped for a Messiah who would be a warlord who would smash their enemies and set up a Jewish state based on Biblical laws. The **Zealots** (p68), who waged guerrilla war against the Roman occupiers and murdered publican collaborators, probably hoped for this sort of Messiah.

Some went further still, hoping for a supernatural king or angelic ruler who would defeat not just the evil empires of the world but the demons that controlled those empires, abolishing war and suffering. The prophet **Daniel** describes the Messiah like this:

> *He was given authority, glory and sovereign power; all nations and peoples of every language worshiped him. His dominion is an everlasting dominion that will not pass away, and his kingdom is one that will never be destroyed* **– Daniel 7: 14**

THE PRIESTLY MESSIAH

In the 1st Century, Jewish priests worked in the Jerusalem Temple (p59). Ordinary Jews had to pay taxes to bring animals for the priests to sacrifice there. The priesthood was seen by many as corrupt and collaborating with the Roman occupiers.

Some Jews looked forward to a messiah who would reform the priesthood, perhaps abolishing the Jerusalem Temple and setting up a better, holier form of worship that was accessible to everyone. The **Essenes** (p66), who lived in desert monasteries and rejected the whole Temple-cult, seem to have hoped for this sort of Messiah.

THE PROPHETIC MESSIAH

The 'Age of the Prophets' seemed to be over by the 1st century, but many Jews hoped for a great prophet who would guide their nation back to God. They lived in confusing times, surrounded by a pagan **Hellenic culture**, ruled over by the Romans and distrusting their own religious and political elites. Moses had promised that God would send another prophet just as great; this prophet would teach people how to be good Jews in these troubled times.

This view was probably popular with many ordinary people and with the **Pharisees** (p64), a religious sect that taught people how to live holy lives by following the Jewish Law closely in every detail of their private lives, rather than waging wars or sacrificing animals.

THE SUFFERING MESSIAH

Christians claim that Jesus was (in a way) ***all of the above*** types of Messiah – a king, a priest and a prophet – but he was also a Suffering Messiah who died an **ATONING DEATH** (a death which makes up for other people's sins). There are passages in the Old Testament that seem to refer to a Suffering Messiah, most famously the **Song of the Suffering Servant** in **Isaiah 53** (p20).

These passages, written 700 years before Jesus, certainly *sound* like a description of a Suffering Messiah. The big debate is, was there actually a belief in a Suffering Messiah in the 1st century? If there was, then Jesus seems to fulfill this prophecy in very precise ways.

> But if there wasn't such a belief, then the "Suffering Messiah" sounds like something Christians came up with later, so that Jesus would "fit the bill" for a Messiah after his unexpected death by crucifixion ruined their hopes that he was going to be a successful king, priest or prophet. We will consider this argument later.

THE MESSIANIC AGE

All of these views share the belief that the arrival of the Messiah would usher in a new age of peace on Earth. There would be an end to war – because a Kingly Messiah had conquered the Roman Empire or perhaps a Prophetic Messiah had taught everybody to be more peaceful. The Jews scattered throughout the world would return to Palestine to worship together. There would be no more suffering or evil. **Isaiah** describes the Messianic Age like this:

> *He will judge between the nations and will settle disputes for many peoples. They will beat their swords into plowshares and their spears into pruning hooks. Nation will not take up sword against nation, nor will they train for war anymore – **Isaiah 2: 4***

And, even more strikingly, with this image of a world where all natural enemies – even carnivorous animals and their prey – are reconciled and live in peace:

> *The wolf will live with the lamb, the leopard will lie down with the goat, the calf and the lion and the yearling together; and a little child will lead them – **Isaiah 11: 6***

> *Jews today still await the Messiah: they look forward to OLAM HA-BA ("the world to come") which is the Messianic Age. Some Christians think the Messianic Age will begin with the second coming of Christ.*

OTHER MESSIAHS

After the death of **Herod the Great** in 4 BCE there were revolts among the Jewish population against his son (also called Herod!). Judas son of Hezekiah led one particularly bloody revolt; Herod the Great's ex-slave Simon of Peraea led another. Both men tried to set themselves up as Kingly Messiahs but their rebellions failed.

The Romans sent a Governor of their own to rule Judea. Naturally, there was a revolt against him too in 6 CE, led by Judas the Galilean. Judas was another failed Messiah but he did found the **Zealot** movement (p68).

About a hundred years after Jesus, the Jews launched a final revolt against the Romans. The leader was **Simon Bar Kokhbar**. Things went well at first and Bar Kokhbar expelled the Romans and ruled as a prince - he declared himself to be the Messiah and was recognised as the Messiah by the leading **Pharisees**. However, in 135 CE the Romans returned in force, led by the Emperor Hadrian. They destroyed the Judean state and massacred Bar Kokhbar's supporters – the Romans suffered heavy losses but half a million Jews were killed and more were sold into slavery and deported. Bar Kokhbar's dreams of an independent Jewish state – and a Kingly Messiah – died with him.

THE IMPORTANCE OF THE LINE OF DAVID

One of the most importance qualifications for someone to be the **Messiah** is that they are descended from the greatest King of Israel: **David**. The Christian claim that Jesus is the Messiah depends upon Jesus being the "*Son of David*" and descended from the Davidic royal line.

King David

David is (after Moses) the main hero of the Old Testament. He lived around 1000 BCE at a time when the Twelve Tribes of Israel were coming together as a kingdom. He began life as a humble shepherd boy from Bethlehem but was taken into the court of Israel's first king, Saul. When the kingdom was split by civil war, David led the resistance against the cruel Saul.

After Saul was murdered, David became king. He founded the United Monarchy, ruling over all the Israelites. David made Jerusalem his capital and brought the Ark of the Covenant there to be a focus for the worship of God. His reign is looked back on as a 'Golden Age' of just rule and pure religion.

David is a sort of ideal: a great warrior, a poet and a musician, a deeply sincere believer and a romantic. He is credited with composing many of the Psalms – the intense religious poems in the Old Testament that are often set to music and sung in churches.

It was not to last. David disgraced himself when he fell in love with a married woman, Bathsheba, and arranged for her husband to die in battle so he could marry her. The Prophet Nathan condemned David for this and, although David repented, his rule was tainted by his selfishness. His family was split by plotting and betrayal, his two sons went to war over his kingdom and David died an unhappy old man.

David is a very attractive figure in the Old Testament. He has huge positive qualities but huge flaws. He is brave and reckless and imaginative; he has a great capacity for repentance when he does wrong and a genuine faith in God.

However, he was a poor father, he could be selfish and destructive and he let power go to his head in the end. Nonetheless, he remains the best king the Jews ever had and was looked back as an ideal warrior, ideal ruler and ideal believer.

David: king, lover, poet, musician...

The Davidic Royal Line

David left behind a united Israelite kingdom that was inherited (after a civil war) by his son **Solomon**. Solomon's rule continued Israel's 'Golden Age' and Solomon built the First Temple in Jerusalem to be the centre of the Jewish religion. Offered any gift he wished for by God, Solomon chose 'Wisdom' and God blessed him for this choice. However, like David, Solomon became corrupted by power and wealth. His death triggered another civil war and the kingdom split into two smaller states: **Judah** in the south, centred on Jerusalem, and **Israel** in the north, centred on Samaria.

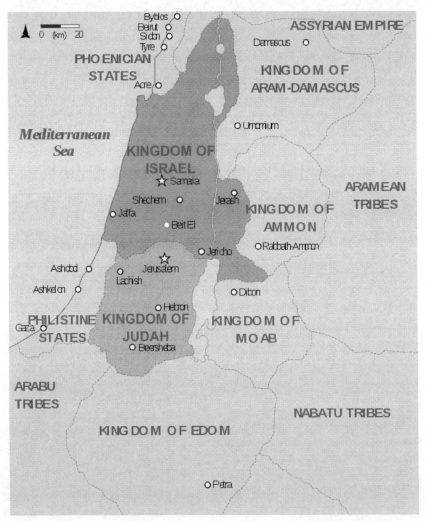

The two Kingdoms continued as neighbours for 200 years. This was the time of the Divided Monarchy. In northern Israel, various families claimed the throne then lost it until, in 722 BCE, the Assyrian Empire invaded northern Israel and destroyed it. Its scattered population became the 'ten lost tribes of Israel' (p47).

Some survivors of the Northern Kingdom became the **Samaritans** who are mentioned in the New Testament. The Samaritans feature in **Topic 6** (where you study the **Parable of the Good Samaritan**) and Jesus seems to have rejected the normal hostility 1st century Jews felt towards their northern neighbours.

The southern kingdom of Judah was much more stable and was ruled for over 300 years by **'the House of David'**, a line of kings descended from David, making it one of the longest reigning dynasties in history. Although there's no direct evidence outside the Bible for David or Solomon, there is some archaeological evidence for the House of David.

The **Tel Dan Stele** is a carved stone with writing on it, set up by a local king to commemorate a victory in battle. It mentions Omri (the king of northern Israel) and an ally "*of the House of David*" ("BYTDWD") – i.e. a king of Judah. It dates from around 800 BCE.

Another carving is the **Moabite Stone** from 850 BCE which also seems to mention the House of David, although the text is damaged (it reads "BT--WD" with a missing portion in the middle but scholars think it reads in full BT DWD, 'House of David').

These carvings tell us that the royal family of Judah in the 9th century called themselves the 'House of David' because they believed David was their ancestor. It doesn't prove David definitely existed – but it does make it more likely that he did.

However, even the House of David could not stand against the great empires that were rising in the ancient world. Judah outlasted the unlucky Kingdom of Israel in the north, but, in 597 BCE, the Babylonians laid siege to Jerusalem, destroyed the city and its Temple and took the citizens away as prisoners of war.

The last Davidic king was **Zedekiah** who had rebelled against the Babylonians (who had replaced the Assyrian Empire). The last thing Zedekiah saw was his children being executed before the Babylonian king Nebuchadnezzar had him blinded and imprisoned.

That was the end of the House of David.

Or was it? We shall see...

The "Son of David"

The Davidic royal line was not a great success. Even while it ruled Judah, it had many bad and weak kings and only a few good ones (Hezekiah and Josiah stand out). Even while the House of David existed, many were dissatisfied and longed for a *true* "Son of David" – somebody who *truly* embodied David's fine qualities – to come to the throne.

After the destruction of Judah, this hope intensified among the exile Jews in Babylon. They believed that the bloodline of David still existed – it had 'gone underground' but it was still there. The Jews returned to Jerusalem and rebuilt their Temple in 516 BCE, but no Davidic king reappeared to sit on the throne. The Jews were ruled by other dynasties, such as the Hasmoneans and after them the hated Herodians. Many Jews felt that these new royal families were illegitimate. The *real* king of the Jews would be a descendant of David.

This wasn't just wishful thinking. The Old Testament reports God making a promise to David:

> *Your house and your kingdom will endure forever before me; your throne will be established forever* – **2 Samuel 7: 16**

*How could Jews make sense of this promise? The House of David had been destroyed in 597 BCE – had God broken his word? You might see a link here to the **problem of evil**: if God is all-good he will want to keep his promise to David and if he is all-powerful he will be able to keep his promise - but it looks like he hasn't kept his promise....*

The Jews believed the answer to this was in two parts. First, God's promise **seemed** to have been withdrawn because the Jewish people had been sinful. God had allowed their enemies to triumph over them to teach them a lesson.

Second, Jews came to believe the line of David *does* "*endure forever*" and a descendant – a 'Son of David' – *will* appear to claim the throne. This Son of David will be a Kingly Messiah. He'll be different from the previous kings of the House of David because his rule will be a success: he'll defeat the enemies of the Jews, make them independent again, and this time the rule of the House of David "*will be established forever*".

The Babylonian Exile, in which the Jewish people were taken from their homeland, left a lasting effect on their religion and their hopes

What was needed for the 'Son of David' to appear? 1ˢᵗ century Jews had differing answers to this:

- **Religious Purity:** Since the destruction of Judah and the House of David had been a punishment for sins, Jews needed to return to the pure worship of God. Only once they had done this would the Son of David appear. However, groups like the **Sadducees** (p63), the **Pharisees** (p64) and the **Essenes** (p66) had different ideas of what 'religious purity' meant (for example, it meant performing sacrifices for the Sadducees and obeying religious laws to the Pharisees)

- **Military Action:** The Jews needed to 'start the ball rolling' by resisting the Romans; once the rebellion was in full swing, the Son of David would appear to lead it. Obviously, this view was popular with the **Zealots** (p68).

Christians developed a different understanding of the 'Son of David' as it applied to Jesus:

- **A Spiritual King:** Various attempts to set up the **'Kingdom of God'** as a political project all failed. God intends his Kingdom on earth to be a different sort of thing: a Spiritual Kingdom where he rules in people's hearts and minds, not a political kingdom imposed by force. Jesus is a spiritual king not a political one and Jesus succeeds where David failed: by dying an atoning death rather than conquering his enemies by force.

The idea of the **Kingdom of God** and Jesus as a spiritual king is explored in **Topic 5**.

Does the Messiah have to be from the line of King David?

YES	NO
Kind David was the original messiah – anointed by God to be the best king. God's promise to David that his line would "*endure forever*" has to be fulfilled. So there has to be a descendant of David who will return to save the Jews from their enemies – the **Messiah**.	It's not proven that 'King David' really existed in history. He might have been a legend like King Arthur in Britain. Even if he did exist, his line was destroyed by the Babylonians and various 'messiahs' who tried to lead the Jews to independence – like Simon Bar Kokhbar – all failed horribly.
The House of David failed because the Jewish people were sinful and turned away from God. When they return to worshipping God again and living morally, the Messiah will restore their kingdom and the line of David will rule it again.	The Messiah is more than just a warlord who wins battles. He's someone who will defeat evil, as God predicts in **Genesis 3: 15**; he might be a prophet as God predicts in **Deuteronomy 18: 15**. He's a wise teacher who will change people's lives, not a king from a failed dynasty.

ISAIAH'S SUFFERING SERVANT

One of the main sources for prophecies about the **Messiah** (p8) is the Old Testament book of **Isaiah** (pronounced EYES-EYE-AH). However, Isaiah contains some passages which describe someone who does not fit the typical picture of a messiah – the **Suffering Servant**.

Isaiah

Isaiah lived in the 8th century BCE. He was probably from the royal family of Judah (the '**House of David**', see p16) and he lived through difficult times. The Assyrian Empire destroyed the northern Kingdom of Israel and dispersed its population. When Judah allied itself with the Egyptians, they were next to be threatened by the Assyrians: Jerusalem was twice attacked by the Assyrian army but miraculously survived. The Jews believed that angels had protected their city from the fate that befell their northern neighbour.

Isaiah's career as a prophet begins in 742 BCE with a shattering **religious experience** in the Temple, Isaiah has a vision of God on his throne, praised by angels while smoke and noise fills the Temple. This is a **numinous experience** for Isaiah – he is gripped by a sense of his own sinfulness and unworthiness. In his vision, an angel brings a fiery coal to his lips to burn away his sin. He hears God saying to his angels "*Whom shall I send*?" and the now-purified Isaiah calls out "*Here I am! Send me!*"

Isaiah has to deliver to the people of Judah a very unpleasant message: God has condemned them for their sinful ways, particularly for their greed and mistreatment of the poor. The Assyrian Empire rising against them is an instrument of God's anger: God is *using* the Assyrians to punish the Jews for their sins. Isaiah predicts military defeat, slavery and humiliation for the people of Judah (in effect, saying that what happened to northern Israel will happen to them too).

> *And Isaiah turns out to be right – although it's the Babylonians rather than the Assyrians who eventually destroy Judah and send the Jews into exile and this happens about a hundred years after Isaiah's death.*

Isaiah is no friend to the Temple priesthood either. He claims that God is sick of their sacrifices of animals and wants them to lead moral lives instead!

> *According to tradition, Isaiah was a vegetarian! In 1st century Palestine, the Essenes had similar criticisms of the priesthood at Herod's temple and the sacrificing of animals there.*

Among all the gloom and doom, Isaiah offers visions of hope. He predicts the future **Messianic Age** when wars between empires will end and the Jews will be able to live in peace in their land, worshiping God properly and leading moral lives.

Isaiah goes beyond just predicting happiness solely for the Jews: he describes a future world where *no one* will have to suffer, a sort of paradise on Earth.

Because of this, Isaiah's prophecies have always been particularly important for people trying to identify the Messiah: what would he be like, what would he do, how could you recognise him? Isaiah seems to hold the answers but his prophecies are like riddles and can be interpreted in many ways.

The Servant Songs

An unusual figure keeps appearing in Isaiah's prophecies. This is the 'Suffering Servant'. The Servant serves God with total selflessness and loyalty. He is given a mission by God to lead the nations of the world. However, the Servant is mocked, abused and attacked by the people God has sent him to help. He endures his sufferings without complaining, intervening on behalf of other people and bearing their sufferings for them. Finally, he is murdered. However, God returns the Servant to life and rewards the Servant in front of the whole world. The people who had mistreated the Servant are stunned and ashamed.

The 19th century German scholar **Bernard Duhm** noticed that the references to the Suffering Servant are grouped together in four places and that these passages are separate poems or songs. They are known as the four 'Servant Songs'.

THE FIRST SERVANT SONG: ISAIAH 42: 1-4

God chooses the Servant who will bring justice to earth. The Servant is a **Kingly Messiah** and a **Prophetic Messiah** who brings about God's will on Earth.

> *Here is my servant, whom I uphold, my chosen one in whom I delight*
> *I will put my Spirit on him, and he will bring justice to the nation* **– Isaiah 42: 1**

- Compare this to the description of Jesus' baptism as described in the Synoptic Gospels e.g. **Matthew 3: 13-17**. Notice how God is pleased with/delights in Jesus and puts his spirit into him. This links Jesus to the Servant in **Isaiah 42**.

THE SECOND SERVANT SONG: ISAIAH 49: 1-6

This Song is from the Servant's point of view. He describes how he was called by God to lead not just the Jews but all the nations. The Servant will not be a political or military ruler but "*a light to the Gentiles*" – a source of inspiration and a moral teacher.

> *I will also make you a light for the Gentiles, that my salvation may reach to the ends of the earth* **– Isaiah 49: 6**

- Jesus gives his disciples the **'Great Commission'** to convert the Gentiles and Paul echoes this passage from Isaiah to justify why he converts Gentiles (non-Jews) to Christianity. For Christians, it's important that Jesus has a message for Gentiles as well as Jews.

THE THIRD SERVANT SONG: ISAIAH 50: 4-9

The Servant describes the abuse he will have to face, but he is confident in God's protection.

I offered my back to those who beat me, my cheeks to those who pulled out my beard; I did not hide my face from mocking and spitting – **Isaiah 50: 6**

- This seems to predict Jesus' famous teaching that his followers should "*turn the other cheek*" (**Luke 6: 29**); it also anticipates Jesus' own abuse at the hands of the soldiers who arrest him

The soldiers torture then mock Jesus (Matthew 27: 27-31)

THE FOURTH SERVANT SONG: ISAIAH 52: 13-53:12

This is the "big one" and the one you will want to show some knowledge of in the exam. It's very famous and the language and phrases from it turn up in church rituals and prayers. There are several quotes here but you don't need to learn them all - but you should learn one or two quotes from Isaiah to support your discussion of the Suffering Servant.

This Song, which takes up all of **Isaiah 53**, probably has the biggest impact. It describes the Suffering Servant as a "*man of sorrows*":

He was despised and rejected by mankind, a man of suffering, and familiar with pain – **Isaiah 53: 3**

- The expression "*man of sorrows*" is commonly applied to Jesus by Christians

The Servant doesn't just suffer for himself – he takes upon himself ***other people's*** pain and suffering, but nobody appreciates it. Instead, people regard the Servant as a victim and an evil-doer.

> *Surely he took up our pain and bore our suffering,*
> *yet we considered him punished by God, stricken by him, and afflicted* – **Isaiah 53: 4**

- Compare this to Christians' beliefs about Jesus' torture and execution. According to the Old Testament, anyone who is hanged or crucified is considered to be cursed by God (**Deuteronomy 21: 23**) but Christians view this as a positive thing.

The Song describes the Servant being put to death, but his death is an ATONING DEATH that brings healing to others.

> *But he was pierced for our transgressions, he was crushed for our iniquities;*
> *the punishment that brought us peace was on him, and by his wounds we are healed* –
> **Isaiah 53: 5**

- The link to Christian beliefs here is pretty clear. Jesus was "*pierced*" by nails for the sake of mankind's "*transgressions*" (sins). Christians believe that Jesus' wounds bring healing from original sin.

The Servant is "*led like a lamb to the slaughter*" (an expression that has entered the English language) but is completely silent: "*he did not open his mouth*".

- Christians regard Jesus as the "*lamb of God who takes away the sins of the world*" (**John 1: 29**). The Gospels present Jesus as remaining silent in the face of his accusers.

After this miserable death, God will restore the Servant to life again. But his sufferings will have saved other people.

> *After he has suffered, he will see the light of life and be satisfied;*
> *by his knowledge my righteous servant will justify many, and he will bear their iniquities* –
> **Isaiah 53: 1**

- For Christians, this predicts Jesus' ATONING DEATH and Resurrection which removes mankind's sins.

Christian vs Jewish Interpretations

For Christians, the Servant Songs predict the **Messiah** – Jesus Christ – but a very different sort of Messiah from the King or Priest or Prophet that were expected by other groups. They predict a **Suffering Messiah** who will die an atoning death then be resurrected.

The specific details in Isaiah struck many Christians as uncanny in their resemblance to Jesus' sufferings and their belief about the meaning behind his death. **Saint Jerome** said that Isaiah *"described all of the mysteries of the church of Christ so vividly that you would assume he was not prophesying about the future, but rather was composing a history of past events"*.

However, there are some problems with this. There's no evidence that Jews of the 1st century believed that the Messiah was going to be a Suffering Messiah or that **Isaiah 53** was supposed to predict the Messiah. The Gospels describe Jesus' Disciples stunned reaction when they learn that he's going to die: they would hardly be so surprised if they believed the Messiah was SUPPOSED to suffer and die.

Modern Jews do *not* regard the Servant Songs as predicting Jesus – they don't accept that Jesus was the Messiah. For them, the Servant is symbolic of *'Israel'* (the entire Jewish nation, not the country, see p47) itself. Earlier in the Book of Isaiah, God refers to *Israel* as his servant:

> *But you, Israel, my servant, Jacob, whom I have chosen, you descendants of Abraham my friend* – **Isaiah 41: 8**

It is Jews who are sent into the world to be a *"light to the Gentiles"* through their religion, but it is Jews who are mocked and abused and tortured and murdered. It is Jews who hope that their sufferings will be vindicated by God and believe that, in some way, the sufferings of their nation will teach a valuable lesson to the rest of the world.

Morna Hooker sums up this interpretation of the Servant as 'Israel' like this:

> *Israel, who has been chosen by [God] as his servant, is to be restored from Exile and will manifest God's glory to all nations* – **Morna Hooker**

In the past, Jews might have thought of various anti-Semitic persecutions in connection with the Servant Songs (culminating in the Holocaust in the 20th century).

- This is a **futurist** interpretation of the Servant Songs – but they refer to the future sufferings of the Jewish people, not Jesus

Many scholars think the section of Isaiah with the Servant Songs was written by somebody else a century or two after the real Isaiah: they call this author 'Second Isaiah'. If this is true, the sufferings might refer to the destruction of the Kingdom of Judah and the Jewish exile in Babylon – with the Jews who were taken into Exile suffering on behalf of the Jews who were left behind in Palestine. When the exiled Jews returned to Palestine in 538 BCE, the mysterious 'Second Isaiah' described their experiences by writing the Servant Songs.

> *Israel had been subjected to terrible humiliation, she was oppressed and afflicted, taken from her own country and led like a lamb to the slaughter: but now her sufferings are over, and she is to return; she will be exalted and know prosperity again* – **Morna Hooker**

- This is a **preterist** interpretation of the Servant Songs – they refer to events going on at the time they were composed

Jews have other interpretations of the Suffering Servant. For some, he represents, not *all* the Jewish people, but the holiest and best, the 'faithful few'. If this is true then the text is saying that anyone who devoutly tries to serve God is bound to suffer in this world – that would apply to the Messiah but it would describe lots of other sincere and good religious people too.

Both of these interpretations (the Jewish nation or the faithful few) treat the Servant as a CORPORATE PERSONALITY: he is a single person who symbolizes the experiences of a big group of people.

However, there are other ancient rabbis (Jewish teachers) who believe the Servant really does represent the Messiah. When the Messianic Age comes, the non-Jewish nations will be ashamed of the way they treated the Jewish people now that their faith in God is backed up by the arrival of the Messiah.

Is the Suffering Servant supposed to be Jesus Christ?

YES	NO
The Servant is identified as the Messiah by several ancient rabbis who believed the Kingly Messiah would suffer. Isaiah links the Servant to the **line of King David**, just like a Kingly Messiah. Jesus is descended from David. The Fourth Song ends with God rewarding the Servant and bringing in the Messianic Age.	The Servant is a corporate personality, representing the whole Jewish nation (called 'Israel') or perhaps just the faithful few among the Jewish people who truly serve God. The Songs describe the sufferings of Jews at the hands of Gentiles (antisemitism), not just the sufferings of Jesus.
The sufferings of the Servant closely fit the sufferings of Jesus, who was rejected by his own people, abused and tortured then painfully executed. This supports the Christian belief that the Servant predicts Jesus and that Jesus' death was an atoning death for the sins of mankind.	Although some later rabbis link the Suffering Servant to the Messiah, there's no evidence that Jews of the 1st century thought **Isaiah 53** described a Suffering Messiah. The link between the Messiah and the Suffering Servant was made by Christians *after* Jesus' crucifixion.

THE MESSIANIC SECRET

In 1901 the German scholar **William Wrede** published a controversial idea based on his study of the **Gospel of Mark**. Wrede proposed that Jesus had *never claimed to be the Messiah* and that his disciples didn't believe he was the Messiah either. Only later, after Jesus' death, did Christians start to think Jesus was the Messiah.

The Gospel of Mark

Mark is the second Gospel in the New Testament, coming after **Matthew**. Most scholars today regard it as the earliest Gospel to be written (the **theory of Markan Priority** is in **Topic 3**, p187), being composed around 65 CE, 30 years after the Crucifixion. It is the shortest Gospel.

It begins with Jesus' baptism by John the Baptist and features many stories of Jesus casting out demons and evil spirits as well as healing people. It ends with the Crucifixion and the women coming to Jesus' tomb on Sunday to find it empty.

There are some distinctive features of Mark's Gospel. Jesus frequently makes people promise to keep his identity secret when they realise he is the Messiah or when he performs miracles.

Here are two examples:

- When Jesus asks his disciples who they think he is, Peter answers, "*You are the Messiah*" and Jesus commands him to keep this a secret **(Mark 8: 27-30)**
- When Jesus heals a leper, he tells the man not to tell anyone about this miracle (but the man disobeys and tells everyone – **Mark 1: 40-45**)

Another feature is that Jesus reveals that he is the Messiah in **Parables** which his disciples cannot understand. For example, the **Parable of the Sower (Mark 4: 1-11** – this Parable is discussed in **Topic 5**) seems to mean that Jesus is the Messiah and his teachings are a "*seed*" that will grow in some people's souls but not in others. Why doesn't Jesus say this more plainly? Jesus explains:

> *The secret of the kingdom of God has been given to you. But to those on the outside everything is said in parables* – **Mark 4: 11**

Wrede thinks that this means Jesus is *deliberately* being mysterious and speaking in Parables because he doesn't *want* ordinary people to know he is the Messiah

> *But why would Jesus not want people to know he was the Messiah?*

The Messianic Secret

Wrede has an explanation for the "Messianic Secret": *Jesus never claimed to be the Messiah.* However the later Christians of the 60s and 70s CE definitely *did* think Jesus was the Messiah. Wrede argues that the early Christians had different beliefs about Jesus from those of Jesus himself and his original followers. **Morna Hooker** explains it by drawing attention to:

> *a tension in the belief of the Early Church of Jesus as Messiah and the unmessianic character of Jesus' ministry* – **Morna Hooker**

The argument goes like this:

- Jesus had an "*unmessianic ministry*" – he didn't set himself up as a King or a Prophet, didn't try to free the Jews from Roman rule; instead he taught a message of God's love and forgiveness and he died a very un-messianic death on the Cross
- Later Christians believed Jesus had been resurrected and that he WAS the Messiah. This meant that the Christians had very different beliefs about Jesus from Jesus' own friends and family and original followers
- When Mark's Gospel was written, those followers and family were still around; they objected to Christians calling Jesus the Messiah because they remembered what Jesus had really been like and they knew he had never made this claim for himself
- So Mark's Gospel argues that Jesus *had* claimed to be the Messiah but he had done so *secretly* - swearing people who were 'in the know' to silence or speaking in Parables that only his 'inner circle' understood

Wrede concludes that the passages in Mark's Gospel where Jesus admits to being the Messiah are fictions – they didn't really happen. Mark invented them and then, when critics pointed out that such things never happened, Mark added more fictional details about Jesus keeping it secret.

Strengths of Wrede's Theory

Wrede's theory is based on **Markan Priority** (p187). Matthew and Luke were written later than Mark (probably in the 80s or 90s CE), so they didn't *have* to keep Jesus' identity a secret since, by that time, the original audience who remembered Jesus' ministry had all died off. Matthew and Luke repeat many of the same stories that are in Mark, but the theme of secrecy is much less important. These later Gospels include other stories where Jesus is quite outspoken about being the Messiah (and if Wrede's theory is correct, these stories must be fictions too).

This theory ties in with the debate about the **Suffering Servant** (p20) being the Messiah. If 1st century Jews did not expect the Messiah to be a Suffering Servant, then that explains why they didn't think Jesus was the Messiah during his lifetime or immediately after his death. It was the Resurrection that made Jesus' followers believe he was the Messiah, so stories about Jesus being recognised as the Messiah before he died cannot be historically true.

Criticising Wrede's Theory

Wrede's theory is an example of **Redaction Criticism** (p201), which is explored in **Topic 3**; it is also an example of the **Historical Approach to interpreting Scriptures**, which is explored in **Topic 4 (Ways of Interpreting the Scripture)**.

Wrede's theory was initially popular but has been challenged in several ways, notably by **Morna Hooker** (1991). Here are the main criticisms:

First, not everyone accepts **Markan Priority** (p187); many Catholics (in particular) continue to believe **Matthew** to be the first Gospel. Matthew does not contain this 'secrecy' theme and, if Matthew is the earliest Gospel, this means the idea of Jesus identifying himself as the Messiah was NOT added in later

Second, there are many good reasons within the story itself for Jesus to keep some things secret. After healing the leper, Jesus is mobbed by crowds and has to stop visiting the big towns. Being famous as a miracle-worker gets in the way of Jesus' real mission, which is spreading his message of love and forgiveness. Jesus doesn't *want* to be a celebrity so he keeps his miracles secret.

> *if he believed himself to be in any sense the Messiah, the last thing he would do was to claim the title for himself* – **Morna Hooker**

Third, people will misunderstand what Jesus means if they hear that he is the Messiah. They will expect him to raise and army or declare himself king. The authorities (who are suspicious of him) will silence him if they believe he is leading some sort of revolution.

> *it would have been misunderstood as a claim to political kingship* – **Morna Hooker**

Jesus distances himself from the idea of the 'Messiah' and uses the term **"Son of Man"** to describe himself (see **Topic 2**, p116 for a discussion of this term).

> *The idea that it might have been politically expedient to arrest and kill someone claiming to be the Messiah is explored in **Topic 5 (Why Did Jesus Have to Die?)***

Jesus' remark about his Parables could be interpreted differently. Jesus might not be trying to hide his identity from ordinary people. Instead, he might be saying that, as a simple matter of fact, some people 'can't handle' the truth about him but others can. He speaks in Parables so that those who are spiritually open to his message will understand but people who are close-minded will not be angered by hearing things they can't accept.

> *the truth about Jesus is at once hidden from view and yet spelt out on every page of the gospel'* – **Morna Hooker**

Finally, there's the **'Triumphal Entry'** when Jesus arrives in Jerusalem and is greeted as a king. This scene is described in **Mark 11: 1-11** and in the other Synoptic Gospels as well as in **John's Gospel**, so it has a good claim to being a historical event.

Jesus enters the city and is met by a huge crowd who wave palms (symbolising liberation from oppression) and declare that he is from **the line of David** (p15).

Jesus rides a donkey to symbolise that he is coming in peace not as a warrior – and fulfilling a prophecy from **Zechariah 9: 9** in the Old Testament about the appearance of the Messiah riding a donkey.

The crowds sing Psalms (Old Testament songs of praise), such as:

> *Blessed is he who comes in the name of the Lord! Blessed is the coming kingdom of our father David!* **– Mark 11: 9-10**

There's no secrecy here and Jesus makes no attempt to silence the crowd. This is a very public claim by Jesus to be the Messiah – somebody who has come *"in the name of the Lord"* and who is going to bring about *"the kingdom of David"* – and this goes completely against Wrede's theory.

Does the Messianic Secret prove that Jesus never claimed to be the Messiah?

YES	NO
The Messianic Secret is a theory which explains why Jesus is so secretive in Mark's Gospel but this secretiveness disappears in the later Gospels. It makes sense of Jesus speaking in Parables that hide his real meaning.	The theory exaggerates the secretiveness in Mark's Gospel. The healed leper doesn't keep the miracle a secret and Jesus is mobbed by crowds. The Triumphal Entry into Jerusalem is a public statement of Messianic identity.
The theory is supported by the view that 1st century Jews did not expect a Suffering Messiah or **interpret Isaiah's Suffering Servant** as a Messiah. Jesus' disciples would not have understood him identifying as the Messiah so these passages must be later fictions.	Not everyone agrees that 1st century Jews didn't expect a Suffering Messiah. There are other plausible explanations for Jesus' secrecy, such as wanting to avoid political entanglements or celebrity that distracted from his mission and message.

THE MESSIAH IN THE NEW TESTAMENT

The New Testament presents a very different view of the Messiah from that found in most of the Old Testament but Matthew's Gospel goes out of its way to identify Jesus as the Messiah predicted in the Old Testament, especially in the story of Jesus' birth. He uses **'Proof-Texts'** which are references back to prophecies in the Old Testament to show that Jesus fulfils these prophecies in unexpected ways.

The Gospel of Matthew

Matthew is the first Gospel in the New Testament. For centuries, Christians believed it was the oldest and original Gospel, with Mark being a sort of edited version and Luke being based on Matthew but with additions. However, most scholars today regard Mark as the earliest Gospel to be written (the **theory of Markan Priority**, p187). Matthew was probably composed in the 80s CE, 20 years after Mark. Matthew begins with Jesus' birth in Bethlehem and features many stories which are linked to prophecies in the Old Testament, proving that Jesus is the Messiah.

There are some distinctive features of Matthew's Gospel. It is a very 'Jewish' Gospel, featuring a lot of detail about Jewish beliefs and a lot of references to the Old Testament. This is why Christians used to think it was the earliest Gospel (since Jesus and his first followers were Jews, it would make sense that the first Christian writings would have a strong Jewish tone). The author of Matthew's Gospel (we don't know if he was really called 'Matthew') seems to have been a Jewish Christian struggling with his Jewish heritage and belonging to a church that had members who were both Jewish Christian and Gentile (non-Jewish) Christians. Jesus is referred to as the "*Son of David*" in the Gospel, which appeals to the Jewish Christians. The Jewish people are referred to as "*Israelites*" up until the Crucifixion; after that they are referred to as "*Jews*" because the *real* children of Israel are the Christians who have faith in Jesus, including the Gentile ones.

The Birth Narrative

Morna Hooker claims that each Gospel has a prologue that works as a "*key*" to "*unlock*" the main themes and teachings about Jesus.

Matthew's Prologue is an extended Birth Narrative that describes the circumstances of Jesus' birth in Bethlehem and how his family ended up living in Nazareth in Galilee. Hooker calls Matthew's Prologue the "*prophetic key*" because it focuses on Jesus being the Messiah and 'second Moses' predicted by the Old Testament prophets. Matthew explains how these prophecies come true in Jesus' life – but in unexpected ways.

Luke's Gospel also has a Birth Narrative that is different from Matthew's. It describes Joseph and Mary coming to Bethlehem in order to take part in a Roman census. Mary puts her newborn baby in a manger and the family are visited by shepherds. Hooker calls Luke's Birth Narrative the "*spiritual key*" because it shows God's Holy Spirit at work through history and in the present – acting, once again, in unexpected ways.

Matthew's Genealogy of Jesus

> *The genealogy isn't part of the Anthology #1 extract, although the rest of the Birth Narrative is. This means you don't need to study the genealogy - but you might find it interesting.*

Matthew's Gospel begins with a **genealogy** (family tree) of Jesus, tracing his family back through the line of David, to King David himself then further back to Abraham (the father of the Jewish nation). **Morna Hooker** points out that that the word Matthew uses for "genealogy" is *Genesis*. So Matthew begins his Gospel with a new 'Genesis', just like the first book of the Old Testament.

The Genealogy in **Matthew 1: 1-17** demonstrates that Jesus is of the royal **line of King David** (p15) – and therefore qualifies to be the Messiah since he is the "*Son of David*".

The Patriarchs	The Kings	After the Exile
Abraham	Solomon, David's son	Jeconiah
Isaac	Rehoboam	Shealtiel
Jacob	Abijah	Zerubbabel
Judah	Asa	Abihud
Perez	Jehoshaphat	Eliakim
Hezron	Joram	Azor
Ram	Uzziah	Zadok
Amminadab	Jotham	Achim
Nahshon	Ahaz	Eliud
Salmon	Hezekiah	Eleazar
Boaz	Manasseh	Matthan
Obed	Amon	Jacob
Jesse	Josiah	Joseph
David, the King	*(The Exile in Babylon)*	**Jesus**

Matthew points out a structure in the family tree: 14 generations between Abraham and David who became king around 1000 BCE, then 14 generations of Davidic kings until the Exile in Babylon in 597 BCE, then 14 more generations bringing us up to the birth of Jesus.

This 3 x 14 pattern suggests that Jesus brings history to an end: a process that began with God promising Abraham that his children were the Chosen People reached its low point with the destruction of the Davidic monarchy but is now complete with the birth of the Messiah. God once promised Abraham that "*all peoples on earth will be blessed through you*" (**Genesis 12: 3**) and the birth of Jesus fulfills that promise.

Raymond E Brown points out that, by linking Jesus back to Abraham, Matthew addresses two audiences: a Jewish audience would be interested in Jesus' descent from King David but a Gentile (non-Jewish) audience would be more interested in Abraham, because God had promised a descendant of Abraham would bring a blessing to "*all peoples on earth*" – including the Gentiles. Jesus is therefore the promised Messiah for ***both*** groups.

Problems with Matthew's Genealogy

The genealogy doesn't match up with the description of the line of David in the Old Testament - several kings have been missed out. Since this ruins Matthew's 3 x 14 pattern, **Raymond E Brown** suggests that Matthew probably didn't notice this; he must have taken this section of the genealogy from another book which already had those mistakes in it (in fairness, these kings' names sound very similar in Greek).

Similarly, there aren't actually 14 generations in each. How Matthew got to be so bad at arithmetic is a bit of a puzzle but a bigger problem is that Luke's Gospel offers another genealogy with *different names in it*.

Perhaps the biggest criticism is that, according to Matthew's own birth-narrative, Jesus isn't descended from these people anyway! He was born of a virgin, with no human father, so Joseph's descent from the line of David is irrelevant. The only human family Jesus is descended from is Mary's!

There are two main solutions to this:

1. Ancient scholars supposed that various adoptions and re-marriages had occurred, with Matthew recording the biological line and Luke the legal one. Others proposed that Luke recorded Mary's family tree. The problem with this view is that ancient Jewish law had no particular word for "step-father" and no concept of tracing the family line through the mother, so these theories cannot be backed up with evidence.

2. **Raymond E Brown** suggests that no Ancient Genealogy tries to be a precise historical document or a biological record. Ancient peoples created genealogies to make political or religious points, not to record the messy business of who had a child with whom – this was an age before marriage or birth certificates or DNA testing. Matthew's Genealogy is a religious claim: that the promises God made about a descendant of Abraham bringing a blessing to all the world and the line of David producing the Messiah had been fulfilled in Jesus.

> *Conservative Christians believe that the genealogies in Matthew and Luke describe actual histories and regard Matthew as Joseph's family tree and Luke as Mary's family tree.*

The objection that Jesus wasn't biologically related to Joseph anyway isn't as important as it seems. Adoption was common in the Ancient World and adopted sons (who were chosen) sometimes were held in higher esteem than biological sons. Legally and politically, an adopted child could be just as much an heir of King David as someone with a biological link back to the Davidic line.

Matthew's Birth Narrative & Proof-Texts

These passages form Anthology extract #1, so you need to be familiar with them all in a general sort of way and you should be able to analyse one or two parts in depth

THE VIRGIN BIRTH

Matthew describes the birth of Jesus from his father Joseph's perspective rather than Mary's (which is described in **Luke's Gospel**). Joseph intends to divorce Mary when he learns she is pregnant but he has a **religious experience** (an angel visits him in a dream) which convinces him to adopt the child as his own.

*In **Philosophy of Religion**, you might come across Thomas Hobbes (1651) questioning whether there's any difference between God speaking to you in a dream – and dreaming that God is speaking to you. This makes a good Biblical link for Hobbes' point*

Matthew makes his point by addressing Joseph as "*Joseph, Son of David*" – emphasizing the Joseph is of the line of David. He also connects the Virgin Birth back to a prophecy by **Isaiah**.

PROOF TEXT 1: ISAIAH 7: 14

> [22] All this took place to fulfil what the Lord had said through the prophet: [23] "The virgin will conceive and give birth to a son, and they will call him Immanuel" (which means "God with us").

This is the first of Matthew's **PROOF-TEXTS**. Proof-texts are references to the Old Testament that attempt to prove that Jesus is the Messiah.

> *Therefore the Lord himself will give you a sign: The virgin will conceive and give birth to a son, and will call him Immanuel* – **Isaiah 7: 14**

This is a much-debated passage. From a **preterist** interpretation, Isaiah is describing a royal birth back in the 8th century BCE – almost certainly Prince Hezekiah, son of King Ahaz. But what about the virgin conceiving? There are two explanations considered by **Raymond Brown**:

1. **The virgin conceiving might be a translation error.** Isaiah's prophecy is in Hebrew and uses the word "*almah*" to describe the mother: *almah* means "young woman" but not necessarily a virgin; Hebrew has another word, "*bethulah*", which means a virgin. However, when the Old Testament was translated into Greek, *almah* was translated as "*parthenos*", a Greek word which definitely means 'virgin'. Matthew used the Greek Old Testament and may have misunderstood what Isaiah had been saying.
2. **The virgin conceiving might not be intended to be supernatural.** After all, virgins conceive all the time. If King Ahaz's young bride was a virgin, then it would be natural to hope that, on her wedding night, she would conceive (losing her virginity in the process) and bear the king a son (and she did – the future King Hezekiah!).

Both of these explanations assume that *Isaiah 7: 14* was never intended to describe a miracle. The line was mistaken for a description of a miracle when it was taken out of its proper context (a royal wedding around 750 BCE) and translated into another language!

However, it's important to remember that *almah* **could** mean 'virgin' in this context and that the Jewish scholars who translated the Old Testament into Greek (200 years before Matthew wrote his Gospel) chose the Greek word *parthenos* so *almah* certainly meant 'virgin' to them! There's also nothing to stop **Isaiah 7: 14** being a DOUBLE-PROPHECY, something that refers to the (perfectly normal) birth of King Ahaz's son long ago and also, 750 years later, to the supernatural birth of Jesus Christ.

You'll notice that the prophecy speaks of a son being called 'Immanuel', (or 'Emannuel') not 'Jesus'. However, it's the MEANING of 'Immanuel' ("God With Us") that matters. **Morna Hooker** explains it like this:

> *The child who is about to be born WILL be known as 'Emmanuel', in the sense that in later days men and women will say that, through him, God was with them* – **Morna Hooker**

Isaiah's prophecy seems doubly-unlucky with names because, 750 years previously, King Ahaz didn't call the newborn prince Hezekiah 'Immanuel' either

THE VISIT OF THE MAGI

In tradition and Christmas carols, they are known as the 'Three Wise Men' or the 'Three Kings'. Tradition even gives them names: Caspar, Balthasar and Melchior. However, the Bible doesn't name them, doesn't number them to be three and they're not kings.

They are *'magi'*, a word meaning a priest of the Persian religion specialising in astronomy and interpreting dreams. We get the modern words 'magic' and 'magician' from the ancient *magi*. The *magi* had a reputation in the Roman Empire for weird and exotic beliefs, occult powers and ancient wisdom (a bit like the druids over at the other end of the Empire in Britain).

Magi should be pronounced MAR-GEE but it people often say it as MAY-GUY or MAY-JYE. Why did readers assume there were three of them? Probably because their three gifts are named: gold, frankincense and myrrh.

The *magi* are not Jews – they are Gentiles. It is significant that the first people to recognise the Messiah are not Jews at all. Once again, this is Matthew indicating that God's promise to Abraham is being fulfilled: Abraham's descendant Jesus will be "*a blessing to all the nations*" rather than just to the Jews.

Matthew goes even further in this analysis. The Jews have the Old Testament Scriptures but refuse to understand what the prophets have said and refuse to worship the Messiah (instead, Herod, the King of the Jews, plots to kill him); it is the Gentiles who understand the truth even though they didn't know the prophecies. This justifies Matthew's claim that the Christians – including the Gentile Christians – are the true followers of the Messiah.

The *magi*'s gifts are symbolic too:

- **Gold** is the gift for a king, representing Jesus as the **Kingly Messiah**
- **Frankincense** was burnt in temples during worship for its sweet smell; it represents Jesus as the **Priestly Messiah**
- **Myrrh** is a medicinal ointment with a bitter flavour; it represents Jesus' suffering and death as the **Suffering Messiah** or the **Suffering Servant** (p20, a "*man of sorrows*")

Raymond E Brown points out some of the problems with this story. Why do the *magi* need to ask where the Messiah would be born, while in **John 7: 42** everyone seems to know about the prophecy that the Messiah would be born in Bethlehem? Why doesn't Herod follow the *magi* on their 5-mile trip to Bethlehem? Why are there no records of the 'star' the *magi* followed, given that the Romans, Greeks and Persians did record a lot of astronomical events – and the Chinese recorded practically everything?

The last point might not be a big criticism. The 'star' might not have been a literal star; it might have been a conjunction of the planets Jupiter and Saturn passing over each other. We know this happened in 7 BCE and would have been incredibly meaningful to ancient astrologers like the *magi* who believed that great events on Earth were announced by the movements of the stars and planets. In fact, since the conjunction happened 3 times in 7 BCE, that would explain the star 'moving' in the sky.

PROOF TEXT 2: MICAH 5: 2-4

> [3] When King Herod heard this he was disturbed, and all Jerusalem with him. [4] When he had called together all the people's chief priests and teachers of the law, he asked them where the Messiah was to be born. [5] "In Bethlehem in Judea," they replied, "for this is what the prophet has written:
>
> [6] "'But you, Bethlehem, in the land of Judah, are by no means least among the rulers of Judah; for out of you will come a ruler who will shepherd my people Israel.'"

The next Proof-Text links Jesus' birth in Bethlehem to the Prophet **Micah**'s prediction that the Messiah would come from King David's home town of Bethlehem.

> *But you, Bethlehem Ephrathah, though you are small among the clans of Judah,*
> *out of you will come for me one who will be ruler over Israel,*
> *whose origins are from of old, from ancient times* **– Micah 5: 2**

Bethlehem had shrunk to a village in the 1st century, about 5 miles south of Jerusalem. It's interesting that Matthew describes Mary and Joseph living here in a house. There's no mention of a stable or a manger and there's no suggestion that Mary and Joseph are just visiting Bethlehem temporarily (which is what Luke's Birth Narrative claims).

Jesus' background was a problem for 1st century Christians – he was from Nazareth in Galilee, about 80 miles to the north. Jesus' Galilean background was well known; he is often referred to as 'Jesus of Nazareth' or 'the Nazarene'. Galilee was a rather backward area of farmlands and fishing villages where the locals had a strong accent: they were regarded as bumpkins and yokels by the sophisticated people of Jerusalem. There are *no* prophecies about the Messiah coming from Galilee.

Matthew's solution is to propose that Jesus' family were really from Bethlehem all along; they moved to Nazareth later (as we shall see). Luke has a different solution: the family was from Galilee but happened to be visiting Bethlehem at the time of Jesus' birth.

> *The story of Mary and Joseph arriving from Nazareth in Galilee because of a Roman census and finding nowhere to stay and putting their baby in a manger (presumably in a stable, although the Bible doesn't say this), comes from Luke's Gospel. The two stories are often combined together (harmonized) but they are originally separate.*

Jesus' Galilean background passes what scholars call the **CRITERION OF EMBARRASSMENT**. In other words, it's a historical detail that was embarrassing for the early Christians because it counted *against* their belief that Jesus was the Messiah. They wouldn't make it up so it's probably historically true. Matthew's story about the family living in Bethlehem *might* be true, but it's also *exactly* the sort of thing Matthew would want to make up.

THE ESCAPE TO EGYPT

Joseph has another prophetic dream, warning him to leave Bethlehem and take his family to Egypt – only a 40 mile trip to get outside the territory controlled by King Herod.

The family stay in Egypt until the death of King Herod – which we know happened in 4 BCE because Herod was a famous person who is described in many other ancient sources.

> *Although the BC/AD dating system is supposed to be based on the year of Jesus' birth, Jesus cannot have been born in 1 CE because that would be **after** the death of Herod. If Matthew's story is historically true, then Jesus must have been born around 7 or 6 BCE.*

PROOF-TEXT 3: HOSEA 11: 1

[14] So he got up, took the child and his mother during the night and left for Egypt, [15] where he stayed until the death of Herod. And so was fulfilled what the Lord had said through the prophet: "Out of Egypt I called my son."

The escape of Mary, Joseph and Jesus into Egypt mirrors ancient history where Joseph (the son of Jacob/Israel) is taken to Egypt in **Genesis 37: 36**. In the Old Testament, the Twelve Tribes of Israel spend generations in Egypt, first as guests then later as slaves. This is known as the Sojourn. Eventually they are led to freedom by **Moses** – this is the **Exodus**.

Matthew connects this journey to a quote from the 8th century BCE prophet **Hosea** (a rough contemporary of Isaiah):

> *When Israel was a child, I loved him, and out of Egypt I called my son* – **Hosea 11: 1**

This prophecy clearly has a **preterist** interpretation. Hosea was writing about the Jewish nation and *'Israel'* is a CORPORATE PERSONALITY representing all Jews. Hosea is recalling the way God rescued 'Israel' from Egypt by sending Moses and he is promising that God will save the hard-pressed Kingdom of Judea from her enemies, the Assyrian Empire. The *'son'* Hosea is talking about is 'Israel' itself.

However, for Matthew, the *'Son'* is the **'Son of God'** (p112), Jesus himself. This is pretty clearly not the meaning Hosea consciously intended, but it could be DOUBLE-PROPHECY, where the passage has a preterist meaning (events in the 8th century BCE) and a futurist meaning (predicting Jesus, 750 years later).

THE MASSACRE OF THE INNOCENTS

To protect his rule against a rival king who might grow up to threaten him, King Herod orders his soldiers to go to Bethlehem and kill all the boys under two years old.

Outside Matthew's Gospel, there's no historical evidence for this massacre. **Josephus Flavius** describes Herod's reign in his *Antiquities of the Jews* (90 CE) but never mentions this atrocity, although he describes how Herod murdered his own sons, wife and mother-in-law!

However, such a murder spree is quite in keeping with Herod's character. Since the population of Bethlehem at this time was about 1000, the massacre could only have involved about twenty children. **R.T. France** explains why the massacre isn't mentioned by historians, saying:

> *the murder of a few infants in a small village [is] not on a scale to match the more spectacular assassinations recorded by Josephus* – **R.T. France**

Raymond E. Brown argues that the story is supposed to echo the story of Moses, where Pharaoh of Egypt gives orders to kill the male children of the Hebrew slaves in **Exodus 1: 22**. Moses narrowly avoided being caught up in this mass-killing and Jesus is presented by Matthew as a "second Moses". Brown believes the story of the massacre is **symbolic**, not historical.

PROOF-TEXT 4: JEREMIAH 31: 15

[16] When Herod realized that he had been outwitted by the Magi, he was furious, and he gave orders to kill all the boys in Bethlehem and its vicinity who were two years old and under, in accordance with the time he had learned from the Magi. [17] Then what was said through the prophet Jeremiah was fulfilled:

[18] "A voice is heard in Ramah, weeping and great mourning, Rachel weeping for her children and refusing to be comforted, because they are no more."

Matthew links the massacre back to another Old Testament prophet, **Jeremiah**. Jeremiah describes the suffering of the Jews of Judah as they are taken away into Exile by the Babylonians in 597 BCE. The prisoners were assembled at a town near Jerusalem called Ramah before being deported. Jeremiah imagines the weeping of the mothers who will be separated fro their children. He compares this to a famous figure from the past, **Rachel** the wife of Jacob and mother of Joseph. Rachel died in childbirth near Bethlehem and is buried there. Dying, she wept that she would never see her sons again.

> *A voice is heard in Ramah, mourning and great weeping, Rachel weeping for her children and refusing to be comforted, because they are no more* – **Jeremiah 31: 15**

This prophecy has a preterist interpretation. 'Rachel' is a CORPORATE PERSONALITY: she represents all the women of the Jewish nation who are grieving throughout history. In this Old Testament passage, 'Rachel' is weeping for the Jews in Exile in Babylon.

Rachel's tears are also tears of joy, because the midwife told her she had delivered a healthy boy. In Jeremiah's prophecy, the tears are also joyful because the Exiled Jews will return to their homeland (which they did, in 539 BCE).

Matthew takes a futurist interpretation, because for him 'Rachel' represents the mothers of Bethlehem weeping for their children, murdered by Herod. Matthew does not tell us that the tears are joyful, but we can interpret them this way because Jesus, the Messiah, has survived and, in the next passage, returns home from exile in Egypt. Like the previous Proof-Texts, this text is a DOUBLE-PROPHECY, describing events from 500 years ago but also (according to Matthew) predicting Jesus' escape and Herod's massacre.

RELOCATION TO NAZARETH

King Herod dies in 4 BCE and Joseph, Mary and Jesus return home. However, Herod's successor is his son (three of them survived their father's rages) and **Herod Archelaus** is just as bloodthirsty as his father. Joseph is advised in another dream not to return to Judea at all, but to go to Nazareth in Galilee.

Bibles usually call this final journey the "return" to Nazareth – but Matthew has never suggested that Joseph and Mary came from Nazareth in the first place. It's Luke's Gospel that describes Joseph and Mary coming from Nazareth to Bethlehem for a census, staying there long enough for Jesus to be born, then going directly home to Nazareth again. For Matthew, Joseph is a citizen of Bethlehem. So why would he go to live in far-away Nazareth?

Avoiding Archelaus would be a reason not to return to Judea. Archelaus certainly existed. He ruled until 6 CE. Sickened of his cruelty, the Jewish subjects complained to the Roman Emperor. Archelaus was deposed and sent into exile; his territory became the Roman province of Judea and a Roman governor was sent out to rule it directly. In the meantime, it makes sense that Joseph wouldn't put his family at risk by returning to a country ruled by Archelaus. However, Galilee was ruled over by King Herod's *other* son, **Herod Antipas**. Antipas wasn't quite as unhinged as Archelaus and he ruled Galilee right through Jesus' lifetime.

> *When the adult Jesus has run-ins with 'King Herod' – for example, the 'Herod' who executed John the Baptist – it is Herod Antipas the Bible is referring to.*

So why avoid returning to one country ruled by an evil son of the king who tried to kill your family, only to go and live in the country ruled by his brother? Why not live in neighbouring Decapolis instead?

Mathew also has a religious reason to locate Jesus in Galilee rather than Judea. Judea is thoroughly Jewish but Galilee is a region of Gentiles where Jewish farmers and fishermen work alongside Romans and Greeks and Syrians and lots of other ethnicities. Matthew calls it "*Galilee of the Gentiles*", echoing **Isaiah** who uses the same phrase. This fits with Matthew's theme that Jesus has come as much for the Gentiles (non-Jews) as for the Jews themselves.

Secondly, the fact that Jesus was a Galilean was too well-known to be ignored by Matthew. Everyone knew Jesus as the preacher and miracle-worker *from Galilee*. This fact passes the CRITERION OF EMBARRASSMENT because it's a biographical detail that Matthew and the other early Christians would probably have ignored if they could.

There are no prophecies about the Messiah coming from Galilee, which is why Matthew has to explain that Jesus was *really* from Bethlehem originally and only *seemed* to be from Galilee.

Joseph, Mary & Joseph's travels in Matthew's Gospel

PROOF-TEXT 5: ISAIAH 11:1

Despite the lack of prophecies linking the Messiah to Galilee, Matthew does make the link in his final Proof-Text.

> [21] So he got up, took the child and his mother and went to the land of Israel. [22] But when he heard that Archelaus was reigning in Judea in place of his father Herod, he was afraid to go there. Having been warned in a dream, he withdrew to the district of Galilee, [23] and he went and lived in a town called Nazareth. So was fulfilled what was said through the prophets, that he would be called a Nazarene.

A 'Nazarene' is somebody from Nazareth... but the Old Testament prophets never said that the Messiah would come from Nazareth or anywhere else in Galilee. What is Matthew talking about?

Raymond E. Brown suggests two possibilities. The first is a word-play. 'Nazarene' sounds like the Hebrew word **NE-TZER** which means "branch". There is a link here back to **Isaiah** who claimed that the Messiah would be of the **line of David** (p15), descended from David's father Jesse:

> *A shoot will come up from the stump of Jesse; from his roots a Branch will bear fruit –*
> **Isaiah 11: 1**

This sounds a bit strained but the prophecy about the messiah being a 'branch' of the Davidic family tree was very famous and so referring to Jesus as ne-tzer ('the branch') might have been recognised by Jewish readers as referring to the prophecy

The second interpretation is that there was an old Jewish sect called the **Nazirites** that included great Old Testament heroes like Samson. The Nazirites were promised to the service of God while still in their mother's wombs, so this reference reinforces the theme that Jesus was born to be the Messiah. Samson was a flawed Nazirite but the TRUE Nazirite – the one who fully dedicates himself to God and does God's work on Earth – is Jesus.

EVALUATING MATTHEW'S BIRTH NARRATIVE & PROOF-TEXTS

On the face of it, Matthew's Birth Narrative seems to be on solid historical ground.

- There are **geographically factual places** (Bethlehem, Egypt, Galilee) and **historical people** (Herod, the *magi* of Persia, Archelaus).
- Compared to Luke's rather more fantastical Birth Narrative, there's **just one miracle** (the Virgin Birth) and the only angels that appear do so in dreams.
- The Virgin Birth might be a mistake based on Matthew misunderstanding **Isaiah 7: 14** and the only other improbable event (the Massacre of the Innocents) is not nearly so improbable once you understand the sort of atrocities King Herod certainly did carry out.

On further investigation, the Birth Narrative looks less plausible. It contradicts Luke's Birth Narrative (no Roman census, Joseph and his family head off to Egypt rather than to Nazareth). More than that, there are wider inconsistencies. Matthew presents the birth of the Messiah as a political event attended by foreign dignitaries and triggering a mass-killing; Jesus' family become political refugees in another country. Yet these events are never mentioned by Luke or the other Gospels. In **John 7: 42**, people say that Jesus can't be the Messiah because he's from Galilee.

Why didn't Jesus just point out that actually, he WAS from Bethlehem originally? Had no one heard of the Messiah being born 30 years previously, the foreign VIPs who came to visit and those poor children who were massacred?

The Proof-Texts have similar problems. At first glance they read like striking predictions of Jesus' early life. On close examination, they are quoted out-of-context and describe events going on in the ancient kingdom of Judah, 750-500 years previously.

There are ways round these problems:

- Conservative Christians HARMONISE the Birth Narratives in Matthew and Luke: Joseph and Mary came from Nazareth to Bethlehem, were visited by the *Magi* AND the shepherds, escaped Herod's massacre **then** returned home to Nazareth
- They interpret the Proof-Texts as DUAL PROPHECIES that have both a preterist meaning (that the prophet consciously intended) and a futurist meaning (that the prophet perhaps did not intend).

These interpretations make some sense, but the immediate simplicity and persuasiveness of Matthew's 'proof' is lost.

Scholars like **Raymond E. Brown** argue that the Birth-Narrative should NOT be regarded as historical and wasn't even intended to be. Instead it is religious **symbolism** conveying Matthew's beliefs about Jesus being the Messiah, the 'new Moses' and the Son of David. It is written to reassure Gentile Christians that the Messiah is important to them too and to answer Jewish criticisms that Jesus did not qualify as being the true Messiah. Brown calls the Birth Narrative *"an attractive drama that catches the imagination"* but concludes that it is probably a PIOUS FICTION.

Morna Hooker regards the Birth-Narrative as a *"key"* that *"unlocks"* the rest of the Gospel, saying, *"the beginning of the story hints at the ideas that will be made plain at the end"*. It tells readers to look for similarities between Jesus and Moses as well as Jesus and King David (in other words, a Prophetic **and** a Kingly Messiah). It hints that the Gentiles will become Jesus' followers but the Jews will reject him. It warns readers that the evil rulers of this world will try to kill Jesus (and later his followers), but promises that their plans will fail because of God's guiding power.

Do the Birth-Narrative and proof-texts in Matthew prove Jesus to be the Messiah?

YES	NO
Matthew shows that Jesus was born in Bethlehem to a family descended from King David, exactly what you'd expect from the Messiah. He only moved to Nazareth in Galilee later and all along the way the key events of his childhood match prophecies from the Old Testament.	Matthew's Genealogy is very flawed and may well be fictional. The Birth-Narrative contains details (like the visit of the *magi*) which are very improbable or (like Herod's massacre of the innocents) are not recorded in independent sources from the time.
The Proof-Texts establish Jesus' Messiah-ship, such as Isaiah's prophecy that he would be conceived by a virgin or Hosea's prophecy that he would be called out of Egypt.	The Old Testament prophecies have preterist interpretations that are much more obvious and plausible, such as Isaiah celebrating the birth of Prince Hezekiah to a young bride or Hosea warning about the attacking Assyrians.

TOPIC 1.2 THE WORLD OF THE FIRST CENTURY

The 1st century CE was a turbulent time in the region known as Palestine, covering the Roman Province of Judea and the neighbouring territory of Galilee. The Jews of this region faced challenges from the wider **Hellenic** (Greek) culture of the Mediterranean world that were both religious and political. They lived under the oppression of the **Roman Empire** and were forced to redefine their religion as a response. Because of this, they divided into many different groups.

> *Note: names can be controversial. The Edexcel specification refers to the region inhabited by the Jews in the 1st century CE as 'Palestine'. This is not a name 1st century Jews themselves used. It's the Greek/Roman term for the region. Today, the name has political connotations that did not exist in the 1st century.*

Life in 1st Century Palestine

Geography

The region the Romans called Palestine is in the Eastern Mediterranean, covering what today is the State of Israel and parts of Lebanon, Syria and Jordan. It is a land of contrasts: rugged mountains which see snow in the winter and scorching deserts that rarely see rain alongside lush farmland where grapes, dates and olives grow and sheep and goats are tended. In the 1st century there are villages of dirt huts built around precious wells, old towns of crumbling stone dating back centuries and new cities in the Greek style with marble columns and paved roads.

In the north is the Sea of Galilee, surrounded by fertile farmland and hills wooded with pine and oak. The Jezreel Valey connects Galilee to the coast. South of this are the highlands of Samaria. A coastal plain stretches all the way to the Egyptian desert, and the valley of the River Jordan slices through the mountains until it flows into the Dead Sea, a lake so salty that plants and animals cannot survive in it (but King Herod made it into a health resort!). The mountains south of Samaria form Judea itself, dominated by the city of Jerusalem. The steep valleys are fertile but south and west of here the land gives way to the Judean Desert.

History & Politics

The southern part of Palestine had been the Jewish kingdom of Judah, until it was destroyed by the Babylonians in 597 BCE. When the Exiled Jews returned here in 539 BCE, they set about rebuilding their homeland, conscious of God's promise in the Old Testament that the entire region was the 'Promised Land' given to the descendants of Abraham.

The Hasmonean family ruled Judea (as it became known) and managed to create a fully independent Jewish kingdom for about 50 years (from 110 BCE to 63 BCE) until **the Roman Empire** invaded the region.

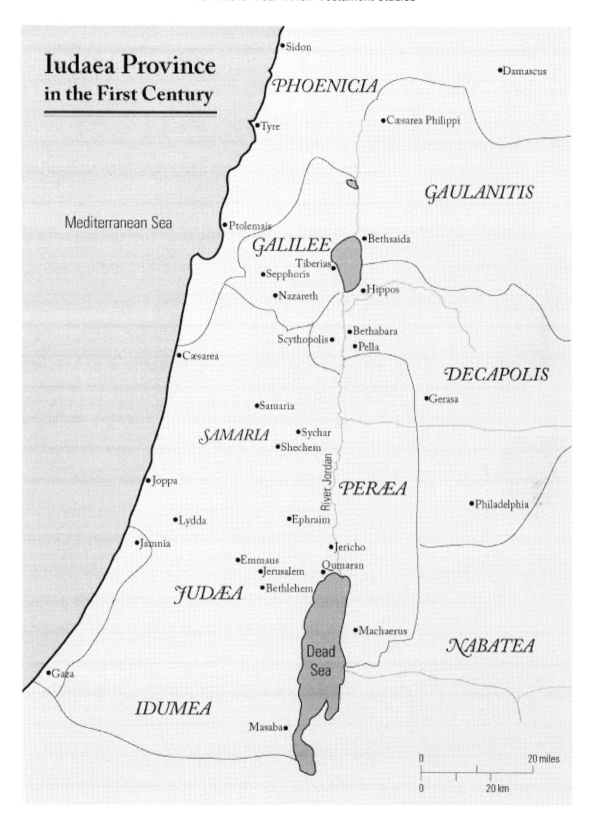

When the Hasmoneans rebelled against the Romans, they were crushed and in 37 BCE another family was installed as rulers who would be more loyal to Rome. These were the Herodians. **Herod the Great r**uled the region for 30 years, with the backing of the Roman Empire. He was unpopular with his Jewish subjects, because his family had only recently converted to Judaism and clearly did not take the religion seriously. Herod murdered many of his family members and oppressed his citizens: his death in 4 BCE came as a relief to the people. However, Herod left a legacy: the magnificent **Temple in Jerusalem** (p61) that he had expanded and lavished gold upon in a bid for popularity.

King Herod – terrible man but great builder

Herod's sons divided up the territory between them, but they were not as successful as their father. **Herod Antipas** ruled Galilee and had a scandalous personal life. **Herod Archelaus** ruled Judea with so much oppression and bloodshed that the Romans had him removed from power. Instead, they made Judea into a Roman province and sent a governor (a Prefect, later a Procurator) to run the territory for them. The governor's main jobs were to collect taxes and keep the peace. The governor was based in the coastal town of Caesarea but would travel 'up country' to Jerusalem for the annual Jewish festival of **Passover**, always a time when rebellions were likely. The Roman governor during Jesus' adult life was **Pontius Pilate**.

There weren't enough Romans to run Judea themselves: they needed helpers (or collaborators) to collect the taxes, report on troublemakers and impose the law. These people were known as PUBLICANS and were widely hated because they often demanded bribes and used their connections with the Romans to extort and bully their neighbours. Jews who became publicans were considered to have 'sold out'. Although Jewish publicans could get rich quick, they risked being ostracized by their community and some were kidnapped and murdered.

The Romans also relied on the Temple Priesthood to run the country on their behalf. The Temple Priests in Jerusalem employed their own soldiers and collected their own taxes and worked closely with the Herodian kings and the Roman governors. In the eyes of some Jews, this made them little better than publicans themselves.

The whole situation was deeply unstable – especially since the governor **Pontius Pilate** was an insensitive and brutal man. Eventually, things came to a head, 30 years after Jesus' lifetime, in the **Great Jewish Revolt** (66-73 CE).

The People

The main distinction in the people was between Jews and **GENTILES** (non-Jews). The Gentiles in Palestine included Greeks and Romans, neighbouring Egyptians, Syrians and Persians as well as people from the Decapolis (the 'Ten Cities'). It also included the Samaritans who considered themselves to be the descendants of the lost tribes of Israel but who were regarded as liars and heretics by the Jews of Judea. These peoples lived side by side, traded with each other and formed friendships. However, Jews who followed their religion strictly could not eat with their Gentile neighbours and certainly couldn't inter-marry with them.

The Romans had mixed feelings about the Jews. On the positive side, they respected the Jewish religion because it was known to be very old and 'old' meant 'good' in the Roman world. They admired Jewish social ethics, such as collecting money for charity and providing healthcare and education for the poor.

However, they found some aspects of Jewish religion irritating, such as resting on the Sabbath every 7 days, the food laws and the way the Jews kept themselves separate. The Jews had a reputation for squabbling with one another and being difficult to govern.

There was a lot of curiosity about Judaism. Gentiles would sometimes attend Jewish Synagogues. The *metuentes* were Gentiles who worshiped the God of Judaism and imitated some Jewish practices, such as keeping the Sabbath and avoiding forbidden meats.

A Jewish preacher like Jesus would have attracted audiences of Gentles as well as Jews.

The 'European' Jesus – probably not accurate

It's difficult to know what the Jewish people of the 1st century looked like. The Old Testament Commandment forbidding images means that the Ancient Jews did not leave behind pictures of themselves. However, many stereotypes about their appearance are certainly wrong.

A lot of European art depicts Jesus and his disciples looking like white Europeans. This is probably wrong. Arab peoples had not spread into the region of Palestine in the 1st century, but Greeks, Romans and Persians had, so it's likely that most of the population looked more like them. Greek and Roman rulers found it difficult to tell who was or wasn't a Jew by appearance alone.

The standard 'look' for men in the Mediterranean world of the 1st century was to keep hair cut short and to shave – no long beards. However, philosophers often defied fashion and stood out by growing beards. Older men would also grow beards.

Religious leaders and people who had taken religious vows let their hair and beards grow. The Jewish sect of the Nazirites refused to cut their hair or shave their beards – but we know Jesus wasn't a strict Nazirite because he drank wine.

The Arab head scarf (*keffiyah*) was NOT worn at this time in history, despite what you see in many films and illustrations. Women grew their hair long (usually with a centre parting) and covered their heads with shawls. However, they did not wear veils over their faces. The standard clothing was a tunic (knee length for men, ankle length for women) with a woollen mantle on top – or two mantles on cold evenings. The mantle was a sort of wrap-around cloak, like a toga. Religious Jews might wear a prayer shawl with tassels over their shoulders. People wore sandals in the dry summer or leather shoes in winter.

Towns & Cities

Most of the Jews in the 1st century were farmers or fishermen (especially on the Sea of Galilee). They lived in small villages. However, these little communities existed alongside bigger towns built by the Greeks and Romans. For example, a couple of miles away from Nazareth was the city of **Sepphoris** with its mosaics and Roman theatres. Jews who moved to these exciting places could get rich and enjoy a much more sophisticated and luxurious lifestyle, but perhaps at the cost of their religious purity. **Tiberias** was considered such a decadent Roman city that strict Jews refused to live there.

Archaeologists have discovered the Synagogue in Capernaum where Jesus would have preached

Capernaum was a fishing village on the north shore of Lake Galilee where Jesus began his Ministry. He preached his first sermons and performed his first miracles there. It was the home of his first disciples: Peter, Andrew, James and John. The tax collector and publican Matthew lived there – tradition claims he is the author of Matthew's Gospel.

The Roman capital was on the coast: **Caesarea** had been built by Herod the Great and named in honour of Caesar Augustus, the first Roman Emperor. The Roman governor of Judea ran the province from here.

Deep in the country and high up in the mountains was **Jerusalem**, the ancient capital of King David. In the past, this had been a remote and rather small city. King Herod had enlarged this place too, rebuilding the Temple on a massive sale and turning Jerusalem into a **Hellenic** city that would be a wonder of the Roman Empire. Jerusalem's population of (perhaps) 50,000 tripled during religious festivals, with pilgrims flooding into the city along with Roman soldiers to police the streets. Jesus came here as a pilgrim for the Festival of Passover at the end of his life. Unfortunately, in 70 CE at the end of the Jewish Revolt, the Romans demolished the city completely and nothing of its grandeur survives in modern Jerusalem except fragments of ancient walls.

> *The Gospels have two main settings: Galilee (especially around Capernaum) and Jerusalem. In the Synoptic Gospels (**Matthew, Mark & Luke**), Jesus' ministry begins in Galilee then moves to Jerusalem, where he is arrested and crucified. **John's Gospel** structures things differently, with Jesus traveling back and forth between Galilee and Jerusalem over a period of 3 years, with tensions escalating until his arrest and death.*

JEWS, ISRAELITES & ISRAEL

'Jewish' refers to a race of people AND a religion. The word comes from the Roman province of Judea ('Jews' are 'Judeans') which gets its name from the earlier Jewish kingdom of Judah.

Jews (and Arabs) claim descent from Abraham, who lived perhaps 1500-2000 BCE. However, a particularly important ancestor for the Jews is Abraham's grandson Jacob, later known as 'Israel'. Jacob had 12 sons, from whom descend the 'Twelve Tribes of Israel' or 'Israelites'. King David ruled over all 12 of these tribes, but, with the later splitting of his kingdom and invasions by Assyrians and Babylonians, 9 of these tribes were 'lost'.

Because 'Israel' is the name of the great ancestor of the Jews, it is often used as a way of personifying the whole Jewish race and religion. When the Bible refers to 'Israel' it often means 'all the Jews'. The **Suffering Servant** (p20) is considered by scholars like **Morna Hooker** to be 'Israel' in this symbolic sense.

To confuse things, Israel was also the name of King David's kingdom and the northern Jewish kingdom that broke away from his dynasty. It's also the name of the modern Jewish state.

HELLENISM

Jews in 1st century Palestine experienced two powerful cultural forces. One was the Jewish religion expressed in the Scriptures along with the festivals and traditions based on it and the strict religious Law taken from it. The other was **Hellenic civilisation**, the international culture that had been brought into Judea by the conquering Greeks and the Roman Empire.

Understanding Hellenism

'*Hellas*' means Greece: 'Hellenic' refers to Greek culture and ideas and 'Hellenism' is the spread of those ideas into other societies. Greek ideas were spread by the conquests of Alexander the Great, who took his Greek armies through Palestine into Egypt, then all across Persia, through Afghanistan and into India. When Alexander died in 323 BCE, his vast empire was carved up by his generals who became kings over Persia, Egypt and Greece itself. One of these founded the Seleucid Kingdom which was based in modern Syria and held power over Palestine and most of the Middle East. The Jews of Palestine found themselves under the control of the Seleucids for 150 years.

The vast kingdoms left behind by Alexander caused mass migration and allowed communication across Asia and the Mediterranean. Distinctive Greek ideas about politics, art, philosophy and religion that had previously been limited to the small Greek city-states like Athens and Thebes were introduced to the wider world along with the Greek language. This language, called *koine* (it's pronounced KOY-NAY), became the international language of business and trade that would be learned by all merchants and diplomats.

> *The term for a second language that people learn for trade and diplomacy is LINGUA FRANCA (because French used to be this sort of language in Europe). Koine Greek was the lingua franca of the ancient world. The New Testament was written in Koine.*

The Impact of Hellenic Civilisation

Hellenic civilisation had a number of distinctive characteristics that were different from the Israelite civilisation the Jews had inherited from the world of the Old Testament. Many Jews resisted **Hellenization** (the spread of Hellenic culture by force) but others cheerfully embraced new fashions, ideas and pastimes as well as new religious beliefs.

Polytheism

Polytheism is the worship of many gods, rather than just one. The Greeks worshiped the Twelve Gods of Olympus (headed by Zeus) along with hundreds of minor gods, demi-gods, nymphs, monsters and heroes. This wasn't unusual – the Jews always had neighbours who were polytheists.

However, the Greek gods differed from the pagan gods of the Middle East in several ways. For one thing, they were very human: they had relationships with humans, took human form, visited Earth and had feuds and romances just like humans did. The myths and legends about the Greek gods were full of psychological symbolism and meaning that made them especially entertaining and thought-provoking. Greek-style religion was adopted by lots of other peoples across the Hellenic world who re-imagined their traditional gods and goddesses in the Greek style, often describing them as local versions of those Greek deities.

For the Jews, this sort of Hellenic religion was very threatening. Their God had no physical appearance: he couldn't be painted or described. The Jews reacted with horror to the appearance of statues of the Greek gods and demi-gods like Hercules in their towns and in their Temple. Back in 168 BCE, the Seleucid king Antiochus had imposed Hellenization by force: he invaded Jerusalem and set up a statue of Zeus in the Temple. This led to a revolt by led the Maccabee brothers and a civil war between Hellenized Jews and the traditionalist Jews. The Maccabees won, reclaimed their Temple and founded the Hasmonean dynasty that ruled Judea for a hundred years.

The Maccabee Revolt was looked back on with great pride by many 1st century Jews, especially those who still opposed Hellenization. King Herod the Great was a keen Hellenizer who set up many pictures of Greek gods in Jerusalem (but not in the Temple itself – he learned THAT lesson) along with a theatre and a circus where wrestling tournaments took place.

Humanistic Art & Leisure

The Greeks had developed striking new art forms that helped spread Hellenic civilisation: theatre and sculpture were the main ones. Of course other civilisations had acting and carved statues (think of the Sphinx!) but the Greeks brought something new to this: **Humanism**, which is a delighted interest in the human situation and the human body. Greek sculpture explored the human body in realistic detail and idealised it – making nakedness into a thing of beauty.

Greek theatre focused on human relationships and human psychology. Greek tragedies explored freewill and what it means to be human; Greek comedies poked fun at sex, religion and politics.

Did Jesus ever visit the theatre in Sepphoris, just an hour's walk away from Nazareth?

Linked to the Hellenic arts were new forms of leisure. Theatre-going became popular but so did the gymnasium. The Greeks obsessed over sport, particularly athletics, and their athletes competed naked. Linked to the gymnasiums were bath houses where the men and women (separately, not together) socialised naked in steam rooms and swimming pools. The Romans carried on this interest in public bathing and public nakedness, inspired by the Hellenic idealisation of the human body.

For the Jews, this was all very shocking. The Second Commandment forbids making "*graven images*" and Jewish culture strongly frowned on nudity. Gymnasiums and bath houses were shameful places for traditionalist Jews. Such believers would not allow their great prophets Moses or Abraham or King David to be played on stage by an actor, especially in a play that presented them as flawed and complex human beings (although, to be fair, the Old Testament itself presents them as flawed on occasions and so does the Jewish storytelling tradition).

Rational Philosophy

The Greeks also developed a powerful philosophical tradition – indeed they invented the *word* "philosophy". This philosophical tradition included the ideas of Socrates which were developed by Plato into a school of philosophy (the 'Academy'). Plato's ideas were taken in different directions by the Stoics and the Cynics who offered codes of living that didn't depend on religion. Plato's student Aristotle rejected Platonism completely and developed his own influential approach to science, ethics and metaphysics.

Stoicism became the unofficial 'religion' of the Roman Empire. Stoics believed in one God, but they were Deists who did not believe God intervened through miracles. Instead they believed everything was predetermined (no freewill) and practised emotional restraint and a strict honour code to make life meaningful. Stoicism recommended suicide as the moral course of action under certain circumstances.

Cynicism was a more unusual philosophy. Today, 'cynicism' means a nasty disbelief in goodness and morality. However, the Ancient Cynics believed that the best life was a life that followed nature rather than social expectations. They recommended giving up material possessions and turned away from society. Cynic philosophers could be very unconventional but people sought them out for advice.

My favourite Cynic anecdote is about Alexander the Great going to visit the famous Cynic philosopher Diogenes. He finds Diogenes sleeping in the sunshine. Diogenes wakes up when the conqueror of the world asks him, "What can I do for you?" The philosopher says, "You can get out of my sun!" and goes back to sleep! Alexander is so struck by the philosopher's total self-sufficiency he says to his courtiers, "If I wasn't Alexander, I would be Diogenes!"

The point about these philosophies was that they had been arrived at by rational thought, not religious **revelation**. This contrasted with the Jewish religion, which came from revelations given by God to Moses and the later prophets. To many Jews, the philosophical basis of their religion seemed weak.

Many of them applied the ideas of Aristotle to their Judaism, linking God to the Unmoved Mover in Aristotle's arguments. However, the Unmoved Mover of Aristotle was very different from the stormy, emotional, intervening God of the Old Testament. **Philo of Aexandria** (20 BCE - 50 CE) applied Greek thought to his Jewish faith. Philo treated the stories in the Old Testament as **allegories** (stories with symbolic meaning that weren't literally true) and applied Aristotle's concept of the **Logos** to Judaism (you will learn more about this in **Topic 2**).

Probably the biggest philosophical idea to affect Judaism was the belief in PERSONAL IMMORTALITY (life after death). The Old Testament barely mentions the Afterlife and most Jews did not believe in a Heaven after death: you had one life to worship God and that was it! Plato's ideas about people having immortal souls that live on after death proved very popular with some Jews.

Cultural Relativism

Perhaps the biggest impact of Hellenism was unintentional. Alexander's enormous empire opened people's horizons. It showed them that they lived in a vast and varied world and brought them into contact with ideas, customs and religions from all across Asia and the Mediterranean. One effect of this was to produce a sense that there's nothing special about your own culture and the customs and beliefs you were brought up with. **Relativism** is the belief that no culture is 'best' and no religion is 'true'.

This view was summed up by the Greek philosopher **Xenophanes** around 500 BCE. Xenophanes pointed out that the Ethiopians in Africa think their gods have black skin and the Thracians in Europe think their gods have white skin. He adds that if cows, horses and lions had hands, they would draw their gods with their animal bodies too.

This was a troubling idea for many Jews. It suggested that their God was really no different from the other gods worshiped by other people: no different from Zeus in Greece or Ahura Mazda in Persia or Ra in Egypt. This would mean there was "nothing special" about Judaism.

The Relationship of Hellenism with Jesus' Life & Work

Jesus grew up in Galilee, a place where Hellenic ideas mixed with Jewish beliefs. Was Jesus a Hellenized Jew?

Clearly, Jesus believed in life after death and personal immortality. These ideas had been growing in importance in Judaism for several centuries but many traditionalist Jews (like the **Sadducees**, p62) still rejected the Afterlife. John's Gospel links Jesus to the **Logos (Word) of God** (p81), which is a Hellenic concept and might have been an idea that Jesus taught to his followers.

Jesus also directs his followers to take his message to the Gentiles as well as the Jews. This 'Great Commission' is in keeping with a Hellenic (universal) outlook rather than a narrow purely-Jewish one.

> *Therefore go and make disciples of all nations, baptizing them in the name of the Father and of the Son and of the Holy Spirit* – **Matthew 28: 19**

> *Although Matthew puts these words into the mouth of the resurrected Christ, we cannot be sure who really said them. During his ministry, Jesus seems to have the opposite view that his mission was solely to the Jews. The 'Great Commission' might reflect the beliefs and priorities of gentile Christians **after** Jesus' time.*

Some scholars go further than this. **John Dominic Crossan** argues that Jesus was in fact a Cynic philosopher. He points out that the **Q Source** (in **Topic 3**, p190) is the oldest account of Jesus' teachings and seems to reflect a Cynic philosophy: give up material possessions, turn your back on the world, live a simple and humble existence. In further support of this, the town of Gadara, 8 miles north of Nazareth, was known to be a centre for Cynic philosophy. Crossan argues that Jesus' Cynic philosophy was ditched by his later followers who came to view him as the Suffering Messiah, which he had never claimed to be (a view shared by supporters of the theory of the **Messianic Secret**, p26).

However, critics of Crossan point out that even in the earliest sources Jesus predicts **the coming Kingdom of God** (*c.f.* **Topic 5**), which is definitely not a Cynic idea. This puts Jesus more in the Prophetic tradition of the Old Testament than the Hellenic tradition of the Cynics. Moreover, Cynics usually behaved in shocking ways, encouraging nudity and sexual shamelessness, but Jesus didn't teach these things. On the contrary, Jesus taught quite a severe sexual ethic about marriage and chastity.

Does Jesus have to be understood in a Hellenic context?

YES	NO
Jesus taught a doctrine of life after death, which is a Hellenic concept not found in the Old Testament. The Sadducees opposed this teaching and believed that life ends at death. Jesus' 'Great Commission' shows that he intended his message for the wider Hellenic world, not just to the Jews.	Although not described in the Old Testament, personal immortality had been taught in Judaism for several centuries and was not viewed as a 'foreign' idea. The 'Great Commission' may tell us more about the Hellenic views of Jesus' Gentile followers than Jesus' own views.
Jesus is best understood as a wandering philosopher of a type that was common in the Hellenistic world, especially among the Cynic philosophers. His teachings about giving away wealth and leading a simple life trusting in God to provide are very similar to Cynic views.	Jesus also opposed certain Cynic views, because he preached about the coming Kingdom of God. Also, Cynics taught people not to be ashamed of nudity and sex, but Jesus taught a rather conservative sexual ethic that sex belonged in marriage.

ROMAN OCCUPATION

Jews in 1st century Palestine lived under foreign rule. The people of Judea were ruled directly by a Roman governor who dealt brutally with dissent; in Galilee and elsewhere, **Herod Antipas** was a client king who ruled because he was backed by Roman military might. Rebellions were always brewing in the provinces of the Empire because of heavy taxes and corrupt officials, but in Galilee and Judea the religious beliefs and Messianic hopes of the Jews produced a particularly dangerous atmosphere.

Judea in the Roman Empire

Understanding the Roman Empire

The Roman Republic flourished in the 1st Century BCE. The Republic was based in Rome in Italy and ruled by a Senate rather than a king (an unusual arrangement for the time) but it had achieved almost total control of Mediterranean trade and dominated the old Hellenistic Kingdoms of Greece and Asia. The Romans enthusiastically absorbed Hellenistic culture (which wasn't very far removed from their own Italian traditions): they identified their own Italian gods with Greek gods (so Jupiter was identified with Zeus, Mars with Ares, Venus with Aphrodite, etc); they adopted public bathing and athletics, theatre and philosophy; they took a relativistic view about religion.

When Julius Caesar was assassinated in 43 BCE, the Roman Republic fell into a civil war which engulfed the whole Mediterranean world for 15 years. Augustus Caesar became the first Emperor of the new Roman Empire, followed in 14 CE by his step-son Tiberius.

> *Augustus was emperor when Jesus was born and Tiberius was emperor when Jesus was crucified.*

The new Emperors took grand titles and Augustus declared himself to be the 'Son of God' (*Divi Filius*). Augustus made sure his statues (such as the one on the left) were placed in temples around the Empire where they were worshiped. Worshiping the Emperor was worshiping the Empire itself – and refusing to worship him was an act of rebellion as well as blasphemy.

The Empire allowed local kings to carry on ruling their populations, so long as they were loyal to the Emperor and paid taxes to Rome. One of these local kings was **Herod the Great**, who wrangled his way through the whole Civil War and stayed in power under the new Emperor. Areas that were too important or too troublesome to be entrusted to some local king were ruled directly from Rome: a governor was sent out to rule the province with the Emperor's authority. This is what happened to Judea. In 26 CE, the new governor was **Pontius Pilate**, a man with a reputation for brutality and arrogance.

> *For most of the people in the Empire, the divine emperor was just one more god to worship. However, the cult of the divine emperor posed a religious problem for Jews (and later for Christians) because their religion forbade them from worshiping any other god.*

So long as taxes were paid and the peace was kept, the Romans largely left their client kingdoms and provinces alone. Some people were 'Roman Citizens' who had particular privileges: they could travel freely within the Empire and they could appeal to Roman law rather than be judged by local kings and magistrates.

Citizens would be spared the most feared punishment dealt out to runaway slaves, outlaws and rebels: death by crucifixion, the victim impaled on a post and dying by slow suffocation in public (usually at the side of the road) as a warning to others (*c.f.* **Topic 5**). At first, all Roman Citizens were actual Italians, but gradually citizenship was given out to more and more people. The Empire didn't impose Latin on everyone: throughout most of the Mediterranean, *koine* Greek remained the *lingua franca* (language of travel and trade).

The Roman legions were the most efficient fighting force in the world at that time and in the 1st century CE they were at their peak. A local governor in a place like Judea couldn't command an elite legion. Instead, the governor would command a force of Auxiliaries: soldiers recruited locally. The governor of Judea employed Syrians and Samaritans to keep the peace in Judea. Just like real legionaries, these soldiers would have to worship the Divine Emperor (which is why no religious Jews ever signed up to serve in the army!). Rome couldn't run the Empire with just soldiers. A civilian 'army' of publicans managed the complicated tax system. These agents had a free hand to demand bribes or impose fines and skim off money for themselves, so long as the Emperor got paid his taxes.

The Impact of Roman Occupation

For many Jews in 1st century Palestine, Roman occupation was fairly distant from their daily lives. In Galilee, where Jesus grew up, the ruler was a client king, Herod Antipas, so many of the magistrates and soldiers would have been locals. However, it was well-known that Antipas was only a puppet for the Roman Emperor and the population resented him and his minions. They also resented the publicans who collected taxes; some publicans were Jews who had turned their backs on their own kind to work with the enemy. These Jews were ostracized by their neighbours, sometimes threatened and killed. Since they had no choice but to socialise with Gentiles (and since some of their fellow-Jews wanted to kill them), many abandoned their Jewish faith altogether.

In Judea, things were more complicated because a Roman governor, **Pontius Pilate**, ruled the province directly. The governor used great brutality to put to riots and protests; troublemakers were crucified along public roads as a lesson for everyone else. Jews had a particular dread of crucifixion because the victim of this punishment is considered cursed by God, according to the Old Testament.

Interacting with the Roman Empire was difficult for Jews because many significant business deals, legal hearings or political meetings would involve a pagan sacrifice to the gods of the Empire or to the Divine Emperor himself (normally burning incense or offering water or milk). Jews could not do this without breaking the First Commandment (which forbids worshipping any other God).

However, Judaism was considered *religio licita* – a protected religion. This meant that Roman officials would go to certain lengths to 'work around' Jewish restrictions about making sacrifices, working on the Sabbath or dining with Gentiles. In return, twice each day, the Jewish priests in the Temple in Jerusalem sacrificed two lambs and an ox for the wellbeing of the Empire and the Emperor.

> *Despite this arrangement, both sides felt irritated and exploited. To the Romans, the Jews seemed unreasonable and troublesome; to the Jews, the Romans seemed to be insulting their faith at every turn.*

The Roman governor (his rank was "Prefect") was **Pontius Pilate**. Pilate was an arrogant man who was very insensitive to the Jewish religion. One of his first acts was to bring banners with pagan symbols into Jerusalem, triggering a riot. Several 1st century writers (including **Flavius Josephus**) describe Pilate's temper and stubbornness. Pilate worked closely with the High Priest of the Temple in Jerusalem, **Joseph Caiaphas**. The High Priest was appointed by the Romans and was expected to keep the Judean population in line.

(The relationship between High Priest Caiaphas and Pontius Pilate is explored in **Topic 5**)

At the annual festival of Passover every Spring, Jerusalem was so crowded with pilgrims that keeping the peace became difficult. Pilate would travel from his coastal base at Caesarea to stay in Jerusalem for 10 days and his soldiers would police the streets. This was a tense time, because any rebellion against the Roman Occupation was probably going to start during Passover.

The Relationship of Roman Occupation with Jesus' Life & Work

One of the main features of Roman occupation in Jesus' Ministry is the appearance of publicans. Jesus tells a **Parable of a Pharisee and a Publican** (Tax Collector), where he praises the humble faith of the publican and condemns the spiritual pride of the Pharisee (p63). It's hard to under-estimate how shocking this contrast would be to Jesus' 1st century listeners.

Jesus didn't just praise the faith of publicans, he socialised with them. **Mark 2: 15-17** describes Jesus being criticised for dining with publicans and replying that these sinners need God's love and forgiveness more than ordinary Jews.

> *Did Jesus tell these publicans to give up working for the Romans? Presumably not, since he wouldn't have been criticised if that's what he did. We can assume his message was that God forgives sinners and that, though the publicans had ruined their relationship with their fellow-Jews, they had not been abandoned by God.*

Jesus made converts of publicans. The Gospels mention Zacchaeus, the chief publican of Jericho, but also Matthew, a tax-collector in Capernaum whom Jesus approached at his money-counting booth and said, "*Follow me!*" According to tradition, this is the very Matthew who wrote **Matthew's Gospel**.

Taxes have an important role in Jesus' life. When asked whether a good Jew should pay taxes to Rome, Jesus cleverly points to the image of Caesar on a coin and says:

> give back to Caesar what is Caesar's, and to God what is God's – **Matthew 22: 21**

> *This seems to be saying, give the Roman Empire the coins it wants but give God the worship and moral living he wants. However, these words are turned around to trap Jesus after his arrest, when he is accused of opposing the paying of taxes to Rome.*

A coin with the Emperor Tiberius' image – Jesus might have held just such a coin

Roman soldiers also appear in the Gospels. In Capernaum, Jesus is asked by a 'Centurion' (army officer) to heal his servant. Jesus praises the faith of the Centurion and announces that Gentiles like this will be rewarded by God alongside Jews.

> *Truly I tell you, I have not found anyone in Israel with such great faith. I say to you that many will come from the east and the west, and will take their places at the feast with Abraham, Isaac and Jacob in the kingdom of heaven –* **Matthew 8: 10-11**

The appearance of publicans and Roman soldiers emphasises the theme in the Gospels that Christ's mission is as much to the Gentiles as to the Jews. Matthew's Gospel often has scenes where Gentiles recognise Jesus' authority as the Messiah but Jews do not.

Of course, the main role the Romans play in Jesus' story is at his execution. Jesus is arrested by the High Priest, but handed over to the governor, Pontius Pilate, to be put to death. Under Roman law, the Jewish authorities could not execute criminals: only the Emperor's official could pass the death sentence on a criminal. All four Gospels present Pilate as strangely unwilling to execute Jesus. However, Pilate asks Jesus an important question:

> *the governor asked him, "Are you the king of the Jews?" "You have said so," Jesus* replied **– Matthew 27: 11**

> *Jesus' reply isn't a weasel-worded attempt to get out of answering: it's the humble way of agreeing, rather like saying "yes indeed!" or "quite so!"*

Luke's Gospel is even more explicit about the accusations leveled against Jesus by the High Priest and his mob:

> *"We have found this man subverting our nation. He opposes payment of taxes to Caesar and claims to be Messiah, a king." –* **Luke 23: 2**

Although Pilate can't have cared much about (or even understood) the title 'Messiah', claiming to be the 'King of the Jews' is a rebellion against Roman rule in Judea. 'King of the Jews' was a title given to Herod the Great by the Emperor: only the Emperor decides who is 'King of the Jews'. Opposing paying taxes to the Roman Empire is very serious. Pilate's main job was to ensure that Rome received its taxes. These crimes amount to SEDITION (trying to overthrow the government) and the Roman punishment for that was crucifixion.

The debate about **why Jesus had to die** and who was responsible is explored in **Topic 5**.

Does the Roman occupation of Palestine make a difference to our understanding of Jesus?

YES	NO
Jesus' Ministry was shaped by the context of occupation: there were two people claiming to be 'Son of God' in the 1st century – Jesus and the Roman Emperor. Jesus' values of love and forgiveness contrast with the violence and brutality of Roman rule. Jesus was executed by the Romans because the values he represented threatened their regime.	Jesus' Ministry is shaped by the Prophetic tradition of the Old Testament, where King David is often referred to as 'Son of God'. Jesus' values are more in contrast with the harsh laws of the Old Testament. Jesus was arrested and sentenced to death by the Jewish priests - and Jesus recognises that the Jews persecute their own prophets without help from the Romans.
Without understanding the Roman occupation, the role of publicans makes no sense. The central question for 1st century Jews was how were they to practise their religion in a world where temporal power rests with an irresistible pagan Empire. Jesus offers an answer to that question that is still relevant for Christians today in a world of unbelievers.	Jesus' teachings about love and mercy and his Parables have lasted down the centuries and still speak to people today. Since Jesus was sent to die an Atoning Death it doesn't matter which regime killed him or which form of execution they used. It would have happened even if Judea was ruled instead by the Persians or by one of Herod's sons.

RELIGIOUS GROUPS IN PALESTINE

A century of rule by foreigners and misrule by Jewish kings who were not of the line of David had left the Jews of 1st century Palestine politically divided. The impact of **Hellenism** (p48) divided them still further. Should they embrace these new beliefs and lifestyles or reject them – and if they rejected them, how should they live as an alternative?

*Most of what we know about these groups comes from a writer called **Flavius Josephus**. Josephus was a Jew who fought in the Jewish Revolt, but after being defeated he changed sides to work for the Romans. His book **Antiquities of the Jews** (c. 95 CE) describes the Sadducees, Pharisees and Essenes as well as the (unnamed) Zealots. Josephus is a fascinating person; it's a shame he isn't one of the key scholars for the course.*

Understanding the Temple

It's not part of the specification, but you won't understand the conflicts within Judaism or the final days of Jesus' ministry unless you understand the role the Temple played in the Jewish religion of the 1st century

The original Temple was built by King David's son Solomon as a place to house the Ark of the Covenant. Over the centuries, Davidic kings of Judah tried to make the Jerusalem Temple the focal point of the national religion. However, in 586 BCE the Babylonians destroyed the Temple and the Kingdom of Judah too. The Ark vanished from history.

When the Babylonian Exiles returned to their homeland, they began building a new Temple, which was completed in 516 BCE. This was the "Second Temple". It was modeled on Solomon's Temple and was a relatively small building.

The priests of this new Temple held a lot of power. The 70 leading priests formed a parliament called the SANHEDRIN that met every day to rule on cases where the Jewish laws were broken. High Priests were appointed by kings and emperors – first the Seleucid kings, then the Hasmoneans and Herodians, eventually the Roman Emperors. Because they were political appointees – and appointed often by Gentiles and foreigners – they were widely distrusted by many Jews.

King Herod the Great, in a bid for fame and popularity, set about rebuilding and enlarging the Second Temple. He coated the walls with gold and built huge columned courtyards for worshipers. He intended the Temple to be one of the Wonders of the Ancient World. However, its association with Herod only tainted the Temple further in the eyes of many Jews.

What went on in the Temple? In a nutshell, animal sacrifice. The Old Testament instructs worshipers to sacrifice various types of animals to God. Ordinary Jews could visit the Temple and pay the priests a Temple Tax to sacrifice animals on their behalf, usually to remove a sin and make themselves pure before God. They were also expected to bring a sacrificial lamb during the Festival of Passover. The animals were killed then burnt on outdoor altars so the smoke could float into the sky. The roasted animal would then be eaten, either by the priests or the worshipers (as part of the Passover meal, in those days).

This wasn't unusual in itself. All ancient pagan temples were sacred abattoirs too. What was unusual about the Jerusalem Temple was the sheer scale of the animal sacrifice that went on every day. Millions of animals were brought to the Temple every year to be slaughtered.

Only 'unblemished' (physically perfect) animals could be sacrificed and selling these lambs and bulls and pigeons to worshipers was a profitable trade. The animal-sellers ran stores in the outer courtyard of the Temple.

In addition, Roman money couldn't be used inside the Temple, because it had pictures of the Emperor on it and he claimed to be a god. Worshipers had to pay the priests their Temple Tax in silver coins called shekels. Money changers operated in the outer courtyard, changing local currency into silver shekels (and making a tidy profit themselves).

A silver half shekel, as used to pay the Temple Tax

Weirdly, the silver shekel had pagan images on it too! Oh well, at least it didn't have the hated Roman emperor on it....

So what with the animal-sellers, the money-changers, the tour guide operators (yes, they had them too), the priests in their tall hats advising people on what sacrifices to offer and the gift shops selling souvenirs (yes, they had them too!), the outer courtyard of the temple was a crowded marketplace.

For some Jews, the Temple seemed to have become a profit-driven business run by politicians rather than a place devoted to the worship of God. Traveling to Jerusalem every year as a pilgrim and paying for a sacrificial lamb at Passover was expensive too – putting the central religious worship of 1st century Judaism outside the reach of many ordinary people.

Reconstruction of what Herod's Temple looked like

Jesus & the Temple

Jesus visited the Temple when he arrived in Jerusalem for Passover. He clearly didn't like what he saw going on. Jesus started a noisy protest, overturning the tables of the money-changers and driving out the animals with a whip. He accused the businessmen and priests of turning the Temple into "*a den of thieves*".

Jesus also made a surprising announcement, claiming, "*Destroy this Temple and I will raise it up in 3 days*" (**John 2: 19-20**). Jesus is taking about *himself* being the true Temple and predicting his Resurrection. However, these words came back to haunt Jesus. At his trial, witnesses were produced who claimed he had said that *he* planned to destroy the Temple (which would have been blasphemy and terrorism). Given the protest Jesus had made with the money-changers, it's understandable how he might have left the impression he wanted to see the Temple destroyed.

> *Some critics argue that the outer court was so huge that Jesus' protest can't have been more than a minor disturbance. Nonetheless, it clearly made a big impression on the people in charge!*

The Sadducees

The **Sadducees** were the most influential religious group among the Jews. They were from the aristocratic families of Judea and they were used to wealth and privilege. They had very conservative (old fashioned) attitudes on many matters. They based their religious beliefs entirely on the **Torah** (the first 5 books of the Old Testament) and they took the laws in these scriptures very literally. For this reason, they concerned themselves with maintaining the Temple in Jerusalem and carrying out sacrifices as detailed in the Old Testament.

The Sadducees controlled the political life of Judea. Not all Temple priests were Sadducees, but the majority was and so were most of the people on the Sanhedrin; almost all the High Priests in the 1st century were Sadducees. The Sadducees were very wealthy and saw the Temple as the source of their power and prestige. The High Priest during Jesus' lifetime was **Joseph Caiaphas**. Caiaphas had been High Priest for 18 years, which suggests he was well-connected and probably a Sadducee.

As religious conservatives, the Sadducees resisted **Hellenic influences** (p48) in the Jewish religion. They did not accept the Greek philosophical notion of the immortal soul and did not believe in life after death. They rejected the idea of a spirit world inhabited by angels and seem to have been quite sceptical about miracles. Some sources suggest they were **Deists**, believing that God does not intervene in history.

> *After the destruction of the Temple in 70 CE, the Sadducees disappear. Without the Temple and its daily sacrifices, their religious code had no meaning.*

Jesus & the Sadducees

The Sadducees came from the opposite end of Jewish society from Jesus and his Galilean followers. Jesus' teachings about life after death bring him into conflict with Sadducees, who ask him awkward questions about the Afterlife. Jesus responds by referring to Moses and the Burning Bush, which is in the Torah (the books of the Old Testament the Sadducees respected most) and argues that the Torah implies there is life after death.

John's Gospel describes an emergency meeting of the Sanhedrin after Jesus raises Lazarus from the dead. The Sadducees seem concerned that the Romans will close down the Temple and destroy the country if Jesus carries on with his activities.

> *This turns out to be true: the Romans DID demolish the Temple when they invaded Judea in 70 CE after the Great Jewish Revolt, but hat had nothing to do with Jesus.*

Possibly, the Sadducees were offended by stories that Jesus could raise the dead – which was impossible according to their beliefs.

These philosophical debates escalate into something more serious when Jesus comes to Jerusalem for Passover – and before the week is over the High Priest has arrested Jesus and put him on trial before the Sanhedrin. The charges against Jesus are that he threatened to destroy the Temple (which would have alarmed the Sadducees), but the main charge that offends High Priest Caiaphas is that Jesus claims to be the Messiah.

The Pharisees

The Pharisees were the group that opposed the Sadducees. They lacked the wealth and political connections, but they were numerous and much more popular among the ordinary people, especially in areas far away from the Temple, like Galilee.

> *However, the two groups weren't entirely opposed. There were Pharisees who were priests at the Temple and some Pharisees were members of the ruling Sanhedrin.*

Whereas the Sadducees thought being a good Jew meant sticking to the rules in the Torah (first 5 books of the Old Testament) and keeping the sacrifices at the Temple going, the Pharisees taught a more personal sort of code. They had built up a huge body of rules that went beyond the Torah, based on traditions, prophets and philosophizing. These laws covered every area of Jewish life, from eating and washing to working, sex and death. The Pharisees' intention wasn't to tie people up in petty rules (though it might feel like that at times), but to provide Jews with a complete code for living which they could adopt in the middle of a pagan world and still remain faithful to their ancient faith.

Since they incorporated teachings that went beyond the Torah, the Pharisees held a number of **Hellenic ideas** (p48, though they perhaps didn't see these ideas as being 'Greek'). They believed in the immortal soul and in life after death. They believed in a spirit world inhabited by angels. However, in other ways they were quite anti-Hellenic: they believed Judaism provided a complete way of life that was superior to what was offered by the surrounding pagan culture.

> *After the destruction of the Temple in 70 CE, the Pharisees gained a lot of authority. Pharisees backed Simon Bar Kokhbar's revolt against the Romans and proclaimed him to be the Messiah. After the Romans destroyed Jerusalem and scattered the Jewish population, Pharisees disappeared but many of their ideas passed into the Rabbinical Judaism that emerged later (and is still around today).*

Jesus & the Pharisees

The Gospels show Jesus clashing with the Pharisees on many occasions. This makes sense, because Jesus travelled around ordinary Jewish towns like Capernaum where the Pharisees were the main religious group in Jewish society, far away from Jerusalem and the Temple.

Jesus condemns the Pharisees on many occasions for being spiritually proud. He accuses them of focusing too much on outward show of 'following the rules' and not enough on the inner state of loving God. He frequently calls them **HYPOCRITES**, meaning that they claim to stand for something good but in their private lives they are completely wicked.

> *Today, the word "pharisee" or "pharisaical" describes someone who is very arrogant and obsessed with imposing petty rules and regulations*

Matthew's Gospel has particularly heated attacks on the Pharisees. Jesus pronounces a series of "*woes*" (curses) on the Pharisees and others like them who treat religion as a set of rules to follow. He calls them "*snakes*" and compares them to "*whitewashed tombs*" that look good on the outside but are full of rot on the inside:

Jesus' criticisms focus on the Pharisees' concern with PURITY. By following the rules of Phariseeism, Jews could keep themselves ritually pure or "clean". If they broke the rules, they became impure. It was important to keep yourself in a state of purity before God, so the rules could become more important than basic values like loving your neighbour. Keeping the rules successfully could lead to spiritual pride, the feeling that you are holier than anyone else. The Pharisees seem to have avoided the company of publicans and the sick, because these people were IMPURE or UNCLEAN. Women were also considered unclean and excluded from Pharisee worship and prayer.

Jesus rejected Pharisee notions of purity and impurity. He associated with publicans and women. He ministered to the sick and the dead. He freely broke rules like the Sabbath restrictions. In the **Parable of the Pharisee & the Publican (Luke 18: 9-14)**, Jesus shows that God prefers a humble publican to a proud Pharisee.

> *The idea that sincerely repenting your sins and throwing yourself on the mercy of God is more important than following religious rules goes straight to the heart of Jesus' disagreements with the Pharisees*

However, Jesus also shared a lot in common with the Pharisees. He believed in many of the things they believed in: that faith was about more than sticking to the Torah and carrying out animal sacrifices in the Temple, that there was life after death. Some scholars argue that Jesus was himself a Pharisee (or a rogue Pharisee) and that his arguments with the Pharisees show that he was part of their group. Even the hostility in Jesus' arguments might show membership of this group because exaggerated arguments are part of the Jewish tradition of debate.

Two Pharisees are mentioned by name in the Gospels and both are influential members of the Sanhedrin. **Nicodemus** visits Jesus by night to learn his beliefs; **Joseph of Arimathea** also became a follower of Jesus. Both men are present at the Crucifixion and provide a burial for Jesus in a nearby tomb. This suggests that Jesus' relations with the Pharisees were not *entirely* hostile.

The Essenes

The Essenes were a smaller Jewish sect. They completely rejected the Temple in Jerusalem and the animal sacrifices that went on there. But they also rejected living in the pagan world, among the Gentiles, and trying to remain ritually pure by sticking to Pharisaical laws. Instead, the Essenes withdrew from the world to live in separate communities. In effect, the Essenes were monks. The sect was found in the 2nd century BCE after the Maccabean Revolt and their writings refer to the sect being inspired by a 'Teacher of Righteousness' who opposes a 'Wicked Priest' who has led mainstream Jews astray. This reflects the Essene belief that the Temple cult led by the Sadducees had become corrupt.

The main Essene communities were out in the Judean desert, far away from corrupt civilisation. However, some Essenes seem to have lived in cities, presumably in 'monasteries' where they could live separately from everyone else. The Essenes were ASCETICS (they gave up worldly pleasure) and they held all their possessions in common; many Essenes were CELIBATE (they gave up sex) but there seem to have been some Essene groups that allowed marriage. They seem to have been pacifists, but they carried weapons to defend themselves from bandits when traveling.

The interesting Essene practice is BAPTISM: a ritual washing away of sins. It seems the Essenes did this daily and preferred to be fully immersed in water (not just sprinkle it on their heads). This leads some scholars to wonder if **John the Baptist** was an Essene – or a rogue Essene leader who started his own movement. All four Gospels describe John the Baptist living an ascetic lifestyle in the desert and baptizing huge crowds in the River Jordan. However, John didn't seem to expect his followers to join a monastery or share his ascetic lifestyle.

The Essenes looked forward to two Messiahs (or perhaps one Messiah with two functions). A Priestly Messiah would restore pure worship to the Jews; a Kingly Messiah would lead a war against pagans and free the Jews from oppression.

The Essenes probably viewed themselves as getting back to a "pure" form of Judaism, but ironically their beliefs and practices were probably influenced by **Hellenism** (p48). Ancient Judaism didn't support celibacy or withdrawing from the world. This asceticism instead resembles the Cynic philosophy of the Greeks.

> *After the destruction of the Temple in 70 CE, the Essenes also faded from history. Without the Temple-cult to oppose, they probably lost their main reason for existing. Also, the Romans seem to have hunted down and destroyed Essene communities in case they were supporting the Zealots.*
>
> *One of these communities was Qumran near the Dead Sea. The people there hid their library in nearby caves and this library - the Dead Sea Scrolls - was discovered in the 1940s, incredibly intact. The DSS show us the earliest versions of the Old Testament and shed some light on the beliefs of the Essenes.*

Jesus & the Essenes

The Bible never mentions the Essenes, but could Jesus have been one? **Barbara Thiering** proposes that Jesus could have been the 'Teacher of Righteousness' described in the Dead Sea Scrolls.

There are problems with Thiering's view. The 'Teacher of Righteousness' would have lived over a hundred years before Jesus' time. But more importantly, the Essenes cut themselves off from the sinful world and kept their purity by living an ascetic lifestyle – whereas Jesus went to the towns of Galilee and to Jerusalem, he went to weddings, he drank wine and attended dinner parties and associated with publicans and other impure people.

On the other hand, Jesus begins his Ministry by being baptized by **John the Baptist**. Jesus' disciples baptized people too. This sounds like an Essene ritual. Moreover, if John the Baptist was an Essene, then if Jesus went to be baptized by John, he must have spent at least *some* time among the Essenes and been sympathetic to their beliefs and practices.

Furthermore, Jesus goes out into the desert to pray and fast for 40 days and night in the famous passage where he is tempted by the Devil. This sort of 'religious retreat' into the Judean desert seems to have been a common thing for religious 1st century Jews – and it seems that such retreats took place at Essene monasteries in the desert. Readers of the Bible often assume that Jesus was alone in the desert, but the Gospels don't say that. It would have been more normal for a pilgrim to go to a desert community to pray and fast alongside the Essenes.

Another interesting link comes from the **John's Gospel**, which frequently refers to Jesus as the **Light of the World** (p90, 123). The Light/Dark motif used to be viewed by scholars as a sign of **Hellenic influence** (p48) in John's Gospel rather than the teaching of a genuine 1st century Jew – in other words, John added this symbolism in but Jesus never really spoke that way.

However, the DSS (Dead Sea Scrolls) reveal that the Essenes referred to themselves as "*Children of the Light*" and the pagans and sinful Jews as "*Children of the Darkness*". So perhaps John's Gospel *does* preserve the way Jesus spoke, using symbolism inspired by the Essenes.

The Zealots

Josephus refers to the Zealots as a "*fourth philosophy*" after the Sadducees, Pharisees and Essenes. The Zealots were a military sect, dedicated to freeing the Jews from Roman occupation by violence. Josephus claims the Zealots were founded in 6 CE, when an uprising was led by Judas of Galilee and a priest named Zadok. However, violent religious fanatics date back before this and the Zealots probably emerged during the Maccabean Revolt in the 2nd century BCE. In the 1st century, the Zealots particularly objected to paying taxes to Rome.

The Zealots were probably a diverse lot. Some of them might have been gangs of bandits who justified their criminal activities with religious claims, but others were genuine freedom fighters who expected a **Kingly Messiah** to lead them in their war against the Roman Empire; most of the time they engaged in guerrilla warfare. Sometimes their targets were other Jews, like the publicans and the Sadducees who collaborated with the Roman regime. Josephus mentions the *sicarii* ("dagger-men") who would hide knives in their robes, mingle with crowds and assassinate Jewish enemies – or even random strangers, in an attempt to spread terror. In 56 CE, they assassinated High Priest Jonathan, right in the middle of the Temple.

The existence of the Zealots explains why the Romans were so nervous about uprisings. Any popular leader who attracted huge crowds was potentially a Zealot recruiter – and large crowds attracted the *sicarii* to do their indiscriminate killings.

> *The Zealots had their moment in 66 CE. Protests against taxes turned into a full scale rebellion that swept the Romans out of Judea. A Jewish government was created in Jerusalem, with many Zealots in top positions. The Romans returned and in 70 CE, Jerusalem was captured. The Temple was demolished. The Zealots had a last stand at the desert fortress of Masada. In 73 CE, these Zealots committed mass suicide rather than surrender to the Romans.*

Jesus & the Zealots

Obviously, Jesus was completely opposed to the Zealots' violent philosophy. Jesus urged his followers to put away weapons and respond to violence with peace:

> *But I tell you, do not resist an evil person. If anyone slaps you on the right cheek, turn to them the other cheek also* – **Matthew 5: 39**

Jesus is questioned on his attitude to paying tax. The Gospels present this question as a 'trap' – if Jesus urges Jews not to pay taxes he is siding with the Zealots but if he supports the Romans then he is an enemy of the Jewish people. Jesus answers carefully, saying that people should give God what God demands (worship and moral living) and give money but not worship to Caesar.

However, one of Jesus' Twelve Disciples was **Simon the Zealot**. Why would Jesus recruit a Zealot to his group? Scholars propose that Simon the Zealot was recruited to balance Matthew the Tax Collector (a publican). These were two people who should hate each other, so their working together would demonstrate the love and forgiveness that Jesus taught exists in the **Kingdom of God**.

Another Disciple was **Judas Iscariot**, who betrayed Jesus. There are many theories about what the name 'Iscariot' means, but one theory is that it means *sicarius* – so Judas was one of the extremist *sicarii* dagger-men. However, this translation isn't certain and Josephus claims the *sicarii* only appeared in the 50s CE, a couple of decades **after** Jesus.

R.F. Brandon argues that Judas was a Zealot assassin and Jesus was a revolutionary political leader who everyone expected would raise an army against Rome. However, Jesus (wisely) rejected a violent revolution, realising military uprisings were doomed, and embraced pacifism instead. Brandon thinks this is why Judas betrayed him – for abandoning the Zealot cause. This is a colourful interpretation, but there's not enough evidence to support it.

What seems more certain is that the Romans **mistook** Jesus' movement for a gang of Zealots. Jesus was crucified between two other prisoners, described as *lestai* by **Mark** and **Matthew** – a word sometimes translated as "thieves" but really meaning "rebels". The same word is used to describe **Barabbas**, the "*notorious prisoner*" being tried at the same time as Jesus for his part in an "*uprising*". The Gospels describe the Roman governor Pontius Pilate releasing Barabbas rather than Jesus at the insistence of a mob.

Can we understand Jesus better by viewing him in the context of these Jewish groups?

YES

As a member of the royal **Davidic line**, Jesus belongs to the class the Sadducees came from, but his opposition to the Temple suggests he was inspired by the Essenes, as does his connection to John the Baptist and habit of retreating into the desert for fasting and prayer. Jesus specifically opposed the legalism of the Pharisees but shared their debating techniques. His enemies persuaded the Romans that he was a Zealot.

NO

Jesus is the **Son of God** and his teaching comes directly from God, not from any human source. Jesus says of himself "*the son can do nothing by himself; he can do only what he sees his father doing, because whatever the father does the son also does*" (**John 5: 19**). Therefore it's a mistake to try to understand Jesus by looking at the flawed or corrupt religious groups surrounding him.

Even if Jesus is the **Son of God**, he has a human and a divine nature. Jesus' humanity will be formed like all human nature, through social relationships and as part of a community. This means that even if Jesus' teachings are divinely inspired, they will have a human side too inspired by the people Jesus knew growing up: certainly the Pharisees and possibly the Essenes too.

The four sects or philosophies in 1st century Judaism were all destroyed before the century ended: they disappeared after the Temple was destroyed in 70 CE. We now know very little about them, except for (probably biased) passages in Josephus. Whereas Jesus' teachings have lasted 2000 years and are witnessed in all four Gospels. The best way to understand Jesus is with reference to the Bible, not Jewish sects.

TOPIC 1 KEY SCHOLARS

Raymond E Brown

Topic: 1.1 Prophecy regarding the Messiah

Raymond E Brown (1928-1998) is an American Roman Catholic priest and Bible scholar whose work features in other topics in this course too **(2.2 Titles of Jesus, 2.3 Miracles & Signs** and **3.2 Purpose & Authorship of the Fourth Gospel)**.

Brown's contribution to this topic comes largely through his last book *Birth of the Messiah* (1998). This massive work examines the birth narratives in Matthew and Luke in close detail. Even though he's a Roman Catholic scholar, Brown's research and even-handedness make this a book Protestant Christians will refer to as well.

However, Brown is a liberal Christian and questions some of the beliefs Christians have taken for granted over the years. He regards the Bible as a human document, not a divine book. He interprets the birth narratives as works of fiction, created by the Gospelists to tell stories that reflect their beliefs about Jesus. For example, Matthew communicates his beliefs about Jesus being the Messiah, the 'new Moses' and the Son of David and writes to reassure Gentile Christians that the Messiah is important to them. Brown calls the Matthean birth narrative *"an attractive drama that catches the imagination."*

An example of the **Matthew's birth-narrative** (p33) being a human document would be the famous proof-text from **Isaiah** about a virgin conceiving and giving birth. Brown identifies the Hebrew word "*almah*" to describe the mother: *almah* means "young woman" but not necessarily a virgin; Hebrew has another word, "*bethulah*", which means a virgin. However, when the Old Testament was translated into Greek, *almah* was translated as "*parthenos*", a Greek word which definitely means 'virgin'. Matthew used the Greek Old Testament and may have misunderstood what Isaiah had been saying.

An example of the birth narrative appealing to different audiences and 'catching the imagination' would be Matthew's genealogy (family tree) which links Jesus back to Abraham as well as King David. Matthew's Jewish audience would be interested in Jesus' descent from King David but a Gentile (non-Jewish) audience would be more interested in Abraham, because God had promised a descendant of Abraham would bring a blessing to "*all peoples on earth*"- including the Gentiles. Jesus is therefore the promised Messiah for **both** groups.

Because of his liberal views on how Matthew's birth narrative came to be written, Brown's conclusions are rejected by fundamentalist and some conservative Christians. These groups regard the Bible as INERRANT (without error). These Christian readers try to HARMONISE the discrepancies between the birth narratives and genealogies in Matthew and Luke into a single story. They also take the Virgin Birth literally and interpret the Old Testament prophecies in a **futurist** sense as referring to the birth of Jesus rather than the events of 600-700 years before.

Morna Hooker

Topic: 1.1 Prophecy regarding the Messiah

Morna Hooker (b. 1938) is a Professor at Cambridge University and a Bible scholar whose work also features in another topic in this course **(2.1 Prologue in John)**.

Hooker wrote a slim (only 80 pages) introduction to New Testament scholarship called **_Beginnings: Keys that Open the Gospels_** (1998). It's a very readable book and available cheap from online booksellers so I'd recommend it for all students. She argues that each Gospel has a prologue that works as a "*key*" to "*unlock*" the main themes and teachings about Jesus. Matthew's prologue describes the circumstances of Jesus' birth in Bethlehem and how his family ended up living in Nazareth in Galilee. Hooker calls Matthew's Prologue the "*prophetic key*" because it focuses on Jesus as the Messiah and 'second Moses' predicted by the Old Testament prophets.

> *If you enjoyed* **Beginnings***, then Hooker's* **Endings: Invitations to Discipleship** *(2003) covers the endings of the 4 Gospels and ties in with the issues raised in Topics 5 and 6 concerning the Resurrection. It's slightly longer than beginnings, but still a very slim book.*

Much of Hooker's career has been taken up with arguing against various theories that try to construct a 'historical Jesus' that is different from the Jesus Christ of Christian faith. In **_The Gospel According to St Mark_** (1993), Hooker demolishes Wrede's famous theory of the **Messianic Secret** (p26). Hooker argues against Wrede, and claims that that the descriptions of Jesus being called the Messiah are historical and were not invented later by Christians. Hooker thinks it is plausible that Jesus would have tried to 'play down' his identity as the promised Messiah, because it was too politically explosive and would have distracted from his mission. She says, "'*if he believed himself to be in any sense the Messiah, the last thing he would do was to claim the title for himself*'.

> *In* **Topic 3.1***, you will learn how Wrede's theory is part of* **Redaction Criticism** *and Hooker's response to it is part of a backlash against this approach to interpreting the texts of the New Testament.*

However, Hooker is not a conservative Christian scholar. In her first book, **_Jesus & the Servant_** (1959), she argues against the view the Suffering Servant in **Isaiah's Servant Songs** (p20) is supposed to predict Jesus. Hooker goes through Isaiah's "Servant Songs" line by line and then goes through the synoptic Gospels (Matthew, Mark and Luke) line by line, looking for links but does not find a definite connection. She ends up placing the Servant Songs within the framework of Isaiah as a whole, arguing the message can be summed up as: "*Israel, who has been chosen by Yahweh as his servant, is to be restored from Exile and will manifest God's glory to all nations*". In other words, the Servant represents the Jewish nation collectively, not the future Messiah.

This is an unpopular view with people who think Isaiah is specifically predicting the death and Resurrection of Jesus, but it links her to **Raymond E. Brown** who also interprets Old Testament prophecies in a preterist rather than a futurist sense.

TOPIC 2: INTERPRETATION OF THE PERSON OF JESUS

The Prologue in John
- The meaning and theological significance, including ideas about the nature and person of Jesus, the Word made flesh, concepts of life, light and dark, belief, children of God, flesh and spirit, law, grace and truth.
- The influences of Judaism and Hellenism and the importance of these themes in understanding the gospel.
- The implication for religious laws and codes for living of different understandings of the identity and message of Jesus, including its influence beyond a religious community.
- With reference to the ideas of C.H. Dodd and Morna Hooker.

Titles of Jesus in the synoptic gospels and selected 'I am' sayings in John
- The meaning and significance of the terms Messiah, Son of God, Son of Man, and 'I am the bread of life/light of the world/good shepherd/true vine'.
- The background and context of these titles, including Old Testament references and symbolism and the importance of these for interpreting and understanding the Gospels.
- The implication for religious laws and codes for living of different understandings of the identity and message of Jesus, including its influence beyond a religious community.
- With reference to the ideas of Raymond E. Brown and C.H. Dodd.

Miracles and signs
- The meaning and significance of the signs in the Fourth Gospel: Turning water into wine, the Healing of the Official's son, the Healing at the pool, the Feeding of the 5000, Walking on water, the Healing of the blind man and the Raising of Lazarus.
- Ideas about the identity and role of Jesus and the importance of these signs for understanding Jesus' ministry.
- The implication for religious laws and codes for living of different understandings of the identity and message of Jesus.
- With reference to the ideas of Raymond E. Brown and C.H. Dodd.

TOPIC 2: INTERPRETATION OF THE PERSON OF JESUS

Who was Jesus - who did he claim to be and what did his followers think this meant? This unit looks at the identity of Jesus as it is explored in **John's Gospel**, a book with particularly intriguing symbols and a number of miracles which reveal more about who Christians believe Jesus to be.

THE PROLOGUE IN JOHN

This topic looks at the first 18 verses in John - the Johannine Prologue - and ideas about **the Word made flesh, light and dark, life, children of God, flesh and spirit, belief** and **law**, and **grace and truth**. The key scholars are **C.H. Dodd** and **Morna Hooker**.

MIRACLES & SIGNS

This topic looks at the 7 'Signs' (miracles) in John: **turning water into wine, healing the official's son, the healing at the pool, feeding the 5000, walking on water, healing the blind man** and **raising Lazarus**. Key scholars are **Raymond E. Brown** and **C.H. Dodd**.

TITLES OF JESUS & THE 'I AM' SAYINGS

This topic looks at the Jesus' titles in the Synoptic Gospels, including **Messiah, Son of God** and **Son of Man** as well as **Johannine "I Am" sayings** like **Bread of Life, Light of the World, Good Shepherd** and **True Vine**. The key scholars are **Raymond E. Brown** and **C.H. Dodd**.

Before you go any further...

... there are some things you need to know.

The Synoptic Gospels

The first three Gospels (**Matthew**, **Mark** and **Luke**) are known as the SYNOPTIC GOSPELS. 'Synoptic' means 'seen together'. These Gospels share many passages which are word-for-word the same and other passages which differ only slightly in wording (usually because sentences have been added in or taken out). These Gospels also present Jesus' story in a very similar way:

- Jesus is baptized by John the Baptist and goes into the desert to be tempted
- Jesus starts a year-long Ministry travelling around Galilee but mostly based in Capernaum
- Jesus performs many miracles, casting out demons from people who are ill or insane
- Jesus preaches about the arrival of the **Kingdom of God** or (as Matthew calls it) the Kingdom of Heaven
- Finally, Jesus travels to Jerusalem for Passover, which is where he is crucified.

In the Synoptic Gospels, Jesus confronts the Devil a lot

In the Synoptic Gospels, Jesus uses a lot of short but memorable sayings and preaches using **Parables** (stories which carry a symbolic meaning).

John AKA 'the Fourth Gospel'

The **Gospel of John** is very different in structure, style and content from the Synoptics. There are many stories in the Synoptic Gospels that don't appear in John and several famous stories in John that appear nowhere else.

Some of the differences in the Johannine version (i.e. John's version) of Jesus' story include:

- No reference to **John the Baptist** baptizing Jesus or the Devil tempting Jesus
- Jesus' Ministry takes place over 3 years with multiple journeys between Galilee and Jerusalem
- Only **7 'Signs'** (John never uses the term 'miracle') and no casting out evil spirits
- Jesus preaches about **Eternal Life** (p87), less about the **Kingdom of God** (c.f. **Topic 5**)
- Jesus is crucified before Passover and John does not describe the **Last Supper**

In John's Gospel, there are no **Parables**. Instead Jesus speaks in lengthy **'Discourses'** full of symbolism and allegory (although some of the ideas from the Parables in the Synoptic Gospels reappear in the Discourses in John). Even where John does contain the same stories or speeches as the Synoptic Gospels, John words them completely differently.

John's Gospel is sometimes called **'The Fourth Gospel'**. This is for two reasons:

- It's only tradition that says the Gospel was written by John (p206); the text doesn't actually name the author
- There are lots of other Johns in the Bible so calling this Gospel 'John' can be confusing. For example, there are three Epistles (letters) in the New Testament called **1 John**, **2 John** and **3 John**; the **Book of Revelation** of written by someone (else) called John; and there is the character of **John the Baptist** who appears in every Gospel

Why the difference?

First of all, there may not *be* a difference. Many Christians HARMONISE the Gospels and assume that the Synoptics and John describe the same story from different viewpoints. So maybe Jesus' Ministry lasted 3 years but the Synoptics only focus on the last year of it; Jesus made several journeys to Jerusalem but the Synoptics are only interested in the last one; John the Baptist *did* baptize Jesus but John's Gospel (*see the problem with calling it 'John'?*) neglects to mention this; and so on.

> *Harmonising John and the Synoptics isn't always easy. For example, John describes Jesus going to the Temple and driving out the money-changers at the START of his Ministry and the Synoptics describe it happening at the END. To harmonise this, you have to conclude Jesus did this twice, three years apart.*

Another view is that **John's Gospel** was written much later than the Synoptics and might be more inaccurate. Scholars who support this view point out the amount of Greek philosophical terminology in **John** and the very developed view of who Jesus is (a "high Christology" – p76) as evidence that it comes from the 2nd century CE, not the 1st century.

However, the discovery of the **Dead Sea Scrolls** (DSS) shows that this sort of philosophical language was being used by other Jewish writers in the 1st century, so John might not be that late after all. Also, John includes many precise details about **1st century Palestine** and expressions from the original Aramaic language that Jesus spoke which lead scholars like **Bishop John Robinson** to conclude there *is* eyewitness testimony in John's Gospel.

A common distinction is that the Synoptic Gospels contain records of the actual sayings of Jesus (the IPSISSIMA VERBA - the 'very word') but that John's Gospel contains a sort of faithful summary which captures the 'voice' or 'meaning' of Jesus (the IPSISSIMA VOX - the 'very voice') even though it isn't historically accurate.

'High' vs 'Low' Christology

'Christology' is a theory about the identity of Jesus.

- Jesus was God himself, incarnated (in human form)

- Jesus is an angel or spirit sent from God who was incarnated (took human form) to look like a human being

- Jesus is a human being who was exalted (raised up to a superhuman state)) by God at the start of his life, to carry out God's work

- Jesus is a human being who was exalted (raised up to a superhuman state) by God after death as a reward for his loyalty and goodness

- Jesus is a human prophet, passing on wisdom revealed to him from God

- Jesus is a wise teacher with many insights into morality and religion

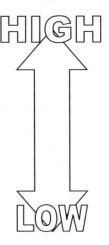

As you can see, 'low' Christology emphasizes how human Jesus is; 'high' Christology emphasizes how divine Jesus is.

Bart Ehrman prefers to use the terms EXALTATION THEOLOGY (to describe the idea that Jesus started out human but got 'promoted' to superhuman status by God) and INCARNATION THEOLOGY (to describe the idea that Jesus was superhuman from birth and existed as a supernatural being before he was born a human).

The **Synoptic Gospels** vary in their Christology, but contain many moments of 'low' Christology (such as showing Jesus making mistakes, losing his temper or behaving in a very human way). **John's Gospel** has a very 'high' Christology; the Johannine Jesus (Jesus as represented in John's Gospel) is a supernatural being who never makes mistakes or loses control of the situation.

> *But what sort of Christology represents the real Jesus?*

TOPIC 2.1 THE PROLOGUE IN JOHN

John's Gospel begins in an unusual way. **Matthew** and **Luke** both begin with Jesus' birth and **Mark** begins later, with Jesus' baptism by **John the Baptist**. But **John's Gospel** begins with the Creation of the Universe and a mystical poem that never mentions Jesus by name, but still links him to God, the events of the Old Testament and John the Baptist.

What is the Prologue in John?

John's Gospel is the fourth and last Gospel in the New Testament. It is very different from the previous three Synoptic Gospels and this becomes apparent straight away with the Prologue. A 'prologue' is an introductory passage at the start of a longer work that sets out the main themes and concerns. The other Gospels have Prologues too (for example, the **Birth Narrative in Matthew**, p33) but John's Prologue is a lengthy (18 verse) poem about Jesus that doesn't mention Jesus by name until the very end.

Morna Hooker claims that each Gospel has a prologue that works as a "*key*" to "*unlock*" the main themes and teachings of the Gospel that follows.

> *The beginning of the story hints at the ideas that will be made plain at the end* – **Morna Hooker**

She calls John's Prologue the "*Glorious Key*" because it focuses on the "*glory*" of Christ – his supernatural character as a divine being on Earth.

Most scholars recognise the Prologue as a hymn that sums up John's view of Jesus Christ. It might have been a hymn that was actually sung at church meetings and was added onto the Gospel later. In support of this view, there is a big change in style from the Prologue itself to the rest of the Gospel story and some of the terms that are important in the Prologue (such as 'Logos') don't actually turn up again in the rest of the Gospel.

However, **Morna Hooker** disagrees with this, arguing that there is a prologue in all four Gospels and a sense of a 'break' or discontinuity where each prologue ends and the main Gospel begins.

> *These passages form Anthology extract #2, so you need to be familiar with them all in a general sort of way and you should be able to analyse one or two parts in depth*

1 In the beginning was the Word, and the Word was with God, and the Word was God. [2] He was with God in the beginning. [3] Through him all things were made; without him nothing was made that has been made. [4] In him was life, and that life was the light of all mankind. [5] The light shines in the darkness, and the darkness has not overcome it.

The Prologue begins with the phrase "*in the beginning*" – repeating the **opening words of the Book of Genesis**. It also introduces the symbol of **Light** (p90), which echoes God's **first creative act in Genesis: creating light**. The author is composing a new Genesis for a new world and a new religion, but one heavily based on the Jewish traditions of the Old Testament. The Prologue also introduces the **Word of God** as a separate force in Creation: a force that is somehow separate from God but also the same as God. The Greek term used for this Word is **'Logos'** (p81). The Prologue doesn't yet link this Logos to Jesus – that will come later.

> ⁶ There was a man sent from God whose name was John. ⁷ He came as a witness to testify concerning that light, so that through him all might believe. ⁸ He himself was not the light; he came only as a witness to the light.

This passage feels like an interruption and some scholars think it originally came from a separate poem and that the two were merged together. This 'John' is not the author of the Gospel, but rather **John the Baptist** (*right*), who is important at the start of all the other Gospels. The author does not refer to John as 'the Baptist' and does not refer to any baptisms. Instead he presents John as a "*witness*" to God's work. The author takes pains to point out that John is NOT the Logos/Light that was being referred to in the previous passage – this is somebody else (it is Jesus of course, as will become apparent later).

The trouble the author takes to play down John's status is interesting. Some scholars think there might have been a rival group that worshiped John the Baptist instead of Jesus. The author makes it clear that John is important, but he's not the star of the show.

> ⁹ The true light that gives light to everyone was coming into the world. ¹⁰ He was in the world, and though the world was made through him, the world did not recognize him. ¹¹ He came to that which was his own, but his own did not receive him. ¹² Yet to all who did receive him, to those who believed in his name, he gave the right to become children of God – ¹³ children born not of natural descent, nor of human decision or a husband's will, but born of God.

We're back to the "*true light*" (as opposed to John the Baptist) and this Light is "*coming into the world.*" This is the key Johannine idea of **INCARNATION** – a **divine force from the beginning of time** entering **the physical world**.

This passage also introduces another key Johannine theme of MISTAKEN IDENTITY – the Light from God is not recognised by people when they meet him. Finally there is the third theme here which is BECOMING CHILDREN OF GOD THROUGH FAITH – the idea that **believing** (p93) in the **Light** (p90) changes humans from **ordinary creatures into divine beings**.

> [14] The Word became flesh and made his dwelling among us. We have seen his glory, the glory of the one and only Son, who came from the Father, full of grace and truth.

The author becomes very explicit here. **The Word of God has become a human being** (p81) and lived a human life on Earth. The author claims people have met this person and recognised him for the divine force he really was in a **life-changing religious experience**. However, although it's becoming really obvious now who this Logos/Light is, the name of Jesus still hasn't been mentioned.

It's interesting that the author says "*we have seen*" rather than "I have seen". Scholars suggest that the Gospel might have been the work of more than one person – a **JOHANNINE COMMUNITY** – and that these people have seen the "*glory*" of Jesus Christ (i.e. they've encountered Christ in religious experiences) but also trace their understanding of Jesus Christ back to someone who actually met him in life. This eyewitness is referred to later in John's Gospel as the BELOVED DISCIPLE (p207).

> [15] (John testified concerning him. He cried out, saying, "This is the one I spoke about when I said, 'He who comes after me has surpassed me because he was before me.'") [16] Out of his fullness we have all received grace in place of grace already given. [17] For the law was given through Moses; grace and truth came through Jesus Christ. [18] No one has ever seen God, but the one and only Son, who is himself God and is in closest relationship with the Father, has made him known.

The different themes in the Prologue are drawn together at last. John the Baptist reappears, reinforcing the idea that Jesus "*surpasses*" him and that Jesus was in some sense "*before*" John even though, historically, Jesus' ministry only began after John the Baptist had been arrested and executed by Herod Antipas. This makes sense if we understand that Jesus is really the Logos/Light who has been around since "*the beginning*".

Finally, the author identifies **Jesus Christ** as the Logos/Light and goes further still: Jesus is the replacement for **Moses**, the greatest Jewish prophet who brought the Law of God down from Mount Sinai. In the Old Testament, Moses was privileged to see a glimpse of God's back, but not the face of God. Jesus however has seen God face-to-face. This means that Moses' understanding of God was imperfect but Jesus offers the **Truth** (p106) – and hence Christianity replaces Judaism as the true religion of God.

Raymond E. Brown speculates that the **Johannine Community** (p208) was a group of Jewish Christians who had been banished from the Jewish Synagogue for their beliefs and put under a curse by their former Jewish friends and neighbours. This traumatic break would explain the hostility towards "*the Jews*" in John's Gospel and the way in which the Prologue radically reinterprets **Genesis** and **Exodus** – the foundational Jewish texts about Creation and God's revelation to **Moses** – to refer to Jesus Christ instead.

Evaluating the Prologue

The Prologue presents a very different perspective on Jesus from the Synoptics. It's not just what is new here (Jesus as the **Word of God made flesh**, p81), but what's missing.

- There's no reference to the **Messiah** (p12) or the **line of David** (p15) – although John does later mention these things, they are much less important in his Gospel.
- You would never know from the Prologue alone that Jesus performed miracles and cast out demons as he does in the Synoptic Gospels – and indeed, there are only 7 miracles in John's Gospel (they are called **Signs**, p135) and there are no references to evil spirits.
- There is no reference to the Kingdom of God arriving on Earth – while John does later mention it, this Gospel is much more concerned with **Eternal Life** (p87).
- There's no **Birth Narrative** like in **Matthew** (p33) and **Luke**; indeed Jesus' mother Mary is never named in John's Gospel and there is no reference to John the Baptist baptizing people.

One explanation for this is that John's Gospel is of late composition: it was written after the original family and friends of Jesus had died, by someone who had never known him in life and who did not share Jesus' original concerns. The Gospel uses **Hellenic terms** (like 'Logos' for the Word of God) which show that it comes from the Greek world rather than the Jewish one that Jesus inhabited.

However, **C.H. Dodd** argues against this view, pointing out the similarity between John's language and the Old Testament; other scholars point out similarities between John's language and the Dead Sea Scrolls as proof that 1st century Jews did think and write this way.

John's ideas have been hugely influential on Christian teaching and John's Gospel is the most loved Gospel by most ordinary Christians, especially Evangelical (Born Again) Christians. However, it can be criticised for its lack of social teaching. The other Synoptic Gospels have a political message for society: Jesus has things to say about poverty, peace and justice. John's Gospel, as the Prologue suggests, is much more **mystical**.

The Word became Flesh

John's Gospel begins with an unusual term not found in the other Gospels. This is the idea of the **Word of God** as a force in the universe that is *separate* from God, but somehow still *the same as* God. John's Gospel claims that this force entered the human world in a special way in the life of Jesus Christ. But what exactly *is* the Word of God and how can it be *the same thing* as a human being?

What is the Word/Logos?

The Prologue starts off by saying that the Word is something that existed "*in the beginning,*" that it was "*with God*" but that it also *"was God."* How can something be *separate from* God and at the same time be *the same as* God?

One way of looking like it is by comparing the Word of God to ordinary human speech or expression. When you say or write things, your words are separate from you, but they are also "you" in an important sense. If you make a promise or a threat, you can't say afterwards "Oh, my *words* said that but it wasn't really *me* saying it." In an important sense, your words ARE you: they express your purposes and feelings. But they also have a 'life of their own': they can be recorded, passed on, translated, even 'used against you'. There is a sense in which your words ARE you and another sense in which they are WITH you, but separate from you.

> *You could compare this to online profiles and avatars. Your online presence in a way is separate from you, but it also IS you - you can be prosecuted for things you say online, for example. (However, you existed before you created your online identity - whereas the Logos seems to have been with God always.)*

The Prologue introduces the idea that God also has a **Word** – an expression of himself – which is part of who God is but which also has a life of its own. This isn't saying that there are two Gods or a split-personality God. It's saying that as well as the remote unchanging God, there is also the activity of God in the world.

The Greek word that John's Gospel uses for 'Word' is **LOGOS**. Logos can mean 'Word' but it also means 'Plan' or 'Thought' or 'Wisdom'. The Logos could be thought of as the 'Mind of God'. The Logos is an aspect of God or an expression of God; in some ways it is less powerful than God, but it's involved with everything that God does in the world. God himself is utterly unknowable and beyond human comprehension, but the Logos can be understood by humans because it was God's Logos that created us.

The idea of separating the concept of 'God' into the **transcendent Deity** who is outside the world and the **Divine Spirit** that creates the world and interacts with the world has several philosophical strengths. It helps explain how a God who is **Eternal and Impassable** can also interact with the world and with humans in time; it explains the point of prayer (the Logos can respond to your prayers but God himself is too far removed for this) and it may help understand the **problem of evil** (because the Logos might respect human freewill even if God himself is capable of overruling it).

> *There is a sense in which we only know people through speech and behaviour, the things they say and do - their personal 'logos'. But there's another sense in which there's more to you than just the stuff you say and do: that's the 'outer you' but there's also the 'inner you' which people never really know directly. Anyone who wants to get to know you properly has to do so through paying attention to your words and actions - your logos - but there's more to you than that: your words and actions point to the 'real you' but they're not the same as the 'real you'. In the same way, God's Logos is the only way we have of knowing what God is like.*

The religious debate about the Logos is whether it should be viewed as an impersonal force - God's blueprint for the universe, rather like a computer program or a string of genetic code – or a spiritual being. Both views existed in the 1st century.

Influences of Hellenism

The word 'Logos' is Greek and the term was used by pagan Greek philosophers. **Heraclitus** coined the term in the 6th century BCE to describe processes in nature that seemed ordered and rational (an early version of the **Design Argument**). **Aristotle** uses 'Logos' to mean the power of reason itself, the ability to change people's minds through logic. The **Stoic philosophers** brought these two ideas together: for them, 'Logos' was **ANIMA MUNDI** (the World Soul) that binds the universe together according to logical principles (the word 'logical' comes from the word 'logos').

The Hellenic concept of the Logos is **IMPERSONAL**. The Logos is not a being or a person; it doesn't have a personality. In modern thought, the Logos would be the scientific laws.

Scholars used to think that the Logos was en entirely Hellenic concept, showing that John's Gospel comes from the world of Greek philosophy, not from the Jewish world of Jesus. However, **C.H. Dodd** challenges this view and shows that the Logos links to the way God is described in the Old Testament too.

Influences of Judaism

The Jews had a different concept of God's Word. God creates the world by *speaking*:

> *God said, 'Let there be light,' and there was light* – **Genesis 1: 3**

It is also God's *words* that Moses hears:

> *God called to him from within the bush, "Moses! Moses!" And Moses said, "Here I am."* – **Exodus 3: 4**

Although it is impossible for human beings to *see* God, the Prophets can *hear God's voice*. This led many Jews to think of God's Word as something separate from God himself and more accessible. They PERSONIFIED this Word of God as the concept of **Holy Wisdom.**

Wisdom is seen as coming from God and sharing his goodness with the world. Two Jewish books written between the end of the Old Testament and the beginning of the New Testament are the **Wisdom of Solomon** and the **Book of Sirach** and they explore this idea further:

> *she is a reflection of eternal light, a spotless mirror of the working of God, and an image of his goodness* – **Wisdom 7: 26**

This quote links Holy Wisdom to **'Light'** (p90) as the first of God's creations

Wisdom is sent by God to make her 'dwelling' among mankind. Specifically, God sends Holy Wisdom to *dwell among* the Jews.

> *Then the Creator of all things gave me a command, and my Creator chose the place for my tent. He said, 'Make your dwelling in Jacob, and in Israel receive your inheritance'* – **Sirach 24: 8**

Philo of Alexandria

Philo (20 BCE - 50 CE) was a **Hellenized** Jew living in Alexandria in Egypt – a great centre of education in the Roman Empire. Philo HARMONISED the Jewish religion with Hellenic philosophy (particularly the ideas of Plato and the Stoics). Philo is the first person to use the word 'Logos' to describe the Holy Wisdom of God.

Philo would have been an older contemporary of Jesus, so it's perhaps unlikely that Jesus or his Disciples used the word 'Logos' the way Philo did. However, by the time John's Gospel came to be written, Philo's ideas were more widely known to educated Jews. Or perhaps the author of John's Gospel chose to use the word 'Logos' independently of Philo to describe the Holy Wisdom of God.

How does the Word "become flesh"?

John's Gospel says that, "*the Word became flesh and made his dwelling among us*". The idea of something spiritual taking on a physical form is known as **INCARNATION**. So John is saying that the Word of God became incarnated as a human being.

The phrase "*made his dwelling*" (i.e. 'came to live') echoes the idea of Holy Wisdom *making her dwelling* on Earth among the Jews. However, Judaism does **not** think of Holy Wisdom becoming a human being. Wisdom *makes her dwelling* on Earth temporarily, to inspire prophets and guide people through prayers. Many Jews would say that the only permanent, physical dwelling place for Holy Wisdom is in the **Torah**, the sacred texts of Judaism. That's why the Torah is a holy book – Wisdom *dwells* (lives) in the words.

The pagan Greeks had no problem with the idea of incarnation. In Greek and Roman myths, gods and goddesses incarnate into human or animal form all the time. **Zeus** often takes physical form to visit his lovers on Earth. Other gods take physical form to visit heroes and pass messages (or threats) on to humans. There are also **demigods**, who are the children of a union between a human and an incarnated god. The most famous demigod is **Hercules** who was born with much of the power of his father, Zeus.

However, the gods only incarnate briefly as a human, then they go back to their life as gods: they are not born as human babies, they don't grow up over many years and they don't die a human death. The demigods live a human life and can die too, However, they are sort of god/human hybrids, half-human and half-god. John's Gospel describes the Word becoming flesh more completely than this: fully human and fully divine at the same time.

There's *no concept* in Hellenic thought of the Logos becoming a human being any more than there is a concept in Judaism of Holy Wisdom becoming a human being, so this idea seems to be entirely new to John's Gospel.

Implications of the Word becoming Flesh

The other Gospels describe Jesus as the 'Son of God' (p112), but they are not always clear about what this means. Is Jesus a holy prophet blessed by God, a 'Second Moses' as Matthew's Gospel presents him? Is he a human being **exalted** (raised up) by God for his loyalty and obedience in going to be crucified?

John's Gospel settles the matter right at the start: Jesus is the incarnated Logos, the Word of God made flesh. He is the being who created the universe, spoke to Moses and inspired the prophets, only now he's here 'in person'. He's not just a 'Second Moses': he's the *source* of Moses' revelation, the voice that spoke out of the Burning Bush and from the thunder on Mount Sinai. Jesus is the plan and the purpose behind the whole Jewish religion, behind all the prophets and behind the Torah; this is what the Logos is – the reason behind everything – only now living on Earth as a human.

Morna Hooker points out how shocking and divisive these views must have been in 1st century Palestine:

> *The followers of Jesus were claiming that what he did and said was nothing less than the works and words of God himself; on the other, their opponents dismissed such claims as blasphemous* – **Morna Hooker**

Morna Hooker explains that it's important not to get confused here. John is *not* saying that the human Jesus of Nazareth existed at the dawn of time and inspired the prophets. He is saying that a divine quality that has always existed (**pre-existent**) became incarnated in Jesus. After the Resurrection, the human person of Jesus becomes divine too. This is **APOTHEOSIS**, a human becoming God. But Jesus himself was not pre-existent (having an existence before he was born); it was the Logos that existed before Jesus.

Further implications: the Holy Trinity

Later Christians had to work out the full implications of this. When Jesus died on the Cross, was that his human nature dying, but did his divine nature survive? Or did the Logos die too – is that even possible? When the **Holy Spirit** visits the Apostles at **Pentecost (Acts 2: 1-12)**, is that the Logos too or another expression of God? Later Christians would work out the concept of the **TRINITY** – God as Three Persons who share One Nature: Father, Son and Holy Spirit – and John's Gospel starts this theological debate but doesn't settle it.

- **THE FATHER:** The transcendence of God; the Father is impassable (nothing can affect him) and ineffable (cannot be described). This is the NECESSARY BEING of the Cosmological and Ontological Arguments. However, the Father cannot be understood as listening to prayers, performing miracles or appearing on Earth.

- **THE SON:** This is the personal expression of the Father's love. The Son *'proceeds'* from the Father (or as some scholars say, *the Son is begotten of the Father* – born from him). This isn't a birth that took place millions of years ago. The Son is ALWAYS proceeding from the Father, going out into the world and then humbly offering himself back to the Father.

- **THE HOLY SPIRIT:** The immanence of God, God's presence in the world; the Holy Spirit is impersonal (it has no personality or human identity) and is present WITHIN human beings and WITHIN the universe. The Holy Spirit performs miracles, answers prayers, grants faith and guides believers.

> *It seems to me that John's Gospel uses the Logos to cover both the Son and the Holy Spirit – but later Christians separated out these ideas.*

The Trinity is a controversial idea. Jews and Muslims reject it because it seems to be saying there's more than one God. Historically, this teaching has been one of the biggest barriers between Christianity and the other monotheistic religions.

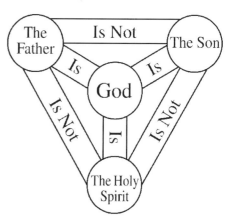

Some Christians called **Universalists** reject the Trinity too, claiming it's a Hellenic pagan concept that doesn't belong in Christianity. However they have to make their own sense of the *Word becoming flesh* in John's Gospel.

These Christological debates continue right through to the present day – all of them are attempts to solve the implications of the tantalizing ideas in John's Gospel.

Is the concept of the "Word made flesh" essential for understanding Jesus' identity?

YES	NO
As the Word of God, Jesus has the authority of God to forgive sins and overrule the Jewish Law in the Torah. Nature obeys him because he created nature. The entire Old Testament refers to Jesus' coming because it was the Logos that inspired the Old Testament, speaking to the prophets through religious experiences.	The idea of the Logos is a Greek term from Hellenic philosophy. Even the way Philo of Alexandria used the term would have been unknown to Jesus and his Disciples. Therefore Jesus cannot have viewed himself as the Logos or taught his followers to view him this way. It must be an idea that came much later, after Jesus' lifetime.
Although the word 'Logos' is Greek, the concept of the Word of God is drawn from Jewish thought and based on the Old Testament. God's Word creates the world in Genesis, speaks to Moses in Exodus and calls to the rest of the Prophets. 1st century Jews would have understood Holy Wisdom dwelling among humans and Jesus' followers understood that he uniquely embodied that Holy Wisdom in his words and actions.	Not all of Jesus' followers viewed him this way; perhaps none did straight away. The earlier Gospels present an Exaltation Theology in which Jesus is a wise prophet who is raised up by God to a divine status *after* his human lifetime. In Mark, this exaltation begins when Jesus is baptized, in Matthew and Luke it begins with his miraculous birth; but none of these Gospels presents Jesus as the incarnation of a divine force that has existed eternally.

Life

⁴ In him was life, and that life was the light of all mankind.

John identifies the **Word/Logos** as the source of Life. However, John doesn't just mean that the Word/Logos created life on Earth (though he certainly thinks that too). John claims that the Life that the Word of God possesses is a **Light for all humanity** (p90). In other words, that this special sort of Life guides and transforms humans. So what is this special sort of Life?

In Greek (the language of the New Testament), there are three words for life: *bios*, *psyche* and *zoë*.

- *BIOS* means biological life. This is all life on Earth as we know it. Biological life comes from the natural world and is always decaying and running down. We need to restore our biological life with 'recharges' in the form of air, water and food, but eventually the decay becomes too much and our bodies age, sicken and die.
- *PSYCHE* is mental life, the life of the soul; it means all your hopes and dreams, your interests and passions: your personality, in a nutshell. However, when our biological life fails our *psyche* dies too. We don't have any way to keep our *psyche* going after we lose our *bios*.
- *ZOË* is a different sort of life: it is spiritual life.

C.S. Lewis describes the difference like this:

> *Bios has, to be sure, a certain shadowy or symbolic resemblance to zoë: but only the sort of resemblance there is between a photo and a place, or a statue and a man* – **C.S. Lewis**

Zoë or spiritual life doesn't run down, decay, sicken or die. It is inexhaustible life that is self-sufficient. It is indestructible life that gives life to other things. Elsewhere, John's Gospel calls it **ETERNAL LIFE**.

So the Life that God possesses and that exists within God's Word is a different *type* of life from the life that plants, animals and humans have. It is *zoë*-life: an **Eternal Life** that would transform any human being who experienced it into a different type of being altogether.

C.H. Dodd makes a distinction between two senses of Eternal Life:

1. **Quantitative:** Eternal Life that is "everlasting" and doesn't end in death. This sort of Life is a hope for the Afterlife. This is the sort of Eternal Life that the **Pharisees** (p64) believed in but the **Sadducees** (p63) didn't.
2. **Qualitative:** Eternal Life that is "timeless" or "divine" but is experienced in the present moment, not in the future. This is life lived in a higher, more fulfilled way: a life of love (*agape*) with no fear of death (but not necessarily a life that lasts longer than a normal sort of life). The Johannine Jesus often talks about Eternal Life this way and **Dodd** argues this is very different from Jewish ideas about Eternal Life in the 1st century.

> *Dodd means spiritual life or zoë is a different quality of life from mere biological life. As different as being awake is from being asleep, or being healthy is from being sick. But even the healthiest, most wide-awake person in the world only has bios. Zoë comes from transformative **religious experience**.*

Implications of Eternal Life

Obviously, *bios* and *psyche* lead to all sorts of dissatisfaction. In fact, *psyche* makes the problems of *bios* worse, because as self-aware creatures we can foresee pain and suffering and our inevitable deaths and this causes us more anxiety. *Zoë* would be the answer to our problems, taking away the fear of death (and perhaps even taking away the FACT of death) and enabling humans to live their lives to the full, without anxiety.

But how can humans acquire *zoë* or **Eternal Life**? This is the question that runs through John's Gospel. John teases the answer in the Prologue: the Word of God has **Eternal Life** and wants to give it to humans too. The details are spelled out later in a very famous passage:

> *For God so loved the world that he gave his one and only Son, that whoever believes in him shall not perish but have eternal life* – **John 3: 16**

> *If you're going to memorize one passage from the New Testament, it should be this one.* **John 3: 16** *is the most succinct summary of Christianity there is. But remember, the eternal life being promised isn't just biological life stretched out forever: it's a new type of life: it's Zoë*

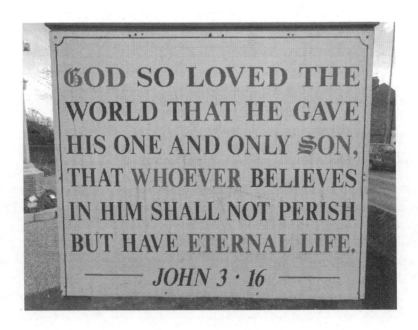

The big debate is whether this new type of Life is something that Christians will receive in the future or in the present. **C.H. Dodd** and **Raymond E. Brown** point out that the Synoptic Gospels treat **Eternal Life** as something believers will enjoy either after they die or when the **Kingdom of God** arrives with Christ's Second Coming; however, John's Gospel seems to view Eternal Life as something that believers can enjoy RIGHT AWAY:

> *Very truly I tell you, whoever hears my word and believes him who sent me has eternal life and will not be judged but has crossed over from death to life –* **John 5: 24**

> *In John's Gospel, Jesus seems to be promising both a future life after death and a transformed life in the present*

However, this focus on Eternal Life in John's Gospel replaces the focus in the Synoptic Gospels on the **Kingdom of God** arriving on Earth. **Eternal Life** seems more like an individual experience, whereas the Kingdom of God is a transformed society run on just and fair principles. However, many Christians HARMONISE both views, arguing that **Eternal Life** involves people treating each other in a loving way and living in the **Kingdom of God** will transform individuals as well.

Is the concept of the "life" or "eternal life" essential for understanding Jesus' identity?

YES

NO

Jesus' mission is entirely about saving humanity from sin and death through his own Atoning Death. He enables those who believe in him to share his own **Eternal Life** (*Zoë*). This is the basis of the Good News (Gospel) he instructs his Disciples to be witnesses to and pass on.

Jesus' mission is better understood in a social sense, to proclaim the **Kingdom of God (*c.f.* Topic 5)** and the transformed way of living this will bring. The Synoptic Gospels were written earlier than John's Gospel and record this original message and mission of justice and social change.

Eternal Life features in the Synoptic Gospels as well (15 references to 37 in John's Gospel). John's Gospel has a *clearer* focus on Eternal Life, but the other Gospels record it as being central to Jesus' mission and identity. Christians throughout the centuries have experienced this Life for themselves in **religious experiences**.

Albert Schweitzer argued that the historical Jesus expected the world to end in his lifetime and died a disappointed man. When believers realized the End Times weren't coming, the Church pushed hopes of the Kingdom of God on Earth or Eternal Life away into the distant future or the afterlife. Christians should focus on moral living instead.

Light & Darkness

⁴ In him was life, and that life was the light of all mankind. ⁵ The light shines in the darkness, and the darkness has not overcome it.

The Word of God/Logos is strongly associated with **light** (Greek *phos*). This is because Light is the first thing to be created in **Genesis 1:3** when God's Word is spoken. God appears to the prophets in light and fire. When Moses comes down from Mount Sinai after meeting God, his face shines with God's reflected light. Light is a **symbol** for the Word of God, because light gives rise to the physical (*bios*) life on Earth and it is through light that we can see the world and understand it, acquiring mental (*psyche*) life. However, the Prologue refers to a more fundamental sort of Light than this: the Light of the true knowledge of God.

This spiritual Light seems to be described in the Old Testament by **Isaiah**:

> *The people walking in darkness have seen a great light;*
> *on those living in the land of deep darkness, a light has dawned* – **Isaiah 9:2**

> *This is one of those passages you often here during carol services at Christmas. Back in the 8ᵗʰ century BCE, Isaiah was describing the Jewish Kingdom of Judah living under threat from the Assyrian Empire and hoping for a king who could save them. For Christians, he's describing the arrival of the light of Christ.*

The world is not all light however. There is **darkness** (Greek *skotos*), which here means **sin**. Sin is a type of blindness – being unable to see the light of God or just refusing to see it. Throughout John's Gospel, Jesus meets many people who have physical (*bios*) sight insofar as their eyes work and some who have intellectual (*psyche*) sight insofar as they are clever and educated. However, these people lack spiritual (*zoë*) sight. They cannot see the spiritual Light in Jesus. They don't realise it, but they live in a darkness more complete than **someone who was born blind** (p155). Jesus sums it up like this

> *I have come into this world, so that the blind will see and those who see will become blind* – **John 9: 39**

Many events in John's Gospel happen during darkness. The Pharisee **Nicodemus** comes "*by night*" to visit Jesus: the darkness of his Pharisee religion prevents him from understanding who Jesus is.

It often seems as if the darkness is stronger than the Light, but John promises otherwise. The darkness never overcomes the spiritual Light. Later on, John's Gospel will describe Jesus' crucifixion and death. This seems to be a complete triumph of darkness over the Light. John's Prologue assures his readers that this isn't the case. The darkness did not overcome Jesus, because he rose from the dead into the **Eternal Life** (p87) he had promised his followers.

[6] There was a man sent from God whose name was John. [7] He came as a witness to testify concerning that light, so that through him all might believe. [8] He himself was not the light; he came only as a witness to the light.

John the Baptist is "*a witness to testify concerning that light*". He has 'seen the light' (as they say) and warns anyone who will listen about the arrival of the **Word of God** (p81). Although the Prologue doesn't say so, John the Baptist stands in a long line of Old Testament prophets who were all 'witnesses testifying concerning the light'. All of them, John's Gospel claims, were testifying about Jesus. But the spiritually blind people living in darkness could not see this.

[9] The true light that gives light to everyone was coming into the world.

The Prologue promises that the Light is coming into the world in the person of Jesus. More than this, the Light of Jesus' message is coming into the world. Centuries of ignorance, superstition and paganism will be replaced by a true knowledge of God. And this isn't just intellectual (*psyche*) knowledge: it's a transforming knowledge that brings about **Eternal** (*zoe*) **Life**.

It's important to understand that the 'Light' is not the same as 'moral behaviour'. Moral behaviour can be mimicked by people who do not truly love God. Satan pretends to be *an 'angel of light'* but as the Devil he lives in darkness. The Light is a spiritual understanding, not just being a good person.

Jesus explains the link between Light (spiritual understanding) and **Life**:

> *I am the light of the world. Whoever follows me will never walk in darkness, but will have the light of life* – **John 8: 12**

Christians receive Eternal Life because they follow Jesus, as opposed to the Pharisees who think salvation comes from following rules.

C.H. Dodd also links Light with "Judgment". He explains that, for John's Gospel, the Light exposes the Darkness and reveals things that were hidden – like sins. Therefore Jesus' coming into the world shows everybody for what they really are: a **Child of God** (p96) who recognises the Light and rejoices in it or a child of the darkness who hates the Light and tries to blot it out.

Implications of Light & Darkness

John's Gospel didn't invent this sort of light/darkness symbolism. The Dead Sea Scrolls record that the **Essenes** (p66) saw themselves as 'Sons of the Light' and their enemies as 'Sons of Darkness', locked in a cosmic war. For John, this war is over and the Light has won, even at the very moment when it seemed to be defeated (Jesus' Crucifixion turns into the Resurrection).

The link between 'Light' and **mystical religious experience** was developed by later believers. The **Gnostics** were Christians who appeared in the 2nd century CE with unusual beliefs. Their name comes from the Greek word *gnosis* which means "secret knowledge". They believed that John's symbolism went much deeper than ordinary Christians realised and that Jesus had left behind a body of secret teachings that could grant **Eternal Life** (p87) to those 'in the know'. The Gnostics saw themselves as superior to the uninformed Christians who believed that **Eternal Life** was based on going to church, praying and leading moral lives. The Gnostics seem to have based their beliefs on John's Gospel but **Raymond Brown** argues they were quickly pushed out of the Johannine churches.

Mainstream Christians still return to John's teachings about the Light. **Friedrich Schleiermacher** in the 19th century argued that **religious experiences** of God matter more than following traditions and rituals. This is based on John's Gospel and its focus on 'seeing the Light' and understanding God on a mystical level. Reformers like **Martin Luther King** have drawn inspiration from the Prologue's image of the beleaguered Light that can never be overcome by the surrounding darkness. This symbolism has always given hope to the underdog.

Is the concept of "Light & Darkness" essential for understanding Jesus' identity?

YES	NO
For Christians, Jesus is not just a wise teacher or the greatest prophet. Every word and action in his life illustrates the power and goodness of God. **C.H. Dodd** argues **that Jesus is the Logos** because his entire life is the Logos in action. This means that Jesus' life is itself a **revelation**. The **symbolism** of the Light draws our attention to this.	Jesus offers challenging moral teachings: give up your possessions, love your enemy, turn the other cheek. This moral living is the most important aspect of Christianity. The Synoptic Gospels recognise this with their proclamation of the **Kingdom of God**. Spiritual understanding will not change the world.
John's Gospel rejects the idea that moral living is central to Christ's message. It's a much more **mystical** Gospel than that, which is why **Morna Hooker** calls the prologue *"the glorious key"* as opposed to **Matthew's Prologue** which is *"the prophetic key"*. John's Gospel promises **Eternal Life** to those who achieve spiritual understanding, not those who live moral lives (but the understanding will lead to moral living too).	This is another example of Johns Gospel being a late addition to the New Testament with a message very far removed from what Jesus himself taught and believed. **Matthew** and **Luke** record the **Beatitudes** (the famous 'Sermon on the Mount') where Jesus blesses people for being humble, merciful, being peace-makers, etc. This seems to be closer to the true message of Christianity than just 'seeing the light'.

Belief

> [11] He came to that which was his own, but his own did not receive him. [12] Yet to all who did receive him, to those who believed in his name, he gave the right to become children of God

'Belief' in John's Gospel means something special. Believing is TRANSFORMATIVE: by believing, humans are transformed into **Children of God** (p96). How can believing do this?

It's worth separating different senses 'belief' and 'believing':

- **Beliefs about:** You can have beliefs *about* things and these beliefs might turn out to be true or false.

> *I have beliefs that the Eiffel Tower is in Paris and that visiting it would be fun. Beliefs like this have consequences - for example, they affect how I plan my holidays - but they don't have deeply personal consequences. If I visit Paris I might see the Eiffel Tower and discover that my first belief is true; if I go up the Tower I might feel dizzy and anxious (I don't like heights) and discover that my second belief was false. I change my beliefs about the Eiffel Tower, but I don't change myself.*

- **Believing in:** You can believe *in* things and this is much more important and personal than beliefs *about* things. I might believe in vegetarianism or pacifism. I might believe in a person that I respect and trust. It's much harder to prove that my believing *in* something is wrong.

> *I will defend the things I believe in passionately; if I believe in a person I will trust them even when the evidence against them mounts up. Believing like this changes the way you live and changes who you are as a person.*

Christians have beliefs *about* Jesus: that he is the **Messiah** (p12), that he is the **Son of God** (p112), that he was crucified and rose from the dead. These beliefs might be right and they might be wrong – but they're not the sort of beliefs that John's Gospel is concerned with.

Christians also believe *in* Jesus: they put all their trust in him, love and obey him, hope to be united with him. This is **transformative believing** because it makes Christians live their lives differently. This is what John's Prologue means by "*believing in his name*" (but see also p216). Another name for this sort of transformative believing is **FAITH**.

> *It's a bit odd that the exam board calls this topic 'belief'. It ought to be called 'believing' because John never uses the word 'belief' once in his Gospel.*

John's Gospel refers to **believing** (the Greek word is *pisteuo*) over 100 times – but always as a verb (**believe** and **believing**) and never as a noun (**belief**). John isn't concerned with 'beliefs' that a person holds – he is concerned with 'transformative believing', a dramatic action that changes people from the inside.

The distinction appears elsewhere. In the Synoptic Gospels, Jesus casts out demons from people who are sick. These demons recognise who Jesus is (because they are supernatural creatures). However, although the demons have (it turns out, correct) beliefs about Jesus being the Son of God, they don't believe *in* Jesus, because they see him as their enemy.

John's Gospel makes this focus on believing very clear. When the crowds ask Jesus what God wants them to do, he replies

> *The work of God is this: to believe in the one he has sent* – **John 6: 29**

> *Notice, not 'live a moral life' or 'give to the poor', not 'pray' or 'worship God'; instead, a transformative act of faith is what God requires*

John's Gospel ends with these words:

> *But these are written that you may believe that Jesus is the Messiah, the Son of God, and that by believing you may have life in his name* – **John 20: 31**

John's Gospel is written to trigger transformative believing in readers - to create religious faith.

Implications of Belief/Believing

Other Christians took their religion in a different direction, focusing on beliefs *about* Jesus instead. This approach is known as **ORTHODOXY** (which means "correct belief"). These Christians composed statements of beliefs *about* God and Jesus that are known as CREEDS (from the Latin *credo* meaning "I believe").

Two famous Creeds are still used today: the **Nicene Creed** of 325 CE and the **Apostles' Creed** of c.390 CE. Both are recited in churches and learned by heart. The Creeds act as a sort of checklist of things Christians agree to, such as there being only one God or Jesus being born of a virgin.

The Johannine church ran into difficulties with its transformative believing, because its congregations filled up with Gnostics who interpreted John's Gospel in very different ways. According to **Raymond E. Brown** the **Johannine Community** (p208) tried to throw out the Gnostics in their midst. At the end of the day, transformative believing turned out to be too unstable to build a community. Orthodoxy was needed so that Christians could agree on what they believed.

However, orthodoxy produced its own problems. Christians who did not agree with orthodox Creeds were labeled HERETICS and in the Middle Ages they were put to death. Reformers who questioned orthodox beliefs were in danger. The pressure to conform meant that scientists like **Galileo** (1564-1642) had to hide some of their discoveries.

There were plenty of critics of this orthodox approach to religion who tried to bring back the sort of transformational believing that John's Gospel celebrates. **St Francis of Assisi** (1181-1226) was a reformer who gave up material possessions to live in 'Holy Poverty' and be close in spirit to Christ. **Martin Luther** started the **Protestant Reformation** by arguing that Christianity should be about **faith (believing)** and not **works** (good deeds and following the church's rules).

Philosophers have also been inspired by the idea of transformational believing in John's Gospel. **Søren Kierkegaard** (1813-1855) writes about the *leap of faith* (or strictly, *"leap to faith"*) that believing involves. **Martin Buber** (1878-1965) was a Jewish philosopher, but he writes about the superiority of an **"I-You" relationship** with the world and with God rather than an **"I-it" relationship**. "I-it" relationships are logical and intellectual, but an "I-You" relationship is personal and involves trust and risk. Buber thinks we should encourage "I-You" relationships with each other, the world and with God.

More recently, many evangelical Christians have returned to the focus on transformational believing; this is the "Born Again" movement that focuses on having a personal relationship with Christ (and a dramatic **conversion experience**) rather than agreeing intellectually to a Creed. Evangelical Christianity has been around for 250 years but the "Born Again" movement has gained popularity and visibility since the 1970s. Just like the Johannine church of the 1st and 2nd centuries CE, Born Again Christians feel that a religion based on mere beliefs is sterile and dead if it doesn't lead to transformation into a **child of God** (p96).

> *It seems that Christianity is always struggling to put the challenge of transformational believing into practice but keeps getting drawn into focusing on orthodox beliefs instead.*

Is the concept of "belief" essential for understanding Jesus' identity?

YES	NO
Not "belief" but BELIEVING. Jesus' identity can only be understood as an act of faith. By believing *in* Jesus as Lord and God, Christians are transformed and receive **Eternal Life**. This is not something that can be understood rationally. It has to be experienced.	If we reject logic and reason, we can end up believing any old nonsense - as the Johannine Church found when the Gnostics turned up in its congregation. Religious belief needs Creeds and orthodoxy otherwise it becomes utterly subjective.
Believing doesn't mean completely rejecting statements of belief. You have to be able to say what it is you believe in. There's a place for Creeds. After all, the Apostles went out and preached about the Resurrection so they had some beliefs *as well as* believing in Christ. It's a matter of priorities and transformation believing is the first priority.	This sort of emotional believing involves putting your rational faculties on hold. That can be very destructive. Religious beliefs only progress because ideas are explored, tested and challenged. This requires "standing back" and being analytical, not jumping in and 'believing'. This is why Born Again Christians tend to be very conservative in their attitudes and politics.

Children of God

> [11] He came to that which was his own, but his own did not receive him. [12] Yet to all who did receive him, to those who believed in his name, he gave the right to become children of God – [13] children born not of natural descent, nor of human decision or a husband's will, but born of God.

The idea of 'children of God' or 'sons of God' recurs throughout the Bible. **Adam** is called a son of God and so are angels; various kings (especially **David**) are called sons of God; the whole Jewish people are children of God. A lot of this language is **symbolic**. Adam is God's 'son' because God created him directly: he didn't have a human father; the same applies to the angels. King David and the Israelites generally are 'sons of God' because they are chosen by God and have a special close relationship with him.

'Children of God' could be taken purely **symbolically**: Christians should be *like children'* since they should trust God like a child trusts a father and be innocent and obedient like children. Many churches have taken this interpretation and it links to a famous passage in the Synoptic Gospels where Jesus says:

> *unless you change and become like little children, you will never enter the kingdom of heaven* – **Matthew 18: 3**

However, John's Gospel seems to be saying something more than that. Christians who **believe in Jesus** (p93) become 'children of God' in a new or special sense: they are "*born of God*". This is different from a physical birth. We are all born physically and have "*natural descent*" (ancestors). We are all products of an ancestral line and the decisions of our parents – stuff we have no control over and cannot change.

> *This is similar to the idea of **contingency** that is important in the **arguments for the existence of God**. As physical children, we are all contingent beings who might not have existed if our ancestors had behaved differently.*

In contrast to this is the idea of **spiritual birth** (or **re-birth**) – something we can choose and that is a gift from God. This spiritual birth is an intense **religious experience**. It is the sense of becoming a new person, making a fresh start. Spiritual birth is linked to **believing in Jesus**: putting your trust in him and acknowledging him as Lord and God.

The concept of spiritual birth is explored further when **Nicodemus the Pharisee** visits Jesus "*by night*". Nicodemus wants to know about the **Kingdom of God**. Jesus' answer to Nicodemus' questions is summed up when he says:

> *no one can see the kingdom of God unless they are **born again*** – **John 3: 3**

The original Greek phrase *gennao anothen* could be translated either as *"born again"* or "*born from above*". Just as physical birth introduces humans to a world of suffering and death, spiritual birth introduces humans to **Eternal Life** (p87).

C.H. Dodd argues that Jews would normally consider themselves to be the Children of God, because they are his Chosen People. **Morna Hooker** describes a *"gigantic take-over battle"*, with the Christians saying that they, not the Jews, are the true Chosen People. Many Christians are not biologically descended from Abraham, like the Jews are, but they a spiritually born from God himself.

Implications of Children of God

John's Gospel isn't the earliest Christian document to discuss spiritual birth. The very earliest Christian texts we have are the **epistles (letters) of Paul** (written in the 50s and early 60s CE). Paul phrases the idea like this:

> *For as in Adam all die, so in Christ all will be made alive* – **1 Corinthians 15: 22**

In Paul's churches, believers who were Born Again experienced the **gifts of the Holy Spirit**: they could speak in tongues, prophesy and experience spiritual healing. This occasionally led to divisions, because some believers experienced these gifts but other believers didn't. The later Christian church downplayed these gifts, perhaps because they were so divisive and unpredictable. The idea of converting to Christianity in a life-changing 'Born Again' experience was replaced by being received into the church when you are born, as part of the 'Christening' ceremony. This enabled Christianity to turn into a powerful worldwide institution.

Various reformers tried to return to the idea of spiritual birth. Christian mystics went to live as monks in the desert to achieve this; later, Christian **mysticism** developed due to the writings of people like **Hildegard of Bingen**, **Francis of Assisi** and **Catherine of Siena**. During the **Protestant Reformation**, reformers like the **Anabaptists** objected to christening babies and brought back adult baptism – the idea that becoming a Christian is a conscious decision to be spiritually reborn and not something your parents can decide for you when you are a child.

Many of these ideas became mainstream in the 20th century. Evangelical Christians exist in most Christian churches and emphasize spiritual birth; the **'Born Again' movement** has become very widespread since the 1970s. **Pentecostalists** are Christians who experience the gifts of the Holy Spirit in their worship and **Baptists** (as their name suggests) practise adult baptism rather than christening children.

However, other churches follow a different tradition: **Catholics** and **Anglicans** still christen their children and downplay the importance of gifts of the Holy Spirit and being Born Again in favour of partaking of the **Sacraments** like **Holy Communion** instead.

Is the concept of "children of God" essential for understanding Jesus' identity?

YES	NO
Jesus is uniquely the **Son of God**, but he also offers to believers the opportunity to become Children of God. This is a spiritual transformation that puts love (*agape*) at the centre of someone's life. Without this transformation, Christianity is just another set of moral rules.	Jesus' moral rules are admirable and worth living by: forgive your enemies, love your neighbour - the world would be a better place if more people did these things. Spiritual transformation is a distraction. Morality matters, not some **mystical experience**.
Putting morality first is no different from the **Law of Moses**. People aren't capable of living truly moral lives and, even if they were, following a bunch of moral rules wouldn't help them do it. People don't need rules: they need inner transformation.	Inner transformation is a very subjective thing. There are lots of examples of people who claimed to be Born Again but then turned out to be cheaters and crooks. It's better to focus on being good because claiming to be a 'Child of God' makes it too easy to *pretend* to be good.

Flesh & Spirit

The Greek word for 'flesh' is *sarx*. At first glance, this only seems to turn up once in the Prologue.

> [14] The Word became flesh and made his dwelling among us.

However, it also occurs in another line but the New International Version (the translation used in the Anthology) misses it out

> *children born not of* sarx, *nor of man, but born of God* **– John 1: 13**

Later on, John's Gospel refers to *sarx* a lot and links it to the Spirit (*pneuma*), as here:

> *Flesh gives birth to flesh, but the Spirit gives birth to spirit* **– John 3: 3**

Both *sarx* and *pneuma* are connected to birth. The Flesh connects to birth in the obvious sense: all human beings are physically born. The Spirit links to the idea of spiritual birth as **Children of God** (p96) – what Christians refer to as being 'Born Again'.

There is also the fact that the Flesh suffers from sickness and has to die eventually, but Spirit never dies. Therefore anyone who is 'Born Again' as a child of Spirit rather than Flesh will have **Eternal Life** (p87). This links to different words for 'life' in Greek: the Flesh has biological life (*bios*) but the Spirit has spiritual life (*zoë*). Jesus explains it like this:

> *The Spirit gives life; the flesh counts for nothing. The words I have spoken to you - they are full of the Spirit and life* **– John 6: 63**

However, the concept of the Flesh goes beyond just our physical bodies. *"According to the flesh"* includes everything that makes us human and of this world. So when the **Word becomes Flesh** (p81), it doesn't just put on a human body like a man putting on a suit. It acquires a human identity, including a racial identity (a Jew of **the line of David**, p15), a political identity (a Galilean, living under **Roman occupation**, p54), a family identity (the son of Mary and Joseph) and friends (Martha, Mary and Lazarus). These relationships are part of the world of the Flesh. Being 'Born Again' into the world of the Spirit doesn't mean fading away and becoming a ghost: it means becoming free of these identities and their 'baggage' and then redefining your relationships.

A New Testament author who has a lot to say about this is **Paul**:

> *There is neither Jew nor Gentile, neither slave nor free, nor is there male and female, for you are all one in Christ Jesus* **– Galatians 3: 28**

The Spirit involves a different way of viewing yourself and your relationships – a view based on love (*agape*). When Jesus criticises the **Pharisees** (p64), he says, *"you judge according to the flesh"* – in other words, they judge people by their worldly identities (lumping people as Jews and Gentiles, discriminating against women, etc) whereas Jesus does not.

Implications of Flesh & Spirit

Many Greek philosophers such as Plato were DUALISTS. This is the belief in two realities: a physical world and a spiritual world. John's Gospel, with its focus on Flesh versus Spirit, seems to share the dualist outlook.

Many pagan dualists viewed the physical world as intrinsically evil and the spiritual world as the source of all goodness. The Jews resisted this conclusion, because the **Book of Genesis** makes it clear that when God created the physical world *"he saw that it was good"*.

However, the Gnostics who appeared in the Johannine churches in the 2nd century CE definitely were dualists. They wanted to escape the 'prison' of physical existence and become purely spiritual beings. They took their hatred of the physical world so far as to suppose it could not have been created by God – they believed a lesser, evil god must have created the physical world.

> *The Johannine Churches treated the Gnostics as HERETICS and drove them out – but you can see how Gnostics arrived at some of their views from the language in John's Prologue.*

Most Christians took a different approach. They regarded the physical world – that is, the Flesh generally – as good but flawed. Writers like **Augustine of Hippo** developed the concept of **ORIGINAL SIN**, which means that, since the Fall of Adam and Eve, sin is passed on down through the generations when human beings are born. This connection between the Flesh and sin is explained by **Paul**:

> *The flesh desires what is contrary to the Spirit, and the Spirit what is contrary to the flesh. They are in conflict with each other* – **Galatians 5: 17**

Over the centuries, some Christians have tried to 'mortify the Flesh' (literally, put it to death) by fasting, going without sleep or even hurting themselves. This distrust of physical bodies certainly encourages some Christians to have very negative attitudes towards sex and pleasure generally.

However, this is only one way of interpreting the Flesh/Spirit **dichotomy** (which means 'split') in John's Gospel. If 'Flesh' is taken in its wider sense to mean relationships and identities which we are born into and have no choice over – and Spirit is the alternative way of living, based on the choice to **love your neighbour (***agape***)** – then the emphasis on evil physical pleasure becomes less important.

'Flesh' might mean attitudes like racism, sexism, greed for money and feelings of resentment and anger rather than 'the body' in a literal sense. Living according to the Spirit rather than the Flesh means breaking away from the difficult relationships, prejudices and grievances you've been born into and starting over 'from scratch' with no ill-will to anyone.

Is the concept of "flesh & spirit" essential for understanding Jesus' identity?

YES	NO
Jesus is a being from the world of the Spirit (*pneuma*) who has come into the world of the Flesh (*sarx*) to save it. In order to understand Jesus, you need to understand the importance of being 'Born Again' into a spiritual life and leaving the life of the Flesh behind. This contrast runs all through John's Gospel and is echoed in the writings of Paul.	This is a dualist outlook that leads to contempt for the physical world and physical pleasure. This seems to be moving away from the Jewish view that the physical world is good. That would be an example of John's Gospel being quite Hellenic and far removed from the actual views of Jesus and his Jewish followers.
This is not a dualist view because the physical world is not evil. Rather, it is a Fallen world and Original Sin is passed through the generations to each child as it is born. Being Born Again of the Spirit sets Christians free from Original Sin and gives them **Eternal Life**.	This view misinterprets 'Flesh' and 'Spirit'. Flesh refers to our worldly identity and all the conflict and prejudice that goes with it; Spirit is freedom from this 'baggage' brought about by the decision to love unconditionally (*agape*). Christians who focus on Original Sin miss out on this.

Law

> [16] Out of his fullness we have all received grace in place of grace already given. [17] For the law was given through Moses; grace and truth came through Jesus Christ. [18] No one has ever seen God, but the one and only Son, who is himself God and is in closest relationship with the Father, has made him known.

In the Bible, "the Law" (in Greek, *ho nomos*) means the Religious Law of the Jews. This body of commandments was given to **Moses** by God, as described in the Old Testament. For this reason, it is known as **'the Law of Moses'** or **'the Mosaic Law'**.

Most of the commandments are in the first 5 books of the Old Testament. For Jews, these 5 books are called the **TORAH** (Hebrew for 'Teaching' or 'Law') and are especially sacred. Supposedly there are 613 commandments (*mitzvot*) in the Torah – not just the Ten Commandments! Some commandments are specifically for priests, or men, or women, but others are commandments all Jews must follow, such as dietary laws (e.g. the *kosher* rules for preparing food and banning pork).

Applying these commandments to daily life could be a complicated business. The **Sadducees** (p63) restricted the commandments to those specifically in the Torah; when new situations came up they worked out new rulings. The **Pharisees** (p64) followed a huge number of commandments that had built up outside the Torah - a whole tradition of laws covering every aspect of life.

*We're inclined to think it bizarre and wearisome to live your life by a huge list of rules, but many 1ˢᵗ century Jews felt otherwise. Following the law could give their lives a structure and a purpose and distinguished them from the pagan Gentiles who seemed to have no plan or purpose to their lives. Nevertheless, obeying the law could be a burden at times and definitely cut Jews off from their neighbours and created conflict under **Roman occupation**.*

There are lots of examples of Jesus in conflict with the Pharisees over their strict interpretation of the Law of Moses. Jesus attacks their **arrogance** in thinking that, because they keep the Laws, they are righteous in the eyes of God. He accuses them of **hypocrisy**, saying that they obey the letter of the Law but they do not obey the spirit of it because they do not love their neighbours.

It's difficult to know how much of this conflict REALLY went on between Jesus and the Pharisees. We know that the early Christian churches were in a bitter conflict with the Jewish leaders in the Synagogues over whether or not Jesus was the Messiah. Some scholars suggest that the writers of the Gospels present Jesus as saying things about the Pharisees which are really things that later Christians wanted to say to their Jewish critics.

John's Prologue admits that the Law was given to **Moses**, but claims that Christians have something better than the Law: Jesus Christ. Christ is presented in the Prologue as an *alternative* to the Law. Like the Law was in the past, Christ is a **grace (gift** or **favour, p106)** from God. The Prologue refers to Moses being allowed only to see God's back – but argues that the Word of God (Jesus) was able to see God face-to-face. This is a much closer relationship than Moses ever had. Therefore, Jesus replaces Moses and the Mosaic Law.

John isn't the only New Testament writer to have problems with the Jewish Law; **Paul** also presents Jesus Christ as a replacement for it. Paul was himself a Pharisee before converting to Christianity. Paul advises Christians like this:

you are not under law but under grace – **Romans 6: 14**

Christian converts don't have to follow the Jewish Law to please God; they receive God's **grace** automatically because they **believe in Jesus** (p93). This links to John's Prologue which claims Christians have "*all received grace*" (forgiveness by God thanks to Jesus' atoning death) instead of the "*grace already given*" (i.e. the Law, which was given to Moses).

The anonymous author of the **Epistle (letter) to the Hebrews** describes the Law as:

a shadow of the good things to come – **Hebrews 10: 1**

This views the Law as a sort of preparation or practice for the life Christians live as **Children of God** (p96).

You could compare the Law to stabiliser wheels on a bicycle: you only need them while you are learning, but once you've learn to ride you take them off and race away.

or you could compare it to taking piano lessons where you learn 'scales', which can be boring and frustrating, but once you've learned to play you can perform for sheer enjoyment and you never have to play scales again..

This is why Paul concludes that selfless love (*agape*) is the *real* way of following the Law:

> *Whoever loves others has fulfilled the Law* – **Romans 13: 8**

Implications of Law

The very first Christians were Jews who continued to follow the Jewish Law. However, when Gentiles (non-Jews) started converting to Christianity (largely due to the efforts of **Paul**), this caused problems. Jewish Christians were forbidden from eating alongside Gentile Christians, which is a problem for a religion whose central act of worship is a meal (the **Eucharist** of bread and wine). The Gentiles were under pressure to convert fully to Judaism (from 'Judaizers') so that they could be 'proper' Christians. Since this involved **circumcision** for men (a dangerous and painful surgical procedure in those days), many converts were unwilling to go through with this. Paul supports the Gentile Christians, arguing that as Christians they don't have to follow the Law.

Raymond E. Brown suggests that the **Johannine Community** (p208, the group that wrote John's Gospel) were in a similar position. They were Jewish Christians but they had been thrown out of the Synagogue for insisting that Jesus was the Messiah. They found themselves cut off from the Jewish religion and the social life that went with it. As a result, they rejected the whole idea of the Law and their Gospel presents Jesus as hostile to "*the Jews*" and the Jewish Law.

> We cannot know if Brown is correct about the Johannine Community, but his theory certainly explains some of the hard feeling towards "*the Jews*" in John's Gospel - for example, even calling Jesus' enemies "*the Jews*" is odd since Jesus was Jewish!

There is a legacy of **anti-Semitism** from John's Gospel, which was used by Christians in later centuries to justify persecuting Jews.

Meanwhile, Christians built up their own lists of laws over the centuries – it seems to be a normal human urge to codify things and turn them into regulations. The Roman Catholic Church developed Canon Law into a complicated legal system for governing its priests and monks and ordinary members.

Other Christians have formed a backlash against this. ANTINOMIANISM is a complete rejection of the Law. The **Gnostic** heretics in the 2nd century were antinomians, whereas the more mainstream Christians still obeyed the Ten Commandments. During the **Protestant Reformation**, various antinomian sects (such as the Quakers) believed that, as Christians, they didn't have to follow any laws at all and their members behaved in shocking ways to make their point.

> Christians remain divided about how much of the Law should be ignored. Surely Commandments like **"Do not murder"** or **"Do not commit adultery"** still apply to Christians? What about Commandments forbidding homosexuality? Debates still go on about why Old Testament laws about (say) sexuality still apply to Christians but laws about (say) food do not.

Is the concept of "Law" essential for understanding Jesus' identity?

YES

If Christians have to follow the Law, then Jesus was just another prophet in the Jewish tradition. However, Jesus came to offer people a new way of living that didn't involve following rules but still involved closeness to God.

In his **'Great Commission'**, Jesus instructs his Disciples to go and convert the Gentiles. Jesus appears to **Paul** to convert him, so the expansion of Christianity among the Gentiles is part of Jesus' plan. This means the Law has been replaced by a new relationship with God based on love.

NO

Jesus was a Jew and so were his Disciples and his first followers. They all kept the Jewish Law. Christians only abandoned the Law when Gentiles started converting to Christianity, thanks to Paul.

Breaking away from the Law seems to be Paul's idea, not Jesus'. It reflects the conflicts of the Early Church with Judaism - such as the Johannine Community being thrown out of the Synagogue - and it was never part of Jesus' own teaching.

Grace & Truth

> We have seen his glory, the glory of the one and only Son, who came from the Father, full of grace and truth.

The Prologue refers to Grace in Greek, (*charis*) and links it to Glory (*doxa*). "*Charis*" means "favour" or "gift" (the word is connected to 'charity') whereas "*doxa*" refers to God's awesome reality which comes across to humans as a **numinous religious experience**.

In the Old Testament, encounters with God are overwhelming for humans. God appears in storms and in smoke and fire and human beings cannot look at him – in fact, it's death to look at God. This is the **Glory of God**. So when John's Gospel claims "*We have seen God's Glory,*" he's claiming something that not even **Moses** could have claimed – because Moses only saw God partially, from behind.

God on Mount Sinai – too much to cope with

How can Christians claim they have seen God's Glory? Because God appeared to them through a human being – through Jesus. This is **Grace** because God reduces himself in stature and becomes something human beings can 'cope with'. Encountering Jesus is still a transformative **religious experience**, but it doesn't kill you!

> [16] Out of his fullness we have all received grace in place of grace already given. [17] For the law was given through Moses; grace and truth came through Jesus Christ.

John links this **Grace** to God's gifts in the past. God graciously (see the connection with 'grace' there?) gave the **Law** to **Moses** (p102). For centuries, this was how Jews could experience God - by keeping the Law and making sacrifices of animals. This Grace was only given to the Jewish people. Now there's a new Grace, given to **everyone**, including Gentiles. This is "*in place of*" the Law – and this new gift comes through Jesus.

The Prologue connects God's Grace to **Truth** (in Greek, *aletheia*). Obviously, this is because Jesus brings the Truth about God – the reality of God, the genuine **revelation** about what God is like that is superior to the Jewish Law. This is summed up in Jesus' statement:

> *I am the way and the truth and the life* – **John 14: 6**

Believing in Jesus (p93) leads to **Eternal Life** (p87) because there is a deeper Truth in Jesus than is found in the Law of Moses (or any other philosophy).

Implications of Grace & Truth

The Hebrew word for Truth is *EMET*. It is made up of the first, middle and last letters of the Hebrew alphabet, symbolising that God was present in the beginning, in the present moment and at the end of time – God is eternally true. The New Testament makes a similar claim about Jesus:

> *I am the Alpha and the Omega, the First and the Last, the Beginning and the End* – **Revelation 22: 13**

Alpha and Omega are the first and last letters of the Greek alphabet. This reference means that Jesus Christ is the new *EMET*, the new Truth.

The Greek philosopher **Plato** tells a famous story about prisoners in a cave to illustrate Truth. The prisoners in the cave mistake the shadows on the cave wall for reality, but only when one prisoner escape and sees real trees and real animals under a real sun does he understand the Truth about reality. However, the other prisoners in the cave do not believe the escapee. They continue to mistake the shadows for reality. Plato's ideas illustrate John's Prologue, because Jesus, being the Logos, has come from the Real World and tries to tell humanity the Truth. However, just like the prisoners in Plato's Cave, Jesus' own people, the Jews, do not believe him.

In John's Gospel, Jesus tells his Disciples:

You will know the truth, and the truth will set you free – **John 8: 32**

Many Christians interpret this as meaning that humans are prisoners of sin and live in a **darkness of ignorance** (p90). The Truth about Jesus will set them free, like the prisoners in the Cave that Plato described. The difference between the Christian view and the Greek philosophers is that for the philosophers, Truth is an intellectual idea, but for Christians it is a person.

Is the concept of "grace & truth" essential for understanding Jesus' identity?

YES	NO
Jesus isn't just another prophet - he's the beginning of a new relationship between humans and God that replaces the old Jewish Law. Jesus is God's Glory - a **revelation** of what God is like – but one that ordinary human beings can encounter and understand on a personal level. That's why he is Grace (a generous gift) and Truth (an insight into divine reality).	Jesus' teachings have a lot of moral sense, but most of what he says is already in the Old Testament: the Jewish Law tells people to forgive their enemies and love their neighbours. There isn't a special sort of Truth in Jesus' teachings that you can't find in other religions like Judaism or in the moral philosophy of **Plato** and **Aristotle**.
Jesus isn't just a teacher of the Truth - he *is* the Truth. His entire life, including his death and Resurrection, reveals the Truth about God. To understand this, you don't just learn Jesus' teachings, you have to **believe in him** and have a personal relationship with Christ.	Truth has to be understood rationally. Reason - and science - is the best tool we have for figuring out Truth. Greek philosophy is might lead people to understand the truth because it's based on reason. Having a relationship with Jesus Christ is a **mystical approach** to Truth which is irrational.

TOPIC 2.2 THE TITLES OF JESUS

The Exam expects you to be familiar with the titles used by and about Jesus in the Synoptic Gospels and the special "I Am" statements in John's Gospel.

What are the Synoptic Gospels?

'Synoptic' means "*seen together*". The Synoptic Gospels are **Matthew**, **Mark** and **Luke** and they are called this because they share a lot of material. There are passages that are word-for-word the same in all three Synoptic Gospels and other passages where it is obvious that one Gospel has taken the text from the other and either added lines to it or taken parts out.

Because of this, the Synoptic Gospels also share a viewpoint and theological position on Jesus Christ, although they have their distinctive differences too. **Matthew** focuses on Jesus as the **prophesied Jewish Messiah**; **Mark** focuses on Jesus as the **Suffering Servant** who moves **in secret** among his people; **Luke** presents Jesus as the Saviour of all people, including Gentiles (non-Jews).

There's also a distinctive style in the Synoptics. They are **descriptive** rather than reflective. The Synoptics describe Jesus *doing things*:

- he performs many miracles and healings;
- he has encounters with the Jewish and Roman authorities, with lunatics and with ordinary people;
- he casts out demons and evil spirits.

Many of his speeches are **short and to-the-point**. In contrast, the **Gospel of John** has far fewer episodes and miracles, no demons and Jesus delivers long speeches (called **'Discourses'**) with a lot of detailed philosophy. The Synoptics also contain records of Jesus' distinctive way of teaching through **Parables**, which are almost entirely missing from John's Gospel.

> *This leads to a debate about which Gospels present the **real** Jesus: was he a storytelling healer and exorcist (Synoptics) or a philosopher who gave long speeches (John)?*

The popular view is that the Synoptics are earlier and record more of the **actual words** – the *IPSISSIMA VERBA* – of Jesus. However, John puts words into Jesus' mouth that he never said, but captures the **distinctive meaning** – the *IPSISSIMA VOX* – of what Jesus was trying to say. Nevertheless, some scholars like **Bishop John Robinson** have made persuasive arguments that John preserves eyewitness testimony about Jesus that is just as old as the Synoptics.

If the Synoptic Gospels are the earliest accounts of Jesus' life and sayings (and many scholars think **Mark** is the first Gospel, perhaps written in the late 60s CE), then the titles used in these Gospels will tell us a lot about what the very first Christians thought of Jesus and perhaps what Jesus thought of himself.

PARALLEL CRUCIFIXION ACCOUNTS IN THE SYNOPTIC GOSPELS

MATTHEW 27	MARK 15	LUKE 23
When morning came, all the chief priests and the elders of the	As soon as it was morning, the chief priests	[66] When day came, the assembly of the elders of the people, both chief priests and scribes,
people conferred together against Jesus in order to bring about his death. [2] They bound him, led him away, and handed him over to Pilate the governor. [11] Now Jesus stood before the governor; and the governor asked him, "Are you the King of the Jews?" Jesus said, "You say so." [12] But when he was accused by the chief priests and elders, he did not answer. [13] Then Pilate said to him, "Do you not hear how	held a consultation with the elders and scribes and the whole council. They bound Jesus, led him away, and handed him over to Pilate. [2] Pilate asked him, "Are you the King of the Jews?" He answered him, "You say so." [3] Then the chief priests accused him of many things. [4] Pilate asked him again, "Have you no answer? See how	gathered together, and they brought him to their council. [23:1] Then the assembly rose as a body and brought Jesus before Pilate. [2] They began to accuse him, saying, "We found this man perverting our nation, forbidding us to pay taxes to the emperor, and saying that he himself is the Messiah, a king." [3] Then Pilate asked him, "Are you the king of the Jews?" He answered, "You say so."
many accusations they make against you?" [14] But he gave him no answer, not even to a single charge, so that the governor was greatly amazed.	many charges they bring against you." [5] But Jesus made no further reply, so that Pilate was amazed.	[4] Then Pilate said to the chief priests and the crowds, "I find no basis for an accusation against this man." [5] But they were insistent and said, "He stirs up the people by teaching throughout all Judea, from Galilee where he began even to this place."
[15] Now at the festival the governor was accustomed to release a prisoner for the crowd, anyone whom they wanted. [16] At that time they had a notorious prisoner, called Jesus Barabbas. [17] So after they had gathered, Pilate said to	[6] Now at the festival he used to release a prisoner for them, anyone for whom they asked. [7] Now a man called Barabbas was in prison with the rebels who had committed murder during the insurrection. [8] So the crowd	LUKE 23 [18] Then they all shouted out together, "Away with this fellow! Release Barabbas for us!" [19] (This was a man who had been put in prison for an insurrection that had taken place in the city, and for

You can see the passages that are the same in Matthew, Mark & Luke's description of Jesus' trial. This is explored further in Topic 3 (Interpreting Texts).

Synoptic Title: Messiah

> *The concept of the Messiah is covered in detail in Topic 1 (Context of the New Testament)*
> *but I will summarise here.*

MESSIAH comes from the Hebrew word, **Mashiach**, meaning *"the anointed one,"* or *"the chosen one."* In Old Testament times, prophets, priests, and kings were anointed when they were given their positions of responsibility. This ceremony involved pouring oil into the hair and beard to make it shine. The anointing was a sign that God had chosen them. Over time, "messiah" stopped meaning *anyone* who had been anointed to be God's chosen leader – it started to mean a *particular* person who was chosen by God for a very special destiny.

1st century Jews believed there would be one particular Messiah, sent by God to free the Jewish people from their oppressors and begin a MESSIANIC AGE, a sort of Golden Age on Earth. This person would be:

- A descendent of King David (**Isaiah 11: 1**)
- Born in Bethlehem in Judea (**Micah 5: 2**)
- Some Jews expected a **Kingly Messiah** who would drive out the occupying Romans from Judea and set up an independent Jewish kingdom
- Others expected a **Priestly Messiah** who would reform the corrupt Temple in Jerusalem and bring back the true worship of God
- Others expected a **Prophetic Messiah** who would arrive before Judgement Day
- There may have been some who expected a **Suffering Messiah** who would die an atoning death for the sake of mankind; this is the Christian view

Christos (Christ) is the Greek equivalent of the Hebrew term, Messiah. Jesus asks his disciples who people think that he is (**Mark 8:27-30**). They reply that some people think he is the prophet Elijah come back to Earth and some that he is John the Baptist restored to life. When he asks them who *they* think he is, Peter says simply: *"You are the* Christos*"* meaning: *"You are the Messiah."*

Matthew's Gospel goes to great lengths to prove that Jesus is the Messiah using **proof-texts**, which are quotes from the Old Testament that apply to Jesus, sometimes in unexpected ways. Matthew has to go to this trouble because Jesus' life doesn't fit the expectations about the Messiah in obvious ways: for example, he is a Galilean from Nazareth, not a Judean from Bethlehem. Scholars call this a CRITERON OF EMBARRASSMENT: we can be very sure the historical Jesus really was from Galilee because the Gospel-writers would never have invented such an embarrassing detail. **Matthew** claims Jesus was born in Bethlehem but his family left because of political persecution by King Herod; **Luke** claims Jesus' family was visiting Bethlehem for a census and Jesus was born there, but then they returned home to Galilee.

The concept of the **Messiah** (p12) is explored more fully in **Topic 1 (Context of the New Testament)**.

Synoptic Title: Son of God

In the Roman Empire, sons of gods were not uncommon. Hercules was a popular demigod worshiped by soldiers and he was the son of Zeus and a mortal woman. It was widely believed that the great heroes of the past had gods for parents. In the Eastern Empire, in places like Egypt, it was common for kings and pharaohs to be descended from gods. This was less common among the Romans themselves, but the first Emperor, Augustus, used the initials **D.F.**, which stand for *divi filius* ('son of the divine one') or *dei filius* ('son of God'). Augustus put this title on his coins and 'son of God' was also used by the next Emperor, Tiberius, who ruled during Jesus' lifetime.

One of Augustus' coins, declaring him to be the son of God

John Dominic Crossan suggests the first Christians deliberately used 'Son of God' to present Jesus as a rival to the Roman Emperor

At the same time as Jesus, another traveling philosopher and miracle-worker lived in Turkey. He was **Apollonius of Tyana** [*right*]. Apollonius had prophecies about his birth and grew up to be a teacher, healer and miracle-worker. After being executed by the Roman Emperor, he is supposed to have appeared to his followers, who believed he was the son of Zeus. Apollonius was another 'son of God' in the Roman Empire of the 1st century.

Jews believe in one God who is a spirit and does not come to Earth to mate with human women. The claim to be 'God' or 'son of God' would be **blasphemy** for Jews.

However, the Old Testament does use the phrase 'son of God' on occasions. **Angels** are called sons of God and so are **kings**. The **Jewish people as a whole** are collectively called 'Israel' and referred to as 'God's son'. **C.H. Dodd** argues that, by the 1st century, many Jews expected the Messiah to be the 'son of God'. These Old Testament titles are **symbolic** and 'son of God' seems to mean someone specially chosen by God, sent by God and blessed by God – not a literal child born to God.

Christians don't believe God had sex with Mary to produce a demigod son. The Christian view is that **Jesus is a human in whom God is uniquely present**.

- This does mean that Jesus **reveals God** in everything he says and does.
- It **doesn't** mean there are two Gods – a powerful father-God and his lesser son-God – because God is indivisible; to be the 'Son of God' is to **be** God
- It does mean that Jesus is someone who perfectly surrenders his will to God's work and who invites God to be present in his soul at all times – the perfect human with a perfect relationship with God (which is why Jesus is called the "*last Adam*" because he is what Adam should have been)
- But it **doesn't** mean that Jesus is 'God in disguise' – God **pretending** to be human or a body with God's spirit **instead of** a human soul

There are a lot of tensions in this view. Some Christians emphasize the divine quality in Jesus and present him as a supernatural being walking the Earth; others emphasize the human quality, presenting him as the perfect embodiment of what all humans try to be. Jesus tells his followers that they too are "children of God" so there is a debate about whether Jesus is the Son of God in a special, unique sense or if **all** humans who **believe in him** (p93) become **Children of God** (p96) just like him.

Implications: Did Jesus call himself 'Son of God'?

Mark's Gospel begins by calling Jesus the "Son of God" and it ends with a Roman Centurion at the foot of the Cross echoing this title:

> *Surely this man was the Son of God!* – **Mark 15: 39**

However, Jesus himself never calls himself 'Son of God' in **Mark's Gospel**, at least not directly. Various demons recognise Jesus as the Son of God and he doesn't deny the title – though he tells the demons to keep it secret. At Jesus' baptism, a voice from Heaven calls Jesus the Son of God.

In **Matthew**, the phrase 'Son of God' is applied to Jesus by his Disciples and Jesus praises them and does not deny it. **Matthew** and **Luke** both begin with Jesus' miraculous birth where an angel reveals that Jesus is the 'Son of God'.

John's Gospel contains the most references to Jesus being God's Son – and the Johannine Jesus (Jesus as he appears in **John's Gospel**) specifically talks about himself this way.

Some scholars conclude that Jesus never referred to himself as the Son of God. However, his later followers did believe that Jesus was divine and so the later Gospels have more references to this. This means the idea of Jesus being the 'Son of God' only formed after Jesus died.

> *The sayings and deeds of Jesus reported in the Gospels have been influenced by hindsight after the Resurrection* – **Raymond E. Brown**

However, even though Jesus might not **call** himself the 'Son of God', he still **acts** like he is. Jesus forgives sins (which only God can do) and he refers to God as 'Father'. This suggests that Jesus thought of himself as God's Son and taught his followers this.

Implications: Low vs High Christology

Christology means a theory about who Jesus Christ is. A 'low' Christology focuses on Jesus as a human being – a great prophet, the **Messiah** – whereas a 'high' Christology focuses on Jesus as being God.

> *"Low Christology" covers the evaluation of him in terms which do not necessarily include divinity, e.g. messiah, rabbi, prophet, high priest, saviour, master. "High Christology" covers the evaluation of Jesus in terms which include* an aspect of *divinity, e.g. Lord, Son of God, God* – **Raymond E. Brown**

As Christianity developed in the 1st century CE, the 'low' Christology that is detectable in the Synoptic Gospels evolved into a 'high' Christology that is obvious in **John's Gospel**.

> However, it's not as simple as that. The earliest Christian documents aren't the Gospels at all - they're the letters of Paul in the New Testament. and Paul seems to have a very 'high' Christology too. So either the first Christians really did have a high Christological view of Jesus - or Paul created this high Christology and gradually the early churches came round to his view.

Some Christians kept to a very low Christology. The Ebionites were an early Christian sect who remained Jewish but believed Jesus was their Messiah but he was not God. The Ebionites disappeared from history as high Christological beliefs took over and became **orthodox**.

Bart Ehrman argues that most early Christians had a **Christology of Exaltation** - they believed that Jesus had been a normal human but that God had **exalted** him (elevated him or raised him up) to divine status. This exaltation takes place when Jesus is raised from the dead. Ehrman thinks this Christology of Exaltation gradually faded as time passed.

A similar idea is that God **adopted** Jesus to be his Son. This is called the ADOPTIONIST MODEL. The moment of Jesus' adoption by God can be seen in his baptism when a voice from Heaven says:

> *You are my Son, whom I love; with you I am well pleased* – **Mark 1: 11**

Jesus' baptism is described almost identically in all three Synoptic Gospels, with **Matthew** feeling the need to explain why a sinless Jesus would need to be baptized at all.

However, Ehrman argues that John's Gospel has a **Christology of Incarnation** – its author believes that Jesus is the **Word made Flesh** (p81), the Logos of God in a human identity. This is why **John's Gospel** never mentions Jesus being baptized (or even calls John the Baptist by the title 'Baptist'): according to this view, Jesus was *always* God's Son.

This shift from a Christology of Exaltation to a Christology of Incarnation might explain why **Matthew** presents John the Baptist as being reluctant to baptize Jesus – Matthew holds to a higher Christology than **Mark** and views Jesus as exalted by God at birth.

Gradually, the high incarnation Christology replaced the low exaltation Christology in most churches. However, there are **Unitarian Churches** today which still believe in a low Christology and interpret 'Son of God' more symbolically. There are also **Jehovah's Witnesses**, who believe that Jesus was the incarnation of an angelic being, but not God.

Is the concept of "Son of God" essential for understanding Jesus' identity?

YES	NO
Jesus is God's **revelation**: God revealed in a human life. Jesus expresses this directly on occasions, but reveals it all the time through his behaviour (commanding demons, controlling nature, forgiving sins). Jesus' atoning death only removes sins if he is God and his Resurrection is explained by the fact that, as God, he can conquer death.	"Son of God" is a **Hellenic** term that crept into Christianity when Gentile converts brought their pagan ideas to their new religion. Jesus himself didn't claim to be the 'Son of God' and, as a Jew, would have found the title offensive. He saw himself, and his first followers saw him, as a teacher and a prophet.
The 'Son of God' isn't a pagan idea; it's a phrase used in the Old Testament and by the 1st century it had become a title for the Messiah. Jesus saw himself as more than a teacher: he cast out demons, raised the dead and – most importantly – forgave sins, which only God can do.	Even if Jesus claimed to be the 'Son of God' it's not clear what he meant. Was he a human adopted by God at his baptism? Exalted by God after his death? Or was he a divine being living a human life? If he was a divine being, was he an angel, the **Logos** or God himself?

Synoptic Title: Son of Man

This is one of the more baffling titles in the Bible. In the New Testament, it occurs 85 times, mostly in **Matthew** and **Luke**, less often in **Mark** and least of all in **John**. It seems to occur nowhere else, though a similar Hebrew expression (*ben-adam*) occurs about 100 times in the Old Testament. The phrase doesn't seem to be Greek or Hebrew originally: it's Aramaic (*bar-nash*) which is the language Jesus and his Disciples actually spoke.

"Son of Man" was one of Jesus' favourite terms for himself. Because the expression is not used in the other New Testament letters and books, nor in any other Jewish or Christian writings from the same time, many scholars believe it to be the IPSISSIMA VERBA – the true voice or actual words – of Jesus. This was how he *actually talked*.

> *the Son of Man did not come to be served, but to serve, and to give his life as a ransom for many* – **Matthew 20: 8**

The phrase is taken to refer to Jesus' humanity, rather than **Son of God** (p112) which describes Jesus' divinity. As 'Son of Man', Jesus is a human being living a human life in a human environment (**1st century Palestine**) with all the troubles, difficulties, joys and challenges that involves. Christians believe Jesus to be both fully God and fully human. As God, Jesus is all-powerful and all-knowing, in control of every situation and assured of what will happen in the future; as a human being, he is frail and limited, powerless in the face of tyranny and troubled by fears and doubts.

For example, when he is waiting for his arrest, Jesus prays to be spared the ordeal ahead. He's in such distress that he sweats blood.

> *And being in anguish, he prayed more earnestly, and his sweat was like drops of blood falling to the ground* – **Luke 22: 44**

Uses of the phrase "Son of Man" fall into three categories in the Synoptic Gospels: the **Coming Son of Man** who will arrive on Judgment Day, the **Suffering Son of Man** who will be tortured and killed and the **Faithful Son of Man** who is God's humble servant.

The Coming Son of Man

Jesus often refers to the Son of Man appearing in the future, on Judgment Day. These are the expressions where it sounds least like he is talking about himself and more like someone else, though the context shows he clearly means himself. This 'Son of Man' is based on a figure described in the Old Testament in the prophecies of **Daniel**:

> *In my vision at night I looked, and there before me was one like a son of man coming with the clouds of heaven* – **Daniel 7: 13**

In Daniel's vision, the Son of Man is led into the presence of God and given the authority to rule the world. This might refer to an angel but for many Jews, this prophecy describes the **Messiah** (p12). By calling himself the Son of Man, Jesus is claiming this authority for himself: he has been given God's authority over the world and he will be the judge on Judgment Day.

Jesus refers to this image again when he is being accused by the High Priest of blasphemy. The High Priests asks Jesus if he is the Son of God and Jesus replies:

> *I am ... And you will see the Son of Man sitting at the right hand of the Mighty One and coming on the clouds of heaven –* **Mark 14: 62**

Notice Jesus answers "I am" - you will meet this meaningful phrase again in John's Gospel

This reply provokes the priests to a fury and they sentence Jesus to death for **blasphemy**. Jesus is claiming to be more than the Messiah: the Son of Man is the Cosmic Judge who arrives on Judgement Day and decides who goes to Heaven and who goes to Hell.

The Suffering Son of Man

Jesus talks about the Son of Man being destined to suffer. This might refer to the idea that humanity in general suffers (and, as a human being, Jesus suffers too), but it also predicts Jesus' own suffering and death:

> *He then began to teach them that the Son of Man must suffer many things and be rejected by the elders, the chief priests and the teachers of the law, and that he must be killed and after three days rise again –* **Mark 8: 31**

The disciples do not understand Jesus when he talks this way (but in the Synoptics, the disciples never seem to understand Jesus). Perhaps they thought by 'Son of Man' he was referring to God's prophets generally - but after the crucifixion they looked back on his words in a new way.

This description of the Son of Man being destined to suffer resembles the **Suffering Servant** from **Isaiah's prophecies** (p20). Isaiah doesn't use the phrase 'Son of Man' so by linking the Son of Man to the Suffering Servant, Jesus is connecting ideas in the Old Testament that weren't ordinarily seen as related: a **Suffering Messiah**.

The Faithful Son of Man

In a rather more cheerful tone, Jesus uses 'Son of Man' to refer to his own Ministry and the work he does preaching and healing. All three Synoptics describe Jesus healing a paralysed man, saying:

> *The Son of Man has authority on earth to forgive sins –* **Mark 2: 10**

Jesus doesn't just heal diseases and broken bodies – he fixes humans' relationship with God by forgiving their sins. Ultimately he does this by dying an atoning death on the Cross – so the Faithful Son of Man is linked to the Suffering Son of Man. This sort of use of 'Son of Man' seems to come from the Old Testament prophet **Ezekiel**. Ezekiel is the book in the Old Testament that contains the most uses of the Hebrew phrase 'Son of Man': it is the way God addresses Ezekiel as his servant. God calls Ezekiel like this:

Son of man, stand up on your feet and I will speak to you – **Ezekiel 1: 2**

The Hebrew phrase here is ben-adam and means "human being". It's a humble title, but it seems to be the inspiration behind Jesus' term for himself doing God's work as "Son of Man"

Ezekiel is a popular Old Testament prophet. He lived in the 6th century BCE, at the time of the destruction of the Jewish Kingdom of Judah by the Babylonians. Ezekiel himself was one of the Jews sent to live in exile in Babylon. His prophecy mixes stark warnings about how God punishes the Jewish people for their sins with hope and yearning for their eventual return to their homeland. This mixture of stern criticism and tender compassion mirrors Jesus' preaching; it makes sense for Jesus to associate himself with Ezekiel by the title 'Son of Man'.

Is the concept of "Son of Man" essential for understanding Jesus' identity?

YES

It's important not to lose sight of Jesus' humanity, especially after reading the **high Christology** of **John's Prologue**. The phrase 'Son of Man' reminds us that Jesus was human and that his sufferings were real, not a pantomime put on by a divine being who cannot feel pain or loss.

'Son of Man' is IPSISSIMA VERBA - Jesus' own actual words. He uses it to mean different things in different places. When he confronts the arrogant priests, he warns them that he is their judge on Judgement Day; to his Disciples, he warns them of his future Resurrection; to ordinary people, he updates **Ezekiel's warnings** about sin and promise of forgiveness.

NO

'Son of Man' seems to be a literary title. It refers to an angelic being or cosmic judge in **Daniel's vision** or else it refers to the long-dead prophet **Ezekiel**. It's not clear why it's been applied to Jesus. Scholars still debate what it means and why Jesus used it.

Even if the phrase 'Son of Man' is an authentic expression of Jesus', its precise relevance has been lost. It's not used by **Paul** (who focuses on the divine Risen Christ) and barely used by **John** (who claims Jesus is the **Word made Flesh**); the other New Testament writers ignore it too. Plainly, it lost meaning for later Christians who still view Jesus as **'Son of God'** instead.

"I Am" Statements in John's Gospel

Throughout **John's Gospel**, when Jesus identifies himself, he uses the phrase **"I Am…"** with great importance. When the priests question Jesus about whom he claims to be, Jesus replies:

before Abraham was born, I am! – **John 8: 58**

On the face of it, this is an absurd thing to say (the Jewish ancestor Abraham lived at least 1500 years before Jesus) but Jesus' remark is so shocking that the priests try to stone Jesus to death there and then. This is because "I AM" is the holy name of God himself. This is the way God identified himself to Moses when he spoke out of the Burning Bush:

I am who I am. This is what you are to say to the Israelites: "I am has sent me to you" – **Exodus 3: 14**

I AM WHO I AM in Hebrew is *ehyeh-asher-ehyeh* but it is normally represented by a four letter code: **YHWH**. This is the name of God. It's pronounced "Yahweh" but religious Jews do not pronounce it – it's too holy to be said by ordinary people. It's too holy to be written down. By Jesus' time, references to YHWH in the Old Testament had been replaced with another word, **ADONAI** ("The Lord"). Modern Jews often use the phrase **Ha-Shem** ("The Name") to refer to God.

Because of this background, there's a huge significance to Jesus' use of the phrase "I Am" when he names himself. He's linking himself to God and taking the holy name of God for himself.

> *The Gospels are written in Greek, so Jesus actually says EGO EIMI, not "YAHWEH". Also, Jesus would have spoken Aramaic, not Hebrew. So Jesus wasn't going around pronouncing the holy name of God out loud. But his listeners would recognise his reference to the name of God - and a claim to __be__ that God.*

There are seven particular occasions when the Johannine Jesus speaks this way:

1. I AM THE BREAD OF LIFE
2. I AM THE LIGHT OF THE WORLD
3. I am the gate for the sheep
4. I AM THE GOOD SHEPHERD
5. I am the resurrection and the life
6. I am the way, the truth, and the life
7. I AM THE TRUE VINE

> *These are the seven "I Am" statements in **John** - but for the exam you only need to be familiar with four (in CAPITALS). These passages form Anthology extract #3, so you need to be able to analyse these in depth*

There are also a few "I Am" statements in the Synoptic Gospels (such as **Mark 14: 62** where the High Priest demands to know if Jesus is the **Son of God** and Jesus replies *"I Am")* and the stunned or angry reaction of listeners shows that Jesus is understood to be making a shocking claim.

"I Am the Bread of Life"

> [35] Then Jesus declared, "I am the bread of life. Whoever comes to me will never go hungry, and whoever believes in me will never be thirsty.

This Discourse is delivered immediately after the **Feeding of the 5000** (p147). The entire Discourse is a *midrash* on the preceding Sign. A *midrash* is a Jewish term for an interpretation of a Biblical passage, explaining its meaning and importance.

This follows a common pattern in John's Gospel: Jesus provides a Sign but the crowds take it at its most literal level, so Jesus has to explain the deeper meaning in the Sign. The crowd has had its physical hunger satisfied by the loaves of bread, but Jesus intends to satisfy their **spiritual hunger** for a closer relationship with God. Bread is essential for life in most cultures – it's the basic foodstuff that poor people depend on. Jesus is offering **spiritual bread** that provides spiritual life instead.

Jesus is contrasted with **Moses**, the greatest Jewish prophet. In the Old Testament, Moses led the Israelites out of slavery in Egypt towards the Promised Land. The Israelites spent 40 years as nomads in the wilderness. When they were starving, God sent them a miraculous food to eat called *manna*.

The Israelites gather manna from heaven in Exodus 16

Jesus explains that the Bread of Life he is offering is superior to the *manna* that Moses provided. The *manna* did not stay fresh: if it was not eaten immediately, it rotted. Jesus declares that his Bread will never spoil. Moreover, although the *manna* kept the Israelites alive for a time, they still died in the wilderness and only their children reached the Promised Land. Jesus declares that those who eat his bread will have **Eternal Life** (p87). He then reveals that the real bread he is offering to his followers is HIMSELF.

Jesus explains that his followers need to **believe in him** (p93) to receive this Bread of Life. More specifically, they need to eat his body and drink his blood. Jesus is referring to his Crucifixion, where he will die an atoning death. More specifically, he is describing the **EUCHARIST**, which is the meal of bread and wine which is the central act of Christian worship. Christians believe that the bread is the body of Christ and the wine is the blood of Christ: by eating and drinking, they commemorate Christ's death and share in his Resurrection.

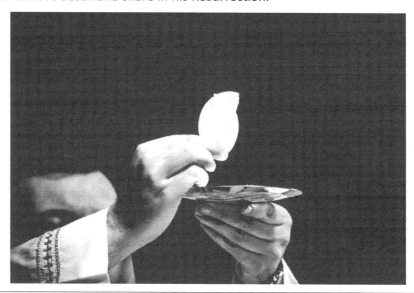

This Eucharistic theme also occurs in the Discourse where Jesus says "I am the True Vine".

Raymond E. Brown argues that this passage has two parts. The SAPIENTIAL (wisdom) THEME involves Jesus' teachings. The bread symbolises his teachings, which will nourish people forever, unlike the Old Testament. The crowd "*grumbling*" about Jesus' teaching echoes the way the Israelites complained about Moses leading them into the desert.

The SACRAMENTAL THEME in this Discourse symbolises the Eucharist. Brown does not think Jesus really said these words, since they would have made no sense to 1st century Jews before the Eucharistic ceremony had been invented; he argues this sacramental theme was added in later by the author of **John**.

Implications

John's Gospel does not contain the **Last Supper**. This is a scene in all three Synoptic Gospels where, the night before his Crucifixion, Jesus shares a Passover meal with his Disciples and instructs them to eat bread and drink wine in memory of him. However, this *midrash* in John's Gospel serves the same function: it sets up the Eucharist (and the **Feeding of the 5000** took place at Passover too).

The Eucharist is also known as **Holy Communion** or the **Lord's Supper**. It is a ritual observed by the very earliest Christians and is described by **Paul**, who wrote about it in the late 50s CE:

> *the Lord Jesus on the night when he was betrayed took bread, and when he had given thanks, he broke it, and said, "This is my body which is for you. Do this in remembrance of me"* – **1 Corinthians 11: 23-24**

Paul wrote this description decades before John's Gospel was written, so the Eucharistic meal was very well established by the time John wrote his *midrash* on the meaning of the **Feeding of the 5000** (p147).

Christians are divided on how to interpret the Eucharist. **Roman Catholics** believe that, in a supernatural sense, the bread and wine really becomes Christ's body and blood (this is called TRANSUBSTANTIATION). **Protestant Christians** are more likely to believe that the bread and wine are purely **symbolic**. The debate about the 'Real Presence' of Christ in the bread and wine has escalated into violence and warfare between different Christian groups in the past.

John's Gospel has been used by both sides of the debate to support their view of the Eucharist. However, it's clear that, for John, it is **believing in Jesus** (p93) that is important, not the bread and wine themselves.

Is the concept of "Bread of Life" essential for understanding Jesus' identity?

YES	NO
Without understanding the Bread of Life, Jesus' miracle the previous day is just a party trick! As the true bread, Jesus is essential for our spiritual life: he 'feeds' us through faith. Moreover, this passage explains the importance of the Eucharist as a celebration of Jesus' atoning death and Resurrection.	The Eucharist has been deeply divisive for Christians and has resulted in wars between Catholics and Protestants with different understandings of what it means. It's ironic that the 'Bread of Life' has led to so much death and hatred.
The Bread of Life isn't purely about the Eucharist. It also represents God's **grace** in forgiving sins and offering **Eternal Life** to those who **believe in Jesus**.	As usual, it's unfortunate that Christians focus on spiritual life rather than moral behaviour. Jesus offered moral teachings about love, forgiveness and generosity, but they are missing in this discussion.

"I Am the Light of the World"

8 [12] When Jesus spoke again to the people, he said, "I am the light of the world. Whoever follows me will never walk in darkness, but will have the light of life."

Jesus Heals a Man Born Blind

9 As he went along, he saw a man blind from birth. [2] His disciples asked him, "Rabbi, who sinned, this man or his parents, that he was born blind?"

[3] "Neither this man nor his parents sinned," said Jesus, "but this happened so that the works of God might be displayed in him. [4] As long as it is day, we must do the works of him who sent me. Night is coming, when no one can work. [5] While I am in the world, I am the light of the world."

John's Prologue introduces the theme of **Light and Darkness** (p90) and this passage continues it. **Isaiah 49: 6** prophesied that the Messiah would be a "*light to the Gentiles*" and **Isaiah 42: 7** said he would "*open eyes that are blind*". Jesus here puts these prophecies into action.

The passage concerns **a man who was born blind** (p155). The discussion represents a popular idea in 1st century Judaism that illness was a punishment for sin; illness from birth would therefore be a punishment for the parents' sins (since Jews do not believe in reincarnation).

> *You might see a connection here to **solutions to the problem of evil**: the disciples are inviting Jesus to offer a theodicy explaining why there is suffering in the world.*

Jesus rejects the popular idea that sickness is a punishment for sin. He suggests that sickness is an opportunity for God's works to be displayed.

> *You could link this to the **Irenaean theodicy**, which proposes that God causes (or at any rate, allows) evil and suffering so that goodness might come out of it.*

Raymond E Brown interprets this passage **symbolically**. The man's blindness represents ignorance, in the way that the Gentiles are ignorant of the God of the Old Testament. This is not their fault (which is why Jesus makes it clear that it's not sin that makes them ignorant) unless they insist on remaining ignorant when Jesus arrives to open their eyes. The '*works of God will be displayed*' in them when they convert to Christianity. This will fulfill Isaiah's prophecy about the Messiah *opening eyes* and *being a light*.

So really, this passage is about the first Gentile Christians who **believe** (p93), contrasting them with the Jews who don't believe in Jesus and remain in the **darkness** of ignorance, even though they have the Old Testament scripture to guide them.

> *The blind man knows little and yet learns much; the Pharisees know everything and can be taught nothing* – **Raymond E. Brown**

To add to the irony, this passage takes place during the **Feast of Tabernacles**. This was a Harvest Festival for the Jews and at this time the Temple in Jerusalem was lit up by giant torches. That's why it's appropriate for Jesus to talk about **light** (p90) at this time. The symbolism is that the Temple is brightly lit, but the people worshipping there are in darkness The REAL Temple is Jesus himself and he is giving out light through his teachings.

Other Christian writers have read even deeper symbolism into this passage. For **Augustine of Hippo**, being "*born blind*" is a reference to **original sin**. Since all human beings are born into original sin (according to Augustine) this means that:

> *The blind man is the human race* – **Augustine of Hippo**

Whichever way you interpret the passage, Jesus claims to be the cure for human blindness, both physically and spiritually. Those who believe in Jesus will "*never walk in darkness*" because they will receive **Eternal Life** (p87). Jesus also hints at his own Crucifixion, which is the coming of "*night*". The three Synoptic Gospels describe **darkness** falling over the world for three hours while Jesus dies (e.g. **Mark 15: 33**).

> *Interestingly, John's account of the crucifixion does not mention darkness falling over the world during the Crucifixion. I suspect the rather sophisticated author of John's Gospel found this detail a bit too clumsily literal. The darkness he's talking about is a spiritual darkness of ignorance and moral confusion, not just a solar eclipse.*

Implications

Jesus' identification with the Light of the World inspires the use of candles in Christian worship. In many churches, the PASCHAL CANDLE is lit on Easter Sunday and used at services throughout the year. When people are baptised, they are given a baptism candle that is lit from the Paschal Candle. This symbolizes the **Light** passing out into the world and to the next generation. The Paschal Candle is also lit at funerals, representing the hope of **Eternal Life.**

A year later, on the Thursday night before Good Friday, the candle is extinguished and the church is in darkness for three days, representing Christ's death. A new Paschal Candle is lit on the Sunday to celebrate his Resurrection.

John's Gospel isn't the only place where "Light" is used as a symbol of awakening from ignorance. In the 18th century, the ENLIGHTENMENT was a great transformation in the way Europeans saw themselves, their world and the future.

This involved rejecting tradition and religious authority, putting reason ahead of **revelation**, following science as a means of discovering truth and making human well-being the central concern of morality. The great scholars of the Enlightenment saw human knowledge as a light, pushing back the darkness of superstition.

> *SAPERE AUDE! 'Have courage to use your own reason!' - that is the motto of Enlightenment* – **Immanuel Kant**

Other religions offer different definitions of Enlightenment. In **Buddhism**, Enlightenment means coming to see reality as it really is, free from the distorting patterns of fear, desire and aversion. Instead of pursuing reason and science, Buddhists seek Enlightenment through detachment. Ultimately, complete detachment leads Buddhists to a state of Nibbana, which is blissful but without passion or self-centredness.

The Christian response is that *all* of these forms of Enlightenment are only reflections of the true Light which is Jesus Christ. Whenever human beings understand things clearly, it is Jesus who lights up their minds. This view is sometimes called CHRISTIAN TRIUMPHALISM: it is the belief that even people who don't think they are Christians are being Christians really when they are at their best.

> *To be fair, Christians aren't the only ones who enjoy a bit of triumphalism. Buddhists will tell you that Jesus acted like a Buddhist when he was detached from pain and suffering; Marxists will tell you Jesus was a good Marxist when he cared about the poor. Nevertheless, Jesus seems to go further by saying that, as the Light of the World, he's the inspiration behind <u>every</u> good idea.*

Is the concept of "Light of the World" essential for understanding Jesus' identity?

YES	NO
Jesus is the Light because his teachings are clearer and more illuminating than any sacred scriptures or moral guides. He is the Light OF THE WORLD because his message is not just for the Jews, but for the Gentiles too. The Christian message is **universal**, which is why Jesus' disciples set out to spread the word.	Jesus' message can't be **universal**. He lived at a particular place and time. He was attacking problems with the Jewish religion as it was in the 1st century. For centuries, most people in the world had never heard of Jesus or his message yet they still managed to be good people and treat each other decently.
Jesus is not just a 'man of his time' and his message of forgiveness and love is relevant to everyone. That's why Christian missionaries put themselves at risk to bring the Gospel to everyone. Even people who don't encounter the Christian message answer to their consciences - and the conscience is also the voice of Christ. That's why he's the Light of the World.	Christian missionary work has caused a lot of mischief in the world and put Christians in the position of forcing people to convert to their religion, which is shameful. Christian triumphalism is less dangerous, but it's still arrogant. Jesus wasn't the only moral teacher and there are other ways to Enlightenment than converting to Christianity.

"I Am the Good Shepherd"

In this famous Discourse, Jesus makes three **"I Am" statements** that are linked by the theme of shepherding.

> *The Bible loves sheep - there are over 220 references to shepherds or sheep.*

> [7] Therefore Jesus said again, "Very truly I tell you, I am the gate for the sheep. [8] All who have come before me are thieves and robbers, but the sheep have not listened to them. [9] I am the gate; whoever enters through me will be saved.

Jesus is using imagery very familiar to his listeners in **1st century Palestine**. Peasant shepherds would herd their sheep into a stonewalled yard beside the house or barn. Sheep were the main farming animal in this region (cows need too much water, pigs were off limits for Jews), providing wool and mutton. Robbers who would 'rustle' sheep were a problem as were wolves and even lions who would try to make off with a meal. Meanwhile, the shepherds were the lowest-paid farm workers, with little incentive to risk their lives to protect someone else's flock.

> *Although there are no Parables in John's Gospel, this passage about thieves trying to break into the sheepfold is similar to one - an extended metaphor*

Obviously, the sheep represent the ordinary Jewish people – the *"lost sheep of Israel"* (**Matthew 15: 24**) as Jesus calls them. If Jesus is the gate, then he is the way for the sheep to leave the pen and enter the pastures, which is a **symbol** for **Eternal Life** (p87). This echoes another Johannine "I Am" statement:

> *I am the way and the truth and the life. No one comes to the Father except through me –* **John 14: 6**

Raymond E. Brown suggests that the *"thieves and robbers"* are the Pharisees. These are people who *claim* to offer the way to God through LEGALISM (following rules and laws closely). Jesus implies that these religious teachers have 'hijacked' the Jewish faith: they don't really represent the sort of religion God promised to Abraham. Ordinary people can't keep all the rules the Pharisees lay down (which is why the sheep *"have not listened to them"*) but they can **believe in Jesus** (p93).

> [11] "I am the good shepherd. The good shepherd lays down his life for the sheep.

Unlike the 'hirelings' who only guard the flock because they are (poorly) paid, the Good Shepherd is motivated by love.

Other Bible passages link Jesus to a Good Shepherd who will not allow a single sheep to become lost. In real life, sheep would wander away from the flock and perhaps get trapped in ditches. A dedicated shepherd would go in search of the sheep. This is a reference to **God's Word becoming flesh** (p81) – coming to Earth to seek out lost souls.

The image of Christ as a shepherd rescuing a sheep is common in the earliest Christian art.

The idea of the heroic shepherd goes back to the story of **King David**. In his youth, David was a shepherd and bravely fought off lions to defend his father's flock. Jesus is of the **line of David** (p15) and, like David, is defending his father's flock - but his father is God and the flock is the entire Jewish people.

When Jesus talks about *'laying down his life for his sheep'*, he is predicting his Crucifixion: David only had to face down lions and survived; Jesus will have to face down the **Sadducees and the Pharisees** and the **Roman Empire**, but he is prepared to die an atoning death to save people from sin.

Early Christian art shows Jesus as the Good Shepherd

The Old Testament often uses the image of God as the Good Shepherd (e.g. **Ezekiel 37: 24**) so by claiming to be the Shepherd, Jesus is identifying himself with God.

> [14] "I am the good shepherd; I know my sheep and my sheep know me – [15] just as the Father knows me and I know the Father – and I lay down my life for the sheep. [16] I have other sheep that are not of this sheep pen. I must bring them also.

Jesus insists that his sheep *'know him'* – that they have a relationship with him because they **believe in him** (p93) rather than just following his rules. Jesus offers a relationship of love with his followers (unlike the Pharisees who offer only rules to follow) and this is the same love that exists between himself and God. This echoes the reference in the Prologue to the **Word of God knowing God** (p81) and bringing this knowledge to humans.

> *If you're doubtful about whether sheep can really know their own shepherd, a **2017 study by Cambridge University** confirmed that sheep can recognise human faces.*

Jesus adds a crucial extra detail: the Good Shepherd has other sheep too and will go in search of them. These *'other sheep'* are the Gentiles. Jesus' atoning death will not just be to save the Jewish people, but all people.

Implications

The earliest Christian leaders were called **pastors** (from the Latin for 'shepherd'). Bishops carried a sign of their authority: a **crozier**, modeled on a shepherd's crook (the stick used by shepherds to 'hook' sheep and pull them out of harm's way).

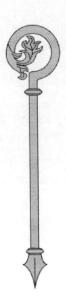

Raymond E. Brown proposes that the **Johannine Community** (p208) didn't have pastors and was more egalitarian than the other Christian churches of the time. Therefore, this passage about Jesus being the Good Shepherd is meant to say that Christ, not any human, is the true 'pastor' of the church.

The freewheeling Johannine Community didn't last and powerful pastors were promoted to be bishops and then Popes. Christianity became a HIERARCHICAL RELIGION, with ranks and power at the top. These leaders have sometimes exploited this power and abused their followers (for example, directing them to war during the Crusades, torturing people for their beliefs during the Inquisition, right up to the recent child sex abuse scandals in the Catholic Church).

Critics say that the imagery of shepherds/sheep is partly responsible for this. Sheep are unintelligent and directionless; they cannot survive in the wild without the shepherd to keep them safe. By viewing Christian believers as 'sheep', Christianity has a low opinion of them and encourages BLIND FAITH.

Is the concept of "Good Shepherd" essential for understanding Jesus' identity?

YES	**NO**
The Good Shepherd puts Jesus in the tradition of the Old Testament, where the original patriarchs like **Abraham** were shepherds and **King David** started life as a shepherd. The image shows Christ's heroic love in coming to Earth and sacrificing himself for humans.	By presenting believers as 'sheep' who needs a 'shepherd', Christianity encourages blind faith rather than reason and judgment. Pastors have often misused their power and silenced believers who ask questions. It's an unfortunate metaphor with nasty consequences in history.
Jesus' original audience understood how maddeningly stupid sheep were. By presenting himself as the Good Shepherd, Christ reassures us that God loves us despite our sinfulness and our failure to follow his commands; it reminds us that we depend on God and cannot survive without him.	Jesus accuses the Pharisees of trying to 'steal' sheep that are rightfully his - but the Pharisees felt that Jesus was the one trying to 'hijack' Judaism and start a new religion of his own. If we're supposed to be sheep, we can't use reason to work out which shepherd to follow.

"I Am the True Vine"

In this Discourse, Jesus compares himself to a vine in a vineyard and God to the gardener. The gardener 'prunes' the vine by cutting away useless branches. In gardening, this makes the plant healthier and the remaining branches grow even more grapes.

The Vine and the Branches

15 "I am the true vine, and my Father is the gardener. [2] He cuts off every branch in me that bears no fruit, while every branch that does bear fruit he prunes so that it will be even more fruitful.

Vines were important crops in **1st century Palestine**. The Jews and the Romans both enjoyed wine which was drunk as a 'soft drink' when water was unhygienic. The Romans had a god of wine called Bacchus. Wine features in the Jewish Passover celebration, when four cups of wine are drunk to remember the Israelites' escape from slavery in Egypt and a fifth cup of wine is set aside (un-drunk) for the **Messiah** (p12).

In claiming to be the True Vine, Jesus identifies himself as the true god of wine instead of the false Bacchus and the real source of the Passover celebration – ironically, although the Jews set aside a cup of wine for the future Messiah, Christians believe the Messiah is already here.

More than that, the Old Testament uses the Vine as a symbol for the Jewish people as a whole – for 'Israel' as the Bible calls them. Religious Jews say these lines as part of their morning prayers:

> *You transplanted a vine from Egypt; you drove out the nations and planted it.*
> *You cleared the ground for it, and it took root and filled the land* – **Psalm 80: 8-9**

Jesus claims to be the root of the Vine, its source. He warns that God will prune the Vine, cutting off the branches that don't "*bear fruit*". This isn't just a warning to sinful Jews who have turned their backs on God; it's directed at the **Pharisees** (p64) and religious leaders who congratulate themselves on their Jewish ancestry but don't show love and humility in their lives.

The Synoptic Gospels echo this warning. In the **Parable of the Tenants (Matthew 21: 33-46)**, Jesus describes a vineyard where the tenant farmers refuse to pay the owner of the vineyard (God) the fruit of the harvest and even murder the owner's son (Jesus). The Parable ends with the owner throwing the tenants off the land and giving the vineyard to someone else - which links to God rejecting the Jews and transferring his blessings to the Gentile Christians.

> [5] "I am the vine; you are the branches. If you remain in me and I in you, you will bear much fruit; apart from me you can do nothing.

Jesus develops this metaphor further. The Disciples are the branches that DO bear fruit. This "*fruit*" is the **Eternal Life** (p87) they receive from God, but also their life of love and morality. Many Christians in the early church faced hardship and persecution, but they would look back upon these words and conclude that God was only 'pruning' them so that they could bear more fruit in future.

> *There are links here to the **Irenaean Theodicy**, which suggests that God causes (or at least, allows) suffering so that a greater good may come from it.*

Raymond E. Brown argues there are two themes here: a SAPIENTIAL theme that focuses on Jesus' teachings of love and a SACRAMENTAL theme that describes the Christian ceremony of the Eucharist.

The sapiential theme becomes clear at the end of the Discourse when Jesus makes clear what the "*fruit*" of his teaching is: LOVE. The Greek word used for 'love' here is ***AGAPE***, which means selfless, compassionate love. This is very different from *eros* (romantic love) or *storge* (the love for children or pets) or even *philia* (the love for friends). *Agape* is a DECISION to love rather than a feeling or an emotion: it is the decision to put other people before yourself. Jesus defines it as 'laying down one's life for one's friends' – self-sacrifice. Of course, this is also a subtle prediction of Jesus' own crucifixion.

The sacramental theme references the wine that is drunk in the **EUCHARIST** (just as the Eucharistic bread is referenced when Jesus claims to be the **Bread of Life**, p120). Christians drink the Communion wine in memory of Jesus shedding his blood when he died for their sins. Catholics believe the wine becomes Jesus' blood and this is what Jesus means when he says "*You remain in me and I in you*". Although John does not describe the **Last Supper**, he outlines the theology behind the Eucharist in passages like this.

Implications

The idea of the "fruits of the Holy Spirit" is developed by **Paul** and Paul also makes it clear that the greatest fruit is Love.

*And now these three remain: faith, hope and love. But the greatest of these is love – **1 Corinthians 13: 13***

Paul's "love is..." speech in *1 Corinthians 13: 1-13* is very popular at weddings. But that's a complete misunderstanding. Paul isn't talking about romantic love (eros). He means agape which is compassionate love, the sort of love you show to strangers, the needy and the poor.

Matthew's Gospel repeats this idea when Jesus is asked which is the 'greatest commandment' in the Old Testament and replies:

Love your neighbour as yourself – **Matthew 22: 39**

The idea that *agape*-love is at the heart of Christian ethics has been influential. In the 1960s, **Joseph Fletcher** developed **Situation Ethics** based on the idea of solving moral problems by putting *agape* into practice and asking "what would be the most loving thing to do?" Fletcher contrasts this **agapeic** approach with the LEGALISM of sticking to fixed moral rules that lead to misery or the ANTINOMIAN confusion of abandoning rules altogether.

However, agapeic ethics have been criticised. Following moral rules is clear-cut and straightforward whereas acting on *agape*-love seems to invite disagreement and confusion. It's not always clear what the most loving course of action is. Often, people confuse different types of love and think they are acting on *agape* when really they are motivated by some non-moral form of love like *eros*.

> *Really, you should give that money to a homeless person, but you buy flowers for your girlfriend instead. Both actions are 'loving', but only the first is really agape-love.*

Most churches reject Fletcher's Situation Ethics. They agree that love ought to characterize our relationships and make us charitable and forgiving, but it shouldn't **replace** moral rules.

Is the concept of "True Vine" essential for understanding Jesus' identity?

YES	NO
As the True Vine, Jesus is the reality behind the Jewish prophecies and rituals: he's the source of all inspiration and comfort, whereas real wine is only a false inspiration and comfort. The Jewish religion did not "*bear fruit*" and God's promises are instead fulfilled in those who **believe in Christ.**	This is another example of CHRISTIAN TRIUMPHALISM, where Christianity claims a sort of monopoly on everything good or wise in other religions. In reality, the Jewish Christians were thrown out of the Synagogues in the 80s and 90s CE but they represent themselves the 'true Jews'.
Jesus' message of *agape*-love is the distinctive feature of Christianity that makes it superior to other religions and philosophies, It replaces the **legalistic** attitudes of the **Pharisees** and the decadent lifestyles of the pagan Romans and continues to inspire people today.	Although lovely in principle, agape-love cannot be the basis of an ethical theory. Christian churches were the first to condemn **Joseph Fletcher**'s **Situation Ethics** when he suggested agape should be more important than moral rules. This is an aspect of Jesus' teaching that most Christians pay only lip-service to.

TOPIC 2.3 MIRACLES & SIGNS

The Exam expects you to be familiar with the miracles performed by Jesus in the New Testament and specifically with the seven 'Signs' performed by Jesus in John's Gospel. You will need to be able to interpret these on different levels. These Signs also comprise **Anthology extract #4**.

What are Miracles?

In the Synoptic Gospels, the Greek word *'dynamis'* is used for miracle it means 'act of power' (think of the word "dynamo" or "dynamic"). Jesus' miracles are public and dramatic: they produce wonder and amazement. These miracles include healing people with visible disabilities, driving out demons and *'unclean spirits'* that shriek and curse (either the spirits make this noise or the possessed lunatics do, it's not clear) and even more astonishing powers over the world around him like multiplying food and walking on water.

These fit the famous definition of miracles by **David Hume**:

a transgression of a law of nature by a particular volition of the Deity **– David Hume**

By breaking the laws of nature, these miracles demonstrate the the Creator and Lord of Nature is present in Christ. According to **H. Van Der Loos** the miracles divide into:

- **miracles of healing** and
- **miracles of control over nature**

The healings also include EXORCISMS (banishing evil spirits possessing a human).

> *Fundamentalist Christians may insist that there really are demons possessing people; liberal Christians argue that this was a pre-modern interpretation of mental illness. Either way, Jesus curing it with a word is a miracle.*

C.S. Lewis divides these miracles into:

- **miracles of the Old Creation:** these represent powers that Jesus has by virtue of being a perfect human (Adam and Eve had these powers and so would all humans if they hadn't Fallen) and
- **miracles of the New Creation:** powers that are a foreshadowing of what the Resurrected life will be like for humans in the Afterlife

Most of the healings are miracles of the Old Creation: God created humans in the Garden of Eden to be immune to illness and death and Jesus restores this status to people temporarily. The nature-miracles are perhaps miracles of the New Creation: in the Afterlife, humans will be able to walk on water like Jesus (as **Peter** can, briefly, before his faith fails him and he sinks, according to **Matthew 14: 25-32**).

Liberal Christians and atheists often look for **naturalistic** (non-supernatural) explanations of these miracles. There are two common interpretations:

Jesus was a hypnotist

Jesus possessed a powerful charisma and had hypnotic powers (either learned or instinctive). Some of his miracles were hallucinations by people who were caught up with the excitement he generated; the healings were examples of the **placebo effect** where the patient's belief in the doctor's power causes them to get better. Many of these illnesses (blindness, lameness, paralysis) could have had a psychological basis rather than a physical cause, so Jesus cured them psychologically. This might apply to the **exorcisms**, because the love and respect Jesus showed sufferers could go a long way to cure them of their mental problems.

Not all the healings and nature miracles can be explained this way. It's not possible to hypnotise everyone in a crowd of (non-consenting) people. Moreover, some of the healings are too dramatic to be placebo effects and some sufferers clearly had disabilities that were not psychological (such as **the man born blind** on p155).

Jesus was an illusionist

Stage magicians *appear* to perform miracles, but it has all been cleverly set up beforehand. If Jesus was an illusionist, then his miracles were really tricks of stage magic. For example, instead of **walking on water** (p152), Jesus was really walking on a sandbank. Many of the lame and blind people he healed were really confederates – they were actors pretending to be ill and pretending to be healed.

This is not the same as claiming Jesus is a **charlatan** who tried to fool people. Jesus wasn't trying to get rich from his miracles (indeed, he made life dangerous for himself instead). The miracles seem to be ENACTED PARABLES: they illustrate Jesus' teachings and this is why he does them: Jesus wants people to understand God through his 'miracles'.

The miracles could be seen as a sort of **'spiritual theatre'** that Jesus provides for the crowds and perhaps were understood as theatrical events by his audiences (the way modern people who go to see a stage magician know it's not really 'magic' but can't explain how it's actually done).

The problem with this view is that Jesus was executed for what he did and his followers went on to become missionaries and martyrs, which they wouldn't have done if they were the knowing accomplices of a (well-meaning) stage magician.

Another problem is that most scholars agree that the earliest Gospel is **Mark**, but, in Mark, Jesus tries to keep his miracles secret. He heals people quietly and asks them to tell no one what he has done (but obviously they do tell: that's why Mark knows about it). This is part of the **Messianic Secret** in Mark's Gospel and it doesn't fit in with Jesus being an illusionist (why perform 'spiritual theatre' if you don't want anyone to find out about it?).

What are the Seven Signs in John?

John's Gospel doesn't call the miracles *dynamis*. Instead it calls them *semeion* (**'Signs'**). Instead of lots of miracles, there are only 7 Signs. There are no noisy exorcisms with demons being cast out of people. Instead, John's Signs are even more outrageously impossible than the miracles in the Synoptic Gospels. It's difficult to explain away these Signs as hypnotism or the placebo effect.

Scholars like **Raymond E. Brown** point out that John's Gospel deliberately makes it hard to take these Signs literally. Jesus doesn't just **turn water into wine** (p136): he creates the best wine anyone has drunk; he doesn't just **raise a dead man to life** (p150): the dead man is rotting and his corpse "*stinks*". John does not want his readers to treat the Signs as literal events because, for John's Gospel, the spiritual meaning is much more important.

> *Be careful. This is not saying that John didn't believe Jesus had supernatural powers. John thought Jesus was the **Word made Flesh** (p81) so obviously Jesus was supernatural. But John is trying to get his readers to look past the supernatural element in the miracles and focus on their meaning.*

This view of John's Signs does link to the idea of Jesus as an illusionist in some ways. Many of the Signs are clearly staged as public theatre. When Jesus **heals the blind man** (p155), he goes through a show of rubbing mud into the man's eyes – even though he can **heal the Official's son** (p140) in another town 20 miles away with just a thought! Similarly, Jesus deliberately delays visiting Lazarus precisely so that Lazarus will die (and rot in the tomb) so that the Sign of **raising Lazarus from the dead** (p150) will be even more meaningful.

> *John would be very irritated by the debate about whether the miracles 'really happened'. John seems to prefer that readers disbelieve the miracle but **believe in Jesus** (p93), rather than people believe the miracles happened but don't appreciate what they mean.*

What should you think?

If God exists then miracles are possible; if God is prepared to intervene in the world, then miracles may even be likely. Of course, some Christians don't believe God would break the laws of nature he has created, so they prefer **naturalistic** explanations of 'miracles' rather than supernatural ones. John's Signs can be taken in different ways:

1. **Supernatural:** the Signs are supernatural miracles but they have an inner meaning to them as well
2. **Naturalistic:** the Signs are non-supernatural 'spiritual theatre' prepared by Jesus to convey spiritual truths
3. **Mythological**: the Signs are fictional and aren't supposed to be treated as historical events: it's only the meaning that matters

> *Take your pick, but defend your choice*

Turning Water into Wine

Links to: I am the True Vine (p129)

John's Gospel presents this as Jesus' first Sign and many Christians (who HARMONISE John and the Synoptics to create a single story) view it as Jesus' very first miracle.

> **2** On the third day a wedding took place at Cana in Galilee. Jesus' mother was there, [2] and Jesus and his disciples had also been invited to the wedding. [3] When the wine was gone, Jesus' mother said to him, "They have no more wine."

A wedding is taking place at **Cana** (probably modern Kefer-Kenna, a few miles from Nazareth) and Jesus is present along with his mother and his Disciples. Weddings in **1st century Palestine** would last several days and the host would be expected to entertain the guests with food and wine, so when the wine runs out the guests are disappointed and the host is humiliated. Jesus' mother asks Jesus to do something.

It's interesting that Jesus' mother (John never refers to her by name) asks Jesus to act. What's it got to do with her? Some scholars propose that Mary was involved in organising the wedding or that it was the wedding of a family member.

- **Bishop John Spong** controversially proposes that this was Jesus' *own* wedding (as the mother of the groom, it would be Mary's responsibility to organise the food and drink) – although most churches teach that Jesus never married.
- Jesus addresses her as "*woman*" which is respectful but distant. This fits John's belief that Jesus is the **Word made Flesh** (p81) and not an ordinary mother's son.

Symbolically, this scene links to the **Genesis** story of the **Garden of Eden** where Christ is the 'new Adam'. The Sign takes place "*on the third day*" which is when God created plants and fertility (**Genesis 1: 11-13**). Addressing **Mary** as "*woman*" links her to **Eve**. As the mother of Christ, Mary is mother to a new perfect Creation just as Eve was mother to an old Fallen Creation. This makes the Wedding at Cana a symbol of the celebration of God's new Creation or the joys of Heaven.

Alternatively, the scene links to Jesus' crucifixion and Resurrection. The "*hour*" that Jesus refers to is his hour of Glory on the cross where Jesus drinks bitter wine, declares "*it is finished*" and dies (**John 19: 28-30**). This s the only other scene in John's Gospel where Jesus' mother is present and Jesus once again addresses her as "*woman*" (**John 19: 26**). On "*the third day*", Jesus is raised from the dead. This makes the Wedding at Cana a symbol for Jesus' Passion and glorious Resurrection, where disappointment turns into rejoicing.

[6] Nearby stood six stone water jars, the kind used by the Jews for ceremonial washing, each holding from twenty to thirty gallons.

[7] Jesus said to the servants, "Fill the jars with water"; so they filled them to the brim.

[8] Then he told them, "Now draw some out and take it to the master of the banquet."

Jesus directs the servants to fill up urns with water then serve the water, which has miraculously become wine. The water was used for ceremonial washing by the Jewish guests, so that they would be pure at the wedding. This introduces another level of symbolism. The water represents the Jewish religion, which only cleanses the body and does not touch the mind or soul. Jesus turns this into sweet and intoxicating wine (the Christian religion) which provides life-altering **religious experiences** and knowledge of God.

The instruction to "*fill the jars*" links to the later **Feeding of the 5000** (p147), which excess food is created. This represents the fullness of **God's grace** (p106), giving human beings more than they need or deserve.

They did so, [9] and the master of the banquet tasted the water that had been turned into wine. He did not realize where it had come from, though the servants who had drawn the water knew. Then he called the bridegroom aside [10] and said, "Everyone brings out the choice wine first and then the cheaper wine after the guests have had too much to drink; but you have saved the best till now."

[11] What Jesus did here in Cana of Galilee was the first of the signs through which he revealed his glory; and his disciples believed in him.

The master of the banquet (equivalent to the Best Man at a modern wedding) tastes the wine and is amazed at its quality. He doesn't "*realise where it had come from*" – he is like the spiritually blind Jews and Gentiles who are in **darkness** (p90) and do not know God. However, "*the servants knew*" because they represent the Christians who are sharing the wine of Christian faith and know it comes from God.

Normally, a party host serves the good wine first then, when guests are a bit tipsy, serves inferior wine because no one will notice or care. However, he tells the groom, "*You have saved the best till now*". Here, the wedding party symbolises the covenant between God and the Jewish people. The previous wine is the **Law of Moses** (p102) and the earlier prophets. The best wine that has been served last is Jesus himself.

A naturalistic explanation of the 'Sign' would be that Jesus' disciples had the wine hidden in the house and substituted it for the water before it was served. This treats the Sign as 'spiritual theatre' rather than a miracle. However, unlike the later Signs, Jesus does not follow the Sign up with a Discourse explaining it (the **"I Am the True Vine"** Discourse comes much later). Instead, Jesus seems unwilling to perform the Sign at first. This is like the **Messianic Secret** in Mark's Gospel (p26): Jesus does not want people to know who he is yet. Jesus' Disciples respond to this Sign by **believing in him** (p93), which is how John wants his readers to respond to every Sign.

Implications

The Sign enacts the teaching in Jesus' **"I Am the True Vine"** Discourse. Here, Jesus is the source of celebration and joy, just as the Word of God is the source of all true happiness, **Light** (p90) and **Life** (p87). This is what **Raymond E. Brown** calls the SAPIENTIAL theme (wisdom teaching).

There is also a SACRAMENTAL theme, referring to Christian worship. Since there is no Last Supper in John's Gospel, this scene establishes the concepts behind the **EUCHARIST**. The Communion wine Christians drink in their worship represents Jesus himself and is both bitter (being the blood he sheds at the Crucifixion) and joyful (being the celebration of his Resurrection). The Wedding at Cana symbolises the Eucharist and the wedding guests are the congregation.

The Sign at Cana is important in another, more day-to-day sense. It represents Jesus as enjoying himself at a wedding where people drink wine and therefore it indicates God's approval of marriage, sex and pleasure. It might seem odd to emphasise this, but many religious groups have rejected these principles. In Judaism, many **Essenes** (p66) were CELIBATE (giving up sex and marriage); the Nazirite sect gave up wine.

Christianity has had a mixed attitude to marriage, sex and pleasure. Paul argues the celibacy is preferable to married life (**1 Corinthians 7: 38**) and many churches inspired by him took this view even further, celebrating virginity and seeing sex as sinful. Many Christian monks were ASCETICS dedicated to a life without physical pleasure; the Roman Catholic Church eventually insisted its priests remain celibate, although Protestant churches do not do this. The Christian Temperance Movement campaigns against alcohol and Methodists do not drink alcohol. Christians who are teetotal claim that the wine Jesus created at Cana was non-alcoholic (though this seems to contradict the Master of the Banquet's assessment of the wine when he drinks it).

Against these views, the Sign at Cana presents marriage (and by extension, sex) and drinking wine (in moderation) as innocent pleasures that Jesus blessed and Christians can enjoy.

Is the sign of Turning Water into Wine essential for understanding Jesus' identity?

YES	NO
The Sign shows that Jesus is the true fulfillment of the Old Testament prophecies: as different from the old prophets and laws as wine is from water. Jesus invites people to become intoxicated by his love rather than going through sterile rituals of cleansing.	This miracle fits in with the nature-miracles of the Synoptic Gospels. Its theme of secrecy resembles the **secret Messiah** in Mark. In the Synoptic Gospels there is a **Last Supper** where Jesus tells his Disciples that the Passover wine is his blood which is clearer than this miracle.
This Sign covers the **Eucharistic** imagery of the Last Supper too. The wine Jesus creates symbolizes his blood shed on the Cross and the party that is suspended then restarted represents his Crucifixion and Resurrection on the third day.	Christians have not been very good at recognising this aspect of Jesus who approves of fun, pleasure, drinking and marriage. For much of history, Christianity has been obsessed with virginity and self-denial. Many Christians have viewed enjoying yourself in this life as sinful.

Healing the Official's Son

Links to: I am the Way, the Truth and the Life

Jesus has been in Jerusalem for the Passover Festival and now returns to his home in Galilee. He stops in Cana (perhaps visiting the family whose wedding he attended when he **turned water into wine**, p136). He is asked for a second Sign.

> [46] Once more he visited Cana in Galilee, where he had turned the water into wine. And there was a certain royal official whose son lay sick at Capernaum. [47] When this man heard that Jesus had arrived in Galilee from Judea, he went to him and begged him to come and heal his son, who was close to death.
>
> [48] "Unless you people see signs and wonders," Jesus told him, "you will never believe."
>
> [49] The royal official said, "Sir, come down before my child dies."
>
> [50] "Go," Jesus replied, "your son will live."

The Royal Official is not identified but, since this is Galilee, he probably works for **King Herod Antipas**. Antipas is the son of Herod the Great who, according to **Matthew's birth narrative** (p33), tried to murder Jesus as a baby. It is ironic that a man whose job is to carry out the evil orders of the Herodian dynasty now comes to Jesus to save *his* young son.

There are parallels with the first **Sign at Cana**: this is again *the third day* and again Jesus seems reluctant to perform the Sign until the petitioner shows his sincerity. As with the previous Sign, Jesus does not have to be physically present to perform the miracle: his word is enough to transform the world.

Jesus' comment about "*signs and wonders*" is important. All of Jesus' Signs in **John's Gospel** are meaningful, but people treat them as 'wonders' to gawp at and be entertained. Jesus is impatient with the 'Sign-seekers' who come to him looking only for stunts and spectacles. Only by understanding the underlying meaning can people move from amazement to **believing in Jesus** (p93).

> The man took Jesus at his word and departed. [51] While he was still on the way, his servants met him with the news that his boy was living. [52] When he inquired as to the time when his son got better, they said to him, "Yesterday, at one in the afternoon, the fever left him."
>
> [53] Then the father realized that this was the exact time at which Jesus had said to him, "Your son will live." So he and his whole household believed.

Jesus has been rejected by the people he has come to save - his Jewish neighbours and the Jewish priests in Jerusalem. However, this enemy *'takes Jesus at his word'*. The Official hasn't come looking for a miracle: he's looking for a Saviour and he believes he has found one. He heads home, a day's journey from the hills of Cana down to Capernaum by the Sea of Galilee. His faith is rewarded: his son recovers.

The Official's "*whole household believed*", which includes his family and servants. This is the sort of **transformative believing** (p93) that turns a person's life around and connects a sinner back to God. John's Gospel isn't saying the Official and his family became Christians – there are no 'Christians' as yet because Jesus hasn't been crucified and risen from the dead yet. Rather, these Jewish people re-connected with God in a state of thankful gratitude.

Jesus' ability to grant the Official's son life – temporary *bios* life, for the child will get sick again and eventually die – is a symbol of Christ's gift of **Eternal Life** (p87) to those who believe in him. The boy returning to life *on the third day* also links to Jesus' own Resurrection on the third day. Like the Royal Official, readers of John's Gospel are looking back on Jesus' words and Signs with hindsight, only realising what they mean later. John's readers are invited to *'take Jesus at his word'* that he is the **Son of God** (p112) and the **Messiah** (p12): if they do, they will receive Life too.

Implications

The Sign seems to relate to **petitionary prayer** – praying for God to do something for you, usually to heal you or save you (or someone you are about). The Royal Official comes to Jesus in person with a prayer, but first has to make a journey up into the hills. By the time John's Gospel was written, Christians were addressing their prayers to Jesus up in Heaven, but hoping that his word could heal them or save them down here on Earth.

This Sign is very consoling: it suggests that Jesus listens and is compassionate, that he can accomplish things that seem impossible and that, even while we are distressed or despairing, God is at work in our lives.

Christianity embeds petitionary prayer in the **LORD'S PRAYER** ("*Give us this day our daily bread ... and deliver us from evil*"). However, the one time Jesus makes a petitionary prayer it is to be spared his upcoming crucifixion – and this prayer is refused (**Matthew 26: 39**).

> *This links to the **problem of evil** - why does God not intervene to save lives and spare people heartbreak? – and the wider question of **divine impassability** - can God's mind be changed by prayers?*

Is the Sign of Healing the Official's Son essential for understanding Jesus' identity?

YES	NO
There is a danger of becoming a 'Sign-seeker': taking an interest in Jesus out of curiosity or selfishness. This Sign reminds Christians that their faith should be in Jesus himself, not his miracles. It also reassures them that their prayers are heard and can be answered, no matter how desperate things seem.	Jesus' early Signs are quite subtle but his later Signs are public and spectacular so he can hardly be THAT opposed to 'Sign-seekers'. The Official's desperation is understandable and quite touching but many people with needs just as heart-wrenching have prayed for help and received none.
Not every prayer is answered Jesus implicitly praises people who believe WITHOUT receiving 'Signs and wonders'. The Official had exemplary faith and, most importantly, his whole household believed as a result. The real reward for faith is **Eternal Life**, not miracles.	Even during his Ministry, Jesus only healed a fraction of the world's population who happen to have been near him at the time. Yet Jesus could have healed every person on the planet by just wishing it. Signs like this raise the **Problem of Evil** because every prayer *could* be answered, but isn't.

Healing at the Pool

Links to: I am the Door

Jesus visits Jerusalem again. At the Sheep's Gate Pool (known as **Bethesda**) there is a superstition that the waters can cure the sick: an invisible angel *'stirs the waters'* and, when this happens, disabled people waiting nearby rush to bathe in the waters and be healed.

> [5] One who was there had been an invalid for thirty-eight years. [6] When Jesus saw him lying there and learned that he had been in this condition for a long time, he asked him, "Do you want to get well?"
>
> [7] "Sir," the invalid replied, "I have no one to help me into the pool when the water is stirred. While I am trying to get in, someone else goes down ahead of me."
>
> [8] Then Jesus said to him, "Get up! Pick up your mat and walk." [9] At once the man was cured; he picked up his mat and walked.

The pool seems to be a real place that archaeologists have discovered in Jerusalem. One theory is that it was an **asclepieion** – a bathing pool sacred to the Greek god of healing, perhaps built for the soldiers in the nearby Roman barracks. That would make it a place of pagan worship. The man in the story seems to be paralysed, which is why he cannot get into the waters to enjoy their (alleged) magical powers.

As with the previous **Sign at Capernaum** (p140), Jesus heals by speaking a word. This demonstrates that he is the REAL god of healing, not the pagan fake that people are depending on out of superstition. As with the previous Sign, Jesus first tests the crippled man's sincerity: does he really want healing or is he just another 'Sign-seeker' looking for something marvelous?

> The day on which this took place was a Sabbath, [10] and so the Jewish leaders said to the man who had been healed, "It is the Sabbath; the law forbids you to carry your mat."
>
> [11] But he replied, "The man who made me well said to me, 'Pick up your mat and walk.'"

The **Sabbath** is the day of rest for Jews. God created the Sabbath when he rested on the 7th Day of Creation (**Genesis 2: 2**). The 4th of the 10 Commandments (**Exodus 20: 8**) orders Jews to keep the Sabbath holy by doing no work on the 7th day.

By healing the crippled man, Jesus is breaking the Sabbath rules and the man himself breaks the rules by carrying his mat. There are 39 rules for things that are forbidden on the Sabbath and the 39th is carrying a burden to your home.

This is the symbolism behind the detail that the man has been sick for 38 years: each year of sickness is a Sabbath rule that has 'paralysed' this man until he breaks the 39th rule at Jesus' command. His ability to walk again is a symbol of his freedom from these rules.

The Sabbath is an example of the **Law of Moses** (p102) that the Jews follow but which **John's Gospel** opposes. Here, Jesus breaks the rule and instructs someone else to break it too: healing people and doing good works is more important than following petty rules. When the Jewish priests question Jesus about this, he replies:

My Father is always at his work to this very day, and I too am working – **John 5: 17**

John is not objecting to the idea of a day of rest, just the way the Jews of his time interpret it. The Sabbath is supposed to be a day off from worldly concerns when people can focus on God and doing God's work: not a day off from doing any work at all.

This Sign shows that people do not need pagan superstitions or the regulations of the Jewish Law: they need to **believe in Jesus** (p93) instead.

The Synoptic Gospels record a similar debate over the Sabbath, with Jesus defending his right to break the Sabbath rules. He calls himself the "*Lord of the Sabbath*" (a title normally associated with God) and says:

The Sabbath was made for man, not man for the Sabbath – **Mark 2: 27**

The statement that '*the Sabbath was made for man*' encapsulates the idea that worshiping God ought to be liberating, not restricting.

Implications

Jews still celebrate Sabbath (Hebrew, *Shabbat*) every week. Since the Jewish day starts at sunset, *Shabbat* lasts from Friday evening through to Saturday night. Observant Jews will clear their work for the day (getting cooking and cleaning done on the Friday so they don't have to do it on the Saturday). Strict Jews won't light a fire (so no smoking!) or even turn on a light switch.

Keeping Sabbath is one of the most obvious and distinctive features of the Jewish religion and, in the 1st century, Jews who 'broke Sabbath' could be ostracized or punished. The Romans found the Jewish Sabbath fascinating and ludicrous in equal measure; they regarded it as Jewish laziness. However, it is the basis for our 7-day week and 'weekend'.

The first Christians were Jews who kept Sabbath too. However, the Gentile converts to Christianity did not keep Sabbath (and their employers and masters wouldn't have let them even if they wanted to). **Raymond E. Brown** argues that the **Johannine Community** (p208) was a group of Jewish Christians who were thrown out of their Synagogue in the 80s-90s CE for claiming that Jesus was God. This left these Christians unable to keep Sabbath with their fellow Jews – and angry and resentful towards their former friends and neighbours. This explains why so much of John's Gospel is hostile to the Jewish Law.

> *The idea is that, because the Johannine Community was excommunicated by the Jewish Law, they convinced themselves that Jesus didn't want them to keep it anyway – and represented Jesus as attacking the Law at every turn in their Gospel. Of course, the other Gospels also present Jesus as criticising the Jewish Law, just not with the intensity of John's Gospel.*

For various reasons, Christian churches abandoned Sabbath-keeping, replacing it with *"the Lord's Day"* which was Sunday. This would be the day they gathered together for worship. Although they didn't ban work, like Jews on the Sabbath, they tried to spend their time on their religious duties instead of their worldly duties. The Christian bishop **Ignatius of Antioch** writes about this in 101 CE and describes Christians as:

> *no longer observing the Sabbath, but living in the observance of the Lord's day on which our life was sprung by him and his death* – **Ignatius of Antioch**

During the **Protestant Reformation**, there was a tendency for Puritan Christians to refer to Sunday as the 'Sabbath' and apply some of the Old Testament rules about not working on the Sabbath to Sundays. This resulted in the status of Sunday in the UK as a day when shops close, buses don't run, pubs have restricted opening hours and employees have the day off. In recent years, many of these practices have faded but the *"Keep Sunday Special"* campaign tries to preserve Sunday as a day of rest when people can spend time with family or be free to worship.

The idea of focusing on the inner meaning of the Jewish Law rather than following it to the letter is summed up when Jesus is asked what the greatest Commandment is. He replies that the entire Law boils down to loving God and loving your neighbour (**Matthew 22: 36-40**). **Joseph Fletcher** calls following the letter of the Law LEGALISM; he proposes **Situation Ethics** which involves acting on *agape*-love even if this means breaking moral rules on occasions. Fletcher argues that this is how Jesus approached moral problems.

Is the Sign of Healing at the Pool essential for understanding Jesus' identity?

YES

NO

Jesus reveals himself here as the *'Lord of the Sabbath'*. Because he is the source of the Jewish Law, he knows when and where to break it. He doesn't just free people from sickness, but also from the distracting burden of the **Jewish Law**.

Jesus and his Disciples were all Jews and the first Christians were Jews who kept the Sabbath. Because of this, it's unlikely that the real Jesus went around breaking the Sabbath rules and encouraging other people to break them.

Jesus is drawing people's attention to the deeper meaning of the Law, when they tend to focus on its superficial meaning. Jesus says the whole Law can be summed up as loving God and loving your neighbour. This is the essence of Jesus' teaching.

Christianity hasn't followed Jesus' example on this, because it has created its own moral rules that are just as inflexible as the Jewish Law; for example, **Roman Catholicism** utterly forbids abortion and many **Protestant Christians** treat Sunday the same way the Jews treat the Sabbath.

Feeding the 5000

Links to: I am the Bread of Life (p120)

This Sign is unusual because it's also described in the Synoptic Gospels with the same details (5000 people, 5 loaves and 2 fish). Jesus is back in Galilee and a huge crowd has come to hear him preach. **Luke's Gospel** locates this at a place called Bethsaida; both **Luke** and **Matthew's Gospel** add a detail that the Disciples want to send the crowd away to buy food in the villages, but Jesus insists they can all be fed here.

> [5] When Jesus looked up and saw a great crowd coming toward him, he said to Philip, "Where shall we buy bread for these people to eat?" [6] He asked this only to test him, for he already had in mind what he was going to do.
>
> [7] Philip answered him, "It would take more than half a year's wages to buy enough bread for each one to have a bite!"
>
> [8] Another of his disciples, Andrew, Simon Peter's brother, spoke up, [9] "Here is a boy with five small barley loaves and two small fish, but how far will they go among so many?"

The barley loaves would have been flat unleavened bread – the staple diet of the poor but also the bread used at the Jewish Passover meal. The fish would probably have been dried or pickled sardines.

On one level, this is a **nature miracle**. The multiplying of bread and fishes happens in nature: wheat is planted and multiplies every harvest; fish spawn and multiply in rivers and seas. This natural fertility was created by God who blessed nature and commanded it to "*be fruitful and increase in number*" (**Genesis 1 22**). Jesus here does the same thing, establishing that he is God.

The bread represents Jesus' body, which is shared by Christians at the **EUCHARIST**. Some commentators think the 5 Loaves symbolise the **5 Wounds** that Christ suffered (nails in the hands and feet and a spear in his side). They could also represent the 5 senses by which believers come to know God's Creation.

The fish link to Jesus' Disciples being fishermen. When Jesus recruits his first Disciples, he tells them:

I will send you out to fish for people – **Matthew 4: 19**

It might be sexist, but I prefer the pun in the older translation: "I will make you fishers of men". fishermen... fishers of men... gedditt?!?!?

The fish represent the souls of people who believe in Christ. The early Christians used the symbol of the Fish as a code because the Greek word for 'fish' is *ichthys* and the Greek letters can stand for **I**esous **Ch**ristos, **Th**eou **Y**ios, **S**oter (JESUS CHRIST, SON OF GOD, SAVIOUR), spelling ICHTHYS..

The important point is that the Disciples think the crowd suffer from physical hunger, which can be dealt with by spending money. Jesus diagnoses them as suffering from **spiritual hunger**. The loaves and fishes that he multiplies symbolise **Eternal Life** (p87) that will truly satisfy them.

[10] Jesus said, "Have the people sit down." There was plenty of grass in that place, and they sat down (about five thousand men were there). [11] Jesus then took the loaves, gave thanks, and distributed to those who were seated as much as they wanted. He did the same with the fish.

[12] When they had all had enough to eat, he said to his disciples, "Gather the pieces that are left over. Let nothing be wasted." [13] So they gathered them and filled twelve baskets with the pieces of the five barley loaves left over by those who had eaten.

It's significant that Jesus gets his Disciples to hand out the bread: this symbolises the way they will go onto to spread his Gospel and convert people to Christianity. The bread symbolises the Christian message, being taken all over the world.

When Jesus takes the bread, gives thanks then distributes it, he is performing the same ritual that the Synoptic Gospels describe at the Last Supper (which doesn't feature in John's Gospel). Christians repeat this ritual in the **EUCHARIST** where the priest will take bread, give thanks, break it then distribute it among the congregation.

The bread created is more than enough. This symbolises God's **Grace** – his generosity (p106). The 12 baskets are symbolic too. The Hebrew numbering system gives every number a meaning. The number 12 symbolises perfection and completion. There were **12 Tribes of Israelites**, but only 2 survived, Benjamin and Judah (perhaps indicated by the 2 fish). Jesus appoints **12 Disciples** to be his team. The 12 baskets full of bread symbolise the entire world 'fed' on Jesus' message and **believing in him** (p93).

John's account of this ends on an unusual event that doesn't feature in any of the Synoptic versions. The crowd wants to make Jesus a king, but Jesus has other plans and escapes. This suggests that people in Galilee wanted Jesus to be a **Kingly Messiah** or perhaps the crowd was actually an army of **Zealots** (p68), not just ordinary civilians expecting a sermon. That might explain why they were camped out in the middle of nowhere. **A.N. Wilson** argues that Jesus' instruction to "*make the men sit down*" is a coded message that the Zealots should abandon their violent rebellion against Rome; the sharing of the loaves and fish symbolises the **Messianic Banquet** and the peaceful unity of all the Jewish people (remember that the Zealots assassinated their fellow-Jews).

If this was an army of rebels and not an ordinary crowd, then Jesus' Sign of peaceful coexistence doesn't seem to have worked: they still want Jesus to be their Kingly Messiah and he has to escape.

Jesus will end up being made King – but not by the crowds or the Zealots. The Roman governor **Pontius Pilate** crucifies Jesus and puts a mocking sign on the cross that reads "*Jesus of Nazareth, King of the Jews*" (**John 19: 19**). This sort of dark humour is typical of **John's Gospel**, where Jesus' enemies say or do things that reveal a truth that they are blind to.

Implications

The implications of the **Eucharist** are discussed as part of the **"I Am the Bread of Life"** Discourse (p120). We know that this ritual was shared by the earliest Christians. **Paul** describes the Eucharist in his first letter to the Corinthian church (54 or 55 CE). He links it to the **Last Supper**:

the Lord Jesus, on the night he was betrayed, took bread, and when he had given thanks, he broke it and said, 'This is my body, which is for you; do this in remembrance of me' – **1 Corinthians 11: 23-24**

The Last Supper is not described in **John's Gospel** but the **Johannine Community** (p208) certainly shared the Eucharist – Signs like this are clearly meant to explain the Eucharist in a coded way. Why does John not describe the Last Supper itself?

- John dates Jesus' death differently from the Synoptics and describes Jesus being executed on the day *before* Passover, so the Last Supper itself cannot take place. John arranges events like this for symbolic reasons: he presents Jesus being crucified at the same time as the **Paschal Lamb** is being sacrificed in the Temple, reinforcing the symbol of Jesus as the "*Lamb of God who takes away the sins of the world*" (**John 1: 29**).
- The Johannine Community perhaps regarded the Eucharist as a sacred mystery that could not be shared with outsiders and unbelievers, so John's Gospel only refers to the Eucharist in a coded way, as in this Sign, **turning water into wine** (p136) and the **Bread of Life** (p120) and **True Vine** (p129) discourses.

A different debate is whether the Sign should be interpreted as a miracle of **multiplication** or of **sharing**. This idea was first raised by **Rudolph Bultmann** who argued that the New Testament needs to be DE-MYTHOLOGISED to get at its original *kerygma* (teaching). For Bultmann, the Sign records something non-supernatural: Jesus shared all his own food and this shamed the people in the crowd into sharing the food that they had brought with them but were planning on keeping for themselves. When everyone shared with everyone else, there was more than enough to go round.

Once it's been de-mythologized like this, the Sign contains a valuable moral lesson rather than a supernatural wonder.

John would certainly agree with Bultmann's method – he wants his readers to penetrate the symbolism rather than focus on the miracle itself - but he probably wouldn't go along with Bultmann's interpretation that the Sign amounts to nothing more than urging people to "pay it forward".

Although many Christians disagree with Bultmann's interpretation of **Feeding the 5000**, it seems to have inspired a sermon about this Sign by the Pope in 2014:

> *This is the miracle: rather than a multiplication it is a sharing, inspired by faith and prayer. Everyone eats and some is left over* – **Pope Francis**

This quote attracted some comments because the Pope *appears* to be agreeing with Bultmann that the Sign wasn't really a supernatural miracle.

However, the Pope might just mean that we can replicate the miracle ourselves by sharing what we have with those who have less: just because WE don't have supernatural powers, it doesn't mean we can't accomplish amazing things when we are generous.

Is the Sign of Feeding the 5000 essential for understanding Jesus' identity?

YES	NO
Jesus reveals himself here as answer to our spiritual as well as our physical needs: as God, he created the world and its fertility; as Christ, he feeds our spiritual hunger. This spiritual nourishment also binds believers into a community.	This miracle occurs in the Synoptic Gospels too, but without the *midrash* on the **Bread of Life** which John's Gospel adds. This suggests John added a lot of extra meaning to an existing miracle story which wasn't about feeding spiritual hunger.
The Sign reveals the meaning behind the **Eucharist**. The version of this miracle in the Synoptic Gospels also has Jesus giving thanks, breaking bread and filling 12 baskets – key parts of the Eucharistic symbolism. John just expands on this meaning.	The Eucharist has been very divisive for Christians. **Catholics** and **Protestants** disagree over whether the 'Real Presence' of Christ is in the bread and wine or whether it just commemorates Jesus' death and Resurrection. This has led to war, not unity.

Walking on Water

Links to: I am the Good Shepherd (p126)

This is another miracle that is described in a similar way in the Synoptic Gospels (**Mark** and **Matthew**, but not **Luke**). The Sea of Galilee is a large freshwater lake, 13 miles long and 8 miles wide. It's a great source of fish, but its position beside mountains to the east mean that it experiences sudden, violent storms and strong winds. Jesus' Disciples are crossing by boat when one of these storms blows in.

[16] When evening came, his disciples went down to the lake,[17] where they got into a boat and set off across the lake for Capernaum. By now it was dark, and Jesus had not yet joined them. [18] A strong wind was blowing and the waters grew rough.[19] When they had rowed about three or four miles, they saw Jesus approaching the boat, walking on the water; and they were frightened. [20] But he said to them, "It is I; don't be afraid." [21] Then they were willing to take him into the boat, and immediately the boat reached the shore where they were heading.

This Sign resembles a **nature-miracle**, with Jesus able to bend the laws of physics to his will – a classic example of **David Hume**'s definition of a miracle as a "*transgression of the laws of nature*". In the Synoptic Gospels, Jesus calms the storm when he enters the boat. John's version is slightly different and more amazing: when Jesus enters the boat they immediately find themselves at the shore they were traveling to.

> *Yes – Jesus **teleports** the boat right across the Sea of Galilee*

Mark includes the detail that the Disciples at first think Jesus is a ghost or spirit. John doesn't mention this directly, but the Disciples are "*frightened*" because Jesus' appearance is **numinous** and they are in awe. This miracle is therefore also a **religious experience** for the Disciples.

Matthew adds another detail which is the famous **'Venture of St Peter'.** When Jesus approaches the boat, Peter gets out and walks on water too ... briefly. When Peter becomes frightened, he starts to sink and Jesus criticises his lack of faith. John doesn't include this story, because (as usual) he wants his readers to focus on the Sign's meaning, not the supernatural details.

The Sign seems to refer to the hardship and persecution experienced by the early Christians. The **boat is the church** and the winds that rock it are the troubles the Christians get from their Jewish critics and the pagan Romans. Christ seems far away and their prayers go unanswered.

These persecutions were real: most of the Apostles were martyred by the Jewish authorities; **Paul** describes being beaten and stoned by the Pharisees on several occasions as well as arrested by the Romans; the **Emperor Nero** blamed Christians for the Fire of Rome in 64 CE and had Christian prisoners burned alive as 'human torches' at his parties.

The Sign reveals Jesus as the Saviour and **Good Shepherd** (p126). It reminds Christians that Christ is always at hand, even when things seem impossible. Believers need to *"take him in"* to their church and their hearts. If they do, they will instantly find themselves at their destination, which is **Eternal Life** (p87).

Meanwhile, the crowds who were present at the **Feeding of the 5000** (p147) are still looking for Jesus. They cross the lake rather comfortably on their own boats: they don't experience a storm but they don't find Jesus either. The symbolism seems to be that people who suffer for the sake of their faith in Jesus will have a deeper **religious experience** than those who don't.

---

*There seems to be a version of **Irenaeus' Theodicy** here, that suffering and persecutions are necessary for people to **believe in Christ***

Implications

As with the other Signs, there are arguments that this should be interpreted **naturalistically** (non-supernaturally). **Albert Schweitzer** suggests that the Disciples saw Jesus walking on the shore and mistook this for him walking on water. Similar arguments claim that Jesus was walking on ice or a hidden sandbank. However, even these explanations don't account for teleporting the boat.

A psychological explanation would be that, in their terror and exhaustion, the Disciples **hallucinated** Jesus walking towards them. Then they passed out and woke up hours later to find the boat had been washed ashore.

John would regard the naturalistic explanations as being just as mistaken as the supernatural ones. With these Signs the reader is not supposed to ask, 'What really happened?' but rather, 'What does this <u>mean</u> for me personally?'

The experience of persecution was common for the early Christians when they refused to make sacrifices to the gods or to the Emperor; the 'Great Persecution' under the Emperors **Diocletian** and **Galerius** came at the end of the 3rd century CE, after 20,000 Christians were executed in grisly ways. These victims were called MARTYRS (which means 'witnesses') and their graves became sites of pilgrimage.

During these persecutions, Christians would meet and worship in secret. One of their hideaways was the **Catacombs** (underground tombs of Rome). In these underground tunnels, Christian art shows Jesus as the protective **Good Shepherd** (p126) more often than any other image. Another popular image is the ship filled with human souls, being rocked by the troubles of this world.

In the 4th century CE, this all changed. The Roman Emperor **Constantine the Great** converted to Christianity and all persecutions stopped; later on, Christianity became the official religion of the Roman Empire.

Unfortunately, once in power, Christians often persecuted other minority groups the way they had once been persecuted themselves: Jews in particular were singled out because they were seen as the people who murdered Christ (a prejudice that was strengthened by the anti-Jewish feeling in John's Gospel, as you will see in the Sign of **Healing the Man Born Blind** on p155). Later on, alternative Christian sects and Protestant reformers were also persecuted.

> *They say that people who are bullied can grow up to be the worst bullies. Did the memory of being victims in the past encourage some Christians to victimize others?*

Is the Sign of Walking on Water essential for understanding Jesus' identity?

YES	**NO**
Jesus is not just a healer - he is the Saviour. Christians need to be prepared to meet opposition for their faith and experience heartache and even danger because of their beliefs, but Jesus Christ is always with them even when things seem to be at their worst.	This Sign is clearly legendary or else has a **naturalistic** explanation, like a hallucination. Even John seems embarrassed by it, cutting out over-the-top details like 'St Peter's Venture', whereas normally John's Signs are MORE extreme than the Synoptics.
There's nothing legendary about this Sign and focusing on 'explaining' it either supernaturally or **naturalistically** is to be blind to its message and meaning. Like the Disciples taking Jesus in to the boat, believers need to take Christ in to their hearts.	The Sign is part of a 'victim mentality' which had a toxic legacy in later centuries. Once the Christian underdogs had power in the Roman Empire, they used it to punish those whom they believed had persecuted them. This Sign encourages such self-righteous thinking.

Healing the Blind Man

Links to: I am the Light of the World (p123)

> *The Edexcel Anthology splits this Sign into two parts. The first part (the actual healing) is in Extract #3 and is covered under **Light of the World**; the second part (the Pharisees investigate the healing) is in Extract #4.*

This healing is unusual because Jesus goes through a strange performance: he makes a mud paste and rubs it into the blind man's eyes and tells him to wash the paste away in the Pool of Siloam. When the man does this, his blindness has been cured.

> *Readers know that Jesus doesn't need to do this sort of thing. He **healed the Royal Official's son** with a word while 20 miles away from Capernaum. The **paralyzed man at Bethesda pool was also healed** with a word from Jesus. So why this unnecessary treatment with mud and washing?*

Jesus making mud might be a reference to God making Adam out of earth (Hebrew, *adamah*) in **Genesis 2: 7**. Jesus isn't just curing this man: he is re-making him as a new human being – as we shall see,

Jesus making a clay paste might be deliberate provocation. This is the Sabbath and making clay counts as 'work' and is forbidden under the **Jewish Law** (p102). As with **the healing at the pool** (p143), Jesus deliberately flouts the Sabbath laws to provoke the **Pharisees** (p64).

Finally, Jesus is sending his patient on a **spiritual journey** that will take him from physical blindness to sight but more importantly from **spiritual darkness** of ignorance to the **Light** (p90). That is why the **Pool of Siloam** features in the story. The name Siloam means **"sent"** and this refers to Jesus (who is SENT by God to Earth) but also to the man born blind (who is SENT by Jesus on a journey of enlightenment). At the start, Jesus acts like a conventional doctor in the 1st century, applying a paste to a blind man's eyes. The patient will realise that Jesus is much more than a doctor, but this is a journey of faith that he must make on his own.

> *The Bible doesn't name this man whom Jesus sends on a spiritual journey, but since he becomes the hero of the story from this point on, he deserves a name. Early Christian tradition names him Celidonius so I'll use that name from now on.*

Celidonius' spiritual journey begins when his neighbours ask him where Jesus is: he doesn't know. He knows that Jesus has cured him, but he doesn't yet **believe in Jesus** (p93): he thinks Jesus is just "*a man*". However, he has begun to change: his neighbours don't recognise him. The next thing is that he is brought before the Pharisees who are investigating Jesus' breaking of the Sabbath Laws.

[13] They brought to the Pharisees the man who had been blind. [14] Now the day on which Jesus had made the mud and opened the man's eyes was a Sabbath. [15] Therefore the Pharisees also asked him how he had received his sight. "He put mud on my eyes," the man replied, "and I washed, and now I see."

[16] Some of the Pharisees said, "This man is not from God, for he does not keep the Sabbath."

The Pharisees are divided because, on the one hand, Jesus breaks the Sabbath rules but, on the other, he performs healing miracles. This doesn't fit into their LEGALISTIC view of God. They question Celidonius and he answers that Jesus is "*a prophet*". Celidonius has more insight now than when he spoke to his neighbours earlier, but he doesn't yet see the truth.

The Pharisees summon Celidonius' parents to question them.

[20] "We know he is our son," the parents answered, "and we know he was born blind. [21] But how he can see now, or who opened his eyes, we don't know. Ask him. He is of age; he will speak for himself." [22] His parents said this because they were afraid of the Jewish leaders, who already had decided that anyone who acknowledged that Jesus was the Messiah would be put out of the synagogue. [23] That was why his parents said, "He is of age; ask him."

> *The author of John's Gospel has a fine gift for comedy and these scenes are very funny. The Pharisees are bumbling investigators like Inspector Clouseau (played by Peter Sellars in a classic series of comedy films). Celidonius and his parents run rings around them and deliver increasingly biting and sarcastic replies to the Pharisees' questions.*

The brief remark about people who believe Jesus to be the Messiah being banned from the Synagogues is significant. **Raymond E. Brown** argues this is exactly what happened to the **Johannine Community** (p208) in the 80s or 90s CE. This group of Jewish Christians was thrown out of the Jewish Synagogues because of their beliefs about Jesus. John's original readers would have identified very strongly with Celidonius. They would have recognised the parents as people who want to 'come out' as Christians but don't dare to. Brown terms these 'shy Christians' as "*crypto-Christians*" and argues that John's Gospel was originally written to encourage them to 'come out' as Christians (p225).

Celidonius himself is going to be braver than his parents.

[24] A second time they summoned the man who had been blind. "Give glory to God by telling the truth," they said. "We know this man is a sinner."

[25] He replied, "Whether he is a sinner or not, I don't know. One thing I do know. I was blind but now I see!"

[26] Then they asked him, "What did he do to you? How did he open your eyes?"

[27] He answered, "I have told you already and you did not listen. Why do you want to hear it again? Do you want to become his disciples too?"

[28] Then they hurled insults at him and said, "You are this fellow's disciple! We are disciples of Moses! [29] We know that God spoke to Moses, but as for this fellow, we don't even know where he comes from."

This time, Celidonius is even more sarcastic. He jokingly asks the Pharisees if *they* want to become Disciples of Jesus. The Pharisees don't know where Jesus comes from. This is another piece of irony from John: the Pharisees are the ones **living in darkness** (p90) who do not realise that Jesus is the **Word made Flesh** (p81) and comes from God because they are spiritually blind. The scene ends with the Pharisees *'throwing him out'*. The phrase echoes the parents' fear that they will be *'thrown out'* of the Synagogue – excommunicated from the Jewish religion.

> *Now here's a strange thing. The Edexcel Anthology extract ends here - but this isn't the end of the story. The most important bit is still to come and without it the Sign makes no sense. I assume the last section has been missed out by accident - so I'll explain it here:*

Jesus reappears and introduces himself to Celidonius. Celidonius realises who Jesus is and completes his spiritual journey.

Then the man said, 'Lord, I believe,' and he worshiped him – **John 9: 38**

Celidonius has moved from believing Jesus to be a human healer, to a prophet, to the **Son of Man** (p116). He is no longer spiritually blind – unlike the Pharisees, who are really the blind ones. Along the way, Celidonius has lost contact with his neighbours (who don't recognise him) and fallen afoul of the Jewish authorities (who have banished him from the Synagogue), which was the fate of many Christian converts.

Implications

This Sign sums up the previous ones. It criticises petty Sabbath rules, like **the healing at the pool** (p143); it shows Jesus is the source of **Life** (p87) who must be **believed in** (p93), like **the healing of the Official's son** (p140). It illustrates the Christian religion growing out of (and replacing) the Jewish religion, like **turning water into wine** (p136). It reassures Christians that their sufferings draw them closer to Christ, like the Sign of **walking on water** (p152). Celidonius worshiping Jesus links to **feeding the 5000** (p147), since Jesus is worshiped through the **Eucharist**.

> *All this, and jokes too!*

All of this is delightful, but there's a darker side to this story, which is the Gospel-writer's hatred of the Jews, which comes from the Johannine Community's own experiences. Once they were thrown out of the Synagogues, the Johannine Christians no longer had the legal protection of being a *religio licita* (a legal religion). Jews could refuse to make pagan sacrifices to the gods of Rome and the Emperor – but Christians had no such exemption now they were a separate religion. Some Johannine Christians were arrested for this refusal and perhaps even executed when their Jewish former-friends informed on them.

This view of the Jews as the enemies of all Christians triggered a tradition of Christian anti-Semitism. **John Chrysostom** wrote a *Homily against the Jews* in 387 CE because the Christians in Antioch were still observing Jewish festivals. He calls the Jews "*dogs*" and "*demons*" and "*assassins of Christ*", saying:

It is the duty of all Christians to hate the Jews – **John Chrysostom**

Augustine of Hippo regarded all Jews as collectively guilty of killing Christ. This perception justified centuries of attacks on Jews in the Christian world and provided the background for the Nazi attempt to exterminate European Jews in the Holocaust.

Is the Sign of Healing the Blind Man essential for understanding Jesus' identity?

YES

NO

The Sign describes the journey of faith made by all believers, from recognising Jesus as a good man, through recognising him as a prophet sent by God, to accepting him as the **Son of God** and Lord. This spiritual journey always comes at a personal cost in terms of ridicule, opposition and sometimes threats and broken relationships.

This spiritual journey comes at the cost of **demonising** the Jews, while forgetting that Jesus was himself a Jew, as were all his Disciples and family and friends. John's Gospel bears a responsibility for the centuries of Christian anti-Semitism that followed and ultimately for the Holocaust, which the Nazis justified with Christian quotations.

Although the experiences of the **Johannine Community** may have coloured the way that John describes his Signs, the hostility is really towards the Jewish leadership, not all Jews. That's why modern translations like NIV-UK use the phrase *'the Jewish leaders'* in passages like this.

This Sign is far more than an attack on the Jewish leadership in the 1st century CE. It's a claim to Christianity's superiority over Judaism; Christians have seen the **Light** while Jews live in darkness. This naturally leads to arrogance and contempt for the Jews, supported directly by the Bible.

Raising Lazarus from the Dead

Links to: "I am the Resurrection and the Life"

This is the greatest of the 7 Signs and the lengthiest. The passage shows John's storytelling at its most powerful, moving from theological discourses to tender human interest to a sort of spiritual horror when the grave is opened and the dead man comes out.

The Sign begins with **Lazarus** dying. Lazarus is the brother of **Martha and Mary**, two friends of Jesus who are also described in the Synoptic Gospels.

> [4] When he heard this, Jesus said, "This sickness will not end in death. No, it is for God's glory so that God's Son may be glorified through it." [5] Now Jesus loved Martha and her sister and Lazarus. [6] So when he heard that Lazarus was sick, he stayed where he was two more days, [7] and then he said to his disciples, "Let us go back to Judea."
>
> [8] "But Rabbi," they said, "a short while ago the Jews there tried to stone you, and yet you are going back?"
>
> [9] Jesus answered, "Are there not twelve hours of daylight? Anyone who walks in the daytime will not stumble, for they see by this world's light. [10] It is when a person walks at night that they stumble, for they have no light."

As with the **Healing of the Blind Man** (p155), there is an element of theatre to Jesus' behaviour. Readers know that Jesus can heal at a distance with just a word (as he did for the **Royal Official's son**, p140) and the distance from the Jordan River to Bethany is about 20 miles, similar to Cana and Capernaum in the earlier Sign. But Jesus does not heal Lazarus and waits 2 more days so that Lazarus actually dies before Jesus reaches Bethany. However, readers have been alerted that Lazarus' story *"will not end in death"* – and neither will Jesus' story. Death is not the end for anyone who **believes in Jesus** (p93) and receives **Eternal Life** (p87).

Jesus states his motives clearly: he has already healed the sick and the blind, but now he has something greater in mind that will glorify God and himself as **Son of God** (p112). This will be the ultimate statement of God's power and love, the most unmistakable expression of who Jesus is.

The Sign will also be the last straw for the Jewish authorities and trigger their determination to execute Jesus. Jesus predicts the coming **Darkness** of his crucifixion and death, when the **Light** (p90) appears to be extinguished (but isn't really).

Jesus is met by **Martha**. John's Gospel presents Martha in the same way as **Luke 10: 38-42**, where Martha is more confident but less insightful than her more spiritual sister Mary.

²¹ "Lord," Martha said to Jesus, "if you had been here, my brother would not have died. ²² But I know that even now God will give you whatever you ask."

²³ Jesus said to her, "Your brother will rise again."

²⁴ Martha answered, "I know he will rise again in the resurrection at the last day."

²⁵ Jesus said to her, "I am the resurrection and the life. The one who believes in me will live, even though they die; ²⁶ and whoever lives by believing in me will never die. Do you believe this?"

²⁷ "Yes, Lord," she replied, "I believe that you are the Messiah, the Son of God, who is to come into the world."

There's a bit of reproach in Martha's greeting (as if she blames Jesus for being late and letting Lazarus die). Martha believes in life after death, because she thinks the dead will come back to life on Judgement Day. This is a belief she shares with the **Pharisees** (p64), but not the **Sadducees** (p63) who believe that death is the end.

Jesus responds with his most famous **"I Am" statement**: *the Resurrection and the Life*, which is read out at Christian funerals. He corrects Martha that **Eternal Life** (p87) is not just to be hoped for in the future; it's available here-and-now for those who **believe in Jesus** (p93). Martha does believe: she's one of only two people who recognise Jesus as the **Son of God** (p112) during his lifetime (the other is **Peter**).

C.H. Dodd argues that Jesus preaches a **'Realised Eschatology'**. Eschatology is beliefs about the end times – Judgement Day, Heaven and Hell. However, Jesus teaches that these things are happening in the present moment, not in the future.

Now Martha's sister **Mary** arrives. She is much more emotionally distressed than Martha.

³² When Mary reached the place where Jesus was and saw him, she fell at his feet and said, "Lord, if you had been here, my brother would not have died."

³³ When Jesus saw her weeping, and the Jews who had come along with her also weeping, he was deeply moved in spirit and troubled.³⁴ "Where have you laid him?" he asked.

"Come and see, Lord," they replied.

³⁵ Jesus wept.

³⁶ Then the Jews said, "See how he loved him!"

³⁷ But some of them said, "Could not he who opened the eyes of the blind man have kept this man from dying?"

This passage contains the shortest verse in the Bible ("*Jesus wept*"). It's an important verse, because it expresses Jesus' humanity. Often, John's Gospel presents Jesus as aloof and ironic, totally in control and untouched by all the strong emotions around him. Here, he is "*deeply moved in spirit and troubled*" (**Raymond E. Brown** argues the phrase could mean 'angry' as well as 'sad') and he openly weeps for the death of his friend.

It's puzzling that Jesus weeps for Lazarus now, but seemed calm about allowing him to die a few days earlier. However, Jesus is not just weeping for Lazarus, but for *all humanity*. God created Adam and Eve to be immortal beings and death entered the world with the Fall, so from Jesus' perspective there's something deeply tragic and unnatural about humans dying. The Jewish bystanders think the weeping shows how much Jesus loved Lazarus but this is Johannine irony: Jesus loves *them too* and is weeping *for them*, but they are spiritually blind to this.

Thomas Browne was a 17th century doctor who summed up the Christian response to death in an interesting way:

I am not so much afraid of death as ashamed of it – **Thomas Browne**

Browne examined dead bodies and was struck by the indignity and horror of death and bodily decay. Christians believe humans are creatures in the **image of God**, so death is an expression of their tragic Fall that leaves them cut off from God, the true source of **Life** (p87). Jesus is here to reverse this arrangement, re-connect humans to God and defeat death itself.

38 Jesus, once more deeply moved, came to the tomb. It was a cave with a stone laid across the entrance. 39 "Take away the stone," he said.

"But, Lord," said Martha, the sister of the dead man, "by this time there is a bad odor, for he has been there four days."

40 Then Jesus said, "Did I not tell you that if you believe, you will see the glory of God?"

41 So they took away the stone. Then Jesus looked up and said, "Father, I thank you that you have heard me. 42 I knew that you always hear me, but I said this for the benefit of the people standing here, that they may believe that you sent me."

43 When he had said this, Jesus called in a loud voice, "Lazarus, come out!" 44 The dead man came out, his hands and feet wrapped with strips of linen, and a cloth around his face.

Jesus said to them, "Take off the grave clothes and let him go."

This is a profound scene. The cave with the stone over it foreshadows the tomb where Jesus will be buried and the stone covering it. Jesus' tomb will be opened after 3 days but Lazarus has been buried for 4 days: he does not have the power to rise from the dead like Jesus does.

John lays on the gory details: the body will stink because it has begun to rot. A popular Jewish belief in the 1st century was that a person's spirit stayed near its corpse for 3 days, but on the 4th day the spirit left and the person was truly and utterly dead. Jesus rejects such superstitions. The tomb is opened. Jesus cries out to Lazarus and summons him back into life.

Raymond E. Brown points out that the expression "*cried out*" is used again when Jesus is being tried by Pontius Pilate and on four occasions the mob "*cry out*" for Jesus to be crucified. There is more Johannine irony here: Jesus cries out for Life but his enemies cry out for Death.

Lazarus has been brought back to life, but it is only physical life (*bios*). This is not like Jesus' Resurrection, where Jesus is raised to a new supernatural life (*zoë*). That's why Lazarus emerges wearing his grave clothes – he will need them again one day when he dies when the Disciples find Jesus' empty tomb in **John 20: 6-7**, they see that the Risen Christ has left his grave clothes behind because he will never need them again.

After this awe-inspiring scene, John moves to a different setting: the sordid political squabbles of the **Sanhedrin**, which is the Jewish council of priests and Pharisees. From Jesus offering **Life** (p87), John shifts to the Jewish leaders plotting death.

[49] Then one of them, named Caiaphas, who was high priest that year, spoke up, "You know nothing at all! [50] You do not realize that it is better for you that one man die for the people than that the whole nation perish."

This is another one of those scenes in John's Gospel where Jesus' enemies say things that are more true than they think, but not in the way they think. The priests and Pharisees really do "*know nothing at all*" because they are spiritually blind. Jesus is the "*one man*" who will die an atoning death "*for the people*" who would otherwise "*perish*" in Hell. Jesus' death really will be for their own benefit, but they "*do not realize*".

Implications

Raymond E. Brown argues that the entirety of John's Gospel has a hidden meaning to it: it refers to the experiences of the **Johannine Community** (p208) in the 80s and 90s CE as well as Jesus' ministry in the 30s CE. The Johannine Community were Jewish Christians who were thrown out of the Synagogues by their fellow-Jews for believing Jesus to be the **Son of God** (p112). This was emotionally distressing, because the Christians were alienated from Jewish friends and family. They were also in danger from the Roman Empire, because they no longer counted as 'Jews' and therefore had to make pagan sacrifices to the Empire's gods like everyone else; when they refused they were imprisoned and executed.

John's Gospel frequently refers to "*the Jews*" as the enemy (for example, in the Sign of **Healing the Blind Man**, p155). This Sign goes even further. Jesus' own Disciples refer to their enemies as "*the Jews*" (even though they were Jewish themselves). At Bethany, Mary and Martha are accompanied by "*the Jews*" (as if Mary, Martha and Lazarus weren't Jewish themselves). John depicts anyone who **believes in Jesus** (p93) as separate from "*the Jews*" who don't.

This is why Lazarus *symbolises the Johannine Community itself*.

- Like Lazarus, the Community was 'sick' when it was just a despised sect within the Jewish community.
- Like Lazarus, the Community 'died' when it was rejected by the Jewish community.
- Like Lazarus, it was cut off from its friends and family (as represented by the stone over the tomb) and it faced actual death (from the Romans).
- However, the Johannine Community's story, like Lazarus', does "*not end with death*". They do not give up or disband.
- Jesus calls the Christians of the Johannine Community to enjoy a deeper, more perfect **Life** of love and truth – a life being experienced at the moment, not in the future on Judgement Day. The Community pulls together and experiences a return to life.

The grave clothes Lazarus is buried in represent the Jewish **Law** (p102). Jesus instructs the grave clothes to be removed. He says, "*let him go*". Without the Jewish Law restricting them, the Johannine Christians are truly free.

These symbolic readings of the Sign lead some scholars to argue that the episode is fictional. This is backed up by the Synoptic Gospels, which mention Martha and Mary, but never mention their brother Lazarus and they do not describe this amazing miracle.

Christians who try to HARMONISE the Synoptic Gospels and John's Gospel argue that this Sign *actually happened* but is missing from the Synoptics because the Synoptics are based on the traditions passed on by **Peter** (the head Disciple) and Peter was not present for this miracle. They also argue that the Synoptics were written while Lazarus was still alive, so this miracle was left out to protect his identity from Jewish enemies who would want to harm him, but **John's Gospel** was written after Lazarus died (for the second time) so his story could be told.

A different view is that the Sign was really "spiritual theatre". Lazarus was not really dead. The whole business was a sort of playacting laid on by Jesus to demonstrate the truths behind his teachings. This view preserves the MEANING of the Sign but avoids the supernatural elements.

> Of course John would resist any attempt to work out what actually happened. John wants his readers to focus on what the sign *means for them* personally.

Is the Sign of Raising Lazarus essential for understanding Jesus' identity?

YES	NO
The Sign reveals the hope of **Eternal Life** that all Christians have: that by **believing in Jesus** they will also be raised from the dead. This Sign is therefore an isolated and temporary example of something that is going to happen to all Christians. Jesus is the giver of this Life which is why he is the Saviour.	Jesus tells Mary that the **Life** he offers is in the here-and-now, not in the future or on Judgement Day. The whole passage is symbolic: Lazarus represents the **Johannine Community** experiencing a new life as Christians in the 90s CE, not some individual man who came back to life around 33 CE.
The story can refer to the Johannine Community *and also* be an event that happened during Jesus' ministry. There are multiple layers of meaning but they are connected by the idea of Jesus as the Saviour who brings hope and comfort to those who are suffering.	This miracle is probably fictional. It is never mentioned in the Synoptic Gospels despite being dramatic and public. The references to "*the Jews*" suggest it was composed by people who no longer viewed themselves as Jewish, not by Jesus' Jewish Disciples and earliest followers.

TOPIC 2 KEY SCHOLARS

Raymond E Brown

Topic: 2.2 Titles of Jesus, 2.3 Miracles & Signs

Raymond E Brown (1928-1998) is an American Roman Catholic priest and Bible scholar whose work features in other topics in this course too **(1.1 Prophecy regarding the Messiah** and **3.2 Purpose & Authorship of the Fourth Gospel**).

Brown carries on the work on John's Gospel started by **C.H. Dodd** and is a big influence on **Morna Hooker**. In *The Gospel & the Epistles of John: A Concise Commentary* (1988), Brown goes through John's Gospel passage-by-passage, exploring the terminology and the symbolism. Brown follows Dodd's concept of 'realised eschatology' – he thinks Jesus' acts and words reveal timeless truths about life and God rather than predicting things that are going to happen after death or at the end of time.

In *The Community of the Beloved Disciple* (1979), Brown explores the background of the **Johannine Community** (p208) and how its situation influences the way John's Gospel presents Jesus. The subtitle of the book is *The Life, Loves and Hates of an Individual Church in New Testament Times*. Notice the word "Hates": Brown focuses on the deep rift between the Johannine Christians and the Jewish Synagogues that expelled them in the 80s and 90s CE.

Brown didn't discover the idea of the Johannine Community. **J. Louis Martyn** was the first to develop this concept, but Brown references Martyn in his book and builds on his scholarship.

Brown argues that the Johannine Christians experienced a deep trauma when they were expelled from the Jewish religion. Not only did they lose friends and family, but they were exposed to danger. Now that they were no longer Jews, they were expected by the Roman authorities to join in pagan sacrifices. Those that refused were arrested and even executed. Brown suspects that the Jewish leaders sometimes informed on these Christians. This explains the 'Hate' felt by the former Jewish Christians towards *"the Jews"* and what he calls *"the deep sense of 'us' against 'them'* in John's Gospel.

Brown also suggests that the entirety of John's Gospel tells a coded story of the Johannine Community's experiences and the development of their faith. For example, **the man born blind** (p155) could also represent the Johannine Community, who started off as Jews thinking Jesus was a wise healer, then a mighty prophet, then (after being *"thrown out"* by the Jewish leaders) worshiping him as God.

Similarly, **Lazarus** (p159) represents the Johannine Community too: being thrown out of the Synagogues seemed to be death for them but they came to see that it was really a calling into spiritual **Life**, once they got rid of the *"grave clothes"* of the Jewish Law.

C.H. Dodd

Topic: 2.1 (Prologue in John), 2.2 (Titles of Jesus in the Synoptics and selected 'I Am' sayings in John), 2.3 (Miracles and Signs)

Charles Harold Dodd (1884-1973) is an Welsh Protestant Bible scholar whose work features in another topic in this course too **(3.1 Purpose & authorship of the Fourth Gospel)**.

Dodd is a very influential figure in Bible scholarship. His work argues against the conclusions drawn by **Albert Schweitzer** and **Rudolph Bultmann**. Both of these scholars tried to analyse the Bible to uncover the historical Jesus by stripping away the supernatural elements. They concluded that Jesus was a rather murky historical figure whose political and religious ambitions were pretty remote from modern life. Dodd argues against this, saying that we can reconstruct details about Jesus' teachings and these are relevant to people in the modern world.

Dodd wrote two books relevant to this part of the course. *The Interpretation of the Fourth Gospel* (1953) goes through all John's key concepts and analyses them in terms of their link to the Old Testament or **Hellenic** philosophy (p48). It's a dense read because Dodd is the sort of scholar who writes 'Logos' as $\lambda o\gamma o\sigma$ and expects you to know your Greek alphabet well enough to understand.

Historical Tradition in the Fourth Gospel (1963) is a little more accessible. Dodd argues that the author of Johns Gospel is a '*historian*' and not a '*chronicler*'. In other words, John's Gospel is interested in the meaning of historical events and freely edits and alters stories and puts speeches into characters' mouths to draw out this meaning. However, Dodd does think there are historical details in the Gospel and that they can be reconstructed by scholars.

Dodd's main contribution is the idea of REALISED ESCHATOLOGY. 'Eschatology' is philosophy about the 'End Times' (from the Greek, *Eschaton*) such as death, Judgement Day and the Afterlife. A typical Jewish eschatology among the Pharisees in the 1st century was that at some point in the future, God would send his Messiah to begin the Messianic Age where God would rule the world, abolishing sin and suffering.

According to Dodd, Jesus taught a 'realised eschatology', that these End Times were **already happening**. This means that Bible passages Heaven, Hell, Judgement Day etc should be interpreted symbolically as religious experiences Christians have in the present.

Dodd's views are popular with Liberal Christians, because they involve focusing on the spiritual meaning of the Bible rather than predictions about the end of the world, the threat of damnation in Hell or a focus on going to Heaven after you die. These views are unpopular with Conservative Christians who prefer to take the supernatural elements in the Bible more literally and have a 'futurist eschatology' (Judgement Day is coming in the future).

Morna Hooker

Topic: 2.1 Prologue in John

Morna Hooker (b. 1938) is a Professor at Cambridge University and a Bible scholar whose work also features in another topic in this course **(1.1 Prophecy regarding the Messiah)**.

Hooker wrote a slim introduction to New Testament scholarship called **_Beginnings: Keys that Open the Gospels_** (1998). It's a very readable book and available cheap from online booksellers so I'd recommend it for students. She argues that each Gospel has a prologue that works as a "*key*" to "*unlock*" the main themes and teachings about Jesus.

Hooker call's John's Prologue the *"glorious key"*. She does not think there is a break between the Prologue and the rest of John's Gospel and rejects the idea that the Prologue was written by someone else and was added onto the Gospel by at a later date. She thinks the Prologue sets out the themes that the Gospel explores in detail later. In fact, she claims the Prologue is a *midrash*, which is a Jewish term for a commentary on an Old Testament passage. The Prologue is a *midrash* on the opening chapter of the **Book of Genesis**, where God creates the world. Johns *midrash* explains the true meaning of Genesis for a Christian audience. This is that the Word of God, which was present at the Creation, is present also in Jesus.

The Prologue also contains a *midrash* on the **Book of Exodus**, where Moses goes up Mount Sinai to meet God and receive the Commandments. John's Gospel presents Jesus as superior to Moses, offering a deeper knowledge of God than Moses did and a more accessible set of Commandments – the commandments to love each other.

Hooker contrasts John's Gospel with the Synoptic Gospels. In the Synoptics, the truth about Jesus' identity is often hidden and is revealed only in hints. In John's Gospel *"the hints become overwhelming"* and Jesus makes *"stupendous claims"*. She argues that, if they have read the Prologue, readers will not be shocked or baffled by these claims and that is why the Prologue is an essential part of John's Gospel.

Hooker also writes about John's Gospel revealing the *"family squabble"* going on between the first Christians and their Jewish friends and neighbours. She says that *"what the parties are squabbling about is their inheritance"* – who are the true children of Abraham, the Jews who follow Moses or the Christians who follow Jesus? She refers to the *"gigantic take-over battle"* going on behind the pages of John's Gospel as the Christians lay claim to the true meaning of the Old Testament and the Jewish **Law** (p102).

Hooker concludes that 'glory' means *"the truth of God revealed"* and that Jesus reveals this truth in his **"I Am" statements** (p119), his miraculous Signs (p135) and, ultimately, in the Crucifixion. Jesus' death on the cross reveals the *'Glory of God'* – the truth about what God is like – more fully than anything else.

TOPIC 3 INTERPRETING THE TEXT

Interpreting the text

- The synoptic problem, source, form and redaction criticism – an examination of the relationship between the synoptic Gospels, including two source hypothesis (priority of Mark and 'Q source'), the idea of proto-Gospels and the four-source hypothesis.
- Units of tradition and their type/form, the way texts appear to have been translated, edited and transmitted.
- The significance of this for understanding the texts.

The purpose and authorship of the Fourth Gospel

- An examination of the different purposes of the Gospel and views of its authorship: Jesus as Christ, Son of God, life in his name, Spiritual Gospel, a Gospel to convert Jews and Gentiles, fulfilment of scripture.
- The strengths and weaknesses of these views based on the text and modern scholarship, and their significance for understanding the text for individuals and communities.
- With reference to the ideas of Raymond E. Brown and C.H. Dodd.

TOPIC 3: INTERPRETING THE TEXT

What's this topic about?

How did the New Testament Gospels come to be written? Who wrote them and who was the intended audience? What were they originally trying to say? These questions are addressed in this topic.

INTERPRETING THE TEXT

This topic looks at the **Synoptic Problem** (including **proto-Gospels**, the **priority of Mark**, *Q* **source**, **2-source** and **4-source solutions**) as well as **source criticism**, **form criticism** and **redaction criticism**

THE PURPOSE & AUTHORSHIP OF THE FOURTH GOSPEL

This topic looks at different theories about John's Gospel, including **purpose** (including **spiritual Gospel**, **life in his Name**, **Christ, Son of God**, **fulfilling Scripture** and **conversion**) and **authorship**. The key scholars are **Raymond E. Brown** and **C.H. Dodd**.

Before you go any further...

... there are some things you need to know.

THE EARLIEST DOCUMENTS

Jesus wrote no books and none of his followers wrote down his sayings or doings during his lifetime. Everything we know about Jesus was written by someone else, a believer living and writing in the decades after Jesus' crucifixion (which was in 30 CE or 33 CE). This means all the New Testament writers view Jesus in the light of the Resurrection (i.e. 'in hindsight').

> *This is an important point. The Gospels are written by people who believe Jesus has been raised from the dead. This changed their view of him from whatever they believed about him during his Ministry in the late 20s and early 30s CE.*

The earliest Christians seemed to believe that the end of the world was imminent. This means that they too did not write down their recollections of Jesus 'for posterity'. They didn't think there was going to *be* any 'posterity'. The earliest Christian documents we have are the **epistles** (letters) of **Paul**. Throughout the 50s CE, Paul founded Christian churches in Turkey and Greece and wrote letters to his congregations, settling disputes and encouraging their faith. However, Paul never knew Jesus during Jesus' lifetime and only mentions the most basic details of Jesus' life and death (e.g. that Jesus was betrayed and crucified, that he had twelve Disciples).

The Gospels were written later, when the generation of Christians who had known Jesus personally started to die. They realised they would need a record of who Jesus was to pass onto a new generations of Christians who had not known Jesus in life – possibly Christians who had never been to Galilee or Judea and knew little or nothing about Judaism.

> *But remember: the Gospels are not just biographies of Jesus. They are written to pass on beliefs about Jesus: that he is the **Messiah**, the **Son of God** and the Saviour of the world.*

The traditional explanation of the Gospels is that they were written ***independently*** by people closely connected to the historical Jesus:

- **Matthew** and **John** were written by Jesus' actual Disciples, Matthew Levi the tax-collector and John son of Zebedee; Matthew was perhaps written in Antioch where there was a large Jewish population, John perhaps in Ephesus (both in modern Turkey).
- **Mark** was written by the secretary of Jesus' chief Disciple, Peter; since Peter was executed in Rome, this Gospel is supposed to have been written there
- **Luke** was written by Paul's traveling companion, a Greek doctor and Christian convert who met with Peter and the other Disciples; it is thought to have been written in Greece, where Paul founded his churches

Traditionally, all the Gospels were written in the 60s CE, before the Jewish Revolt of 67-73 CE and the destruction of the Temple (Jesus predicts this destruction in the Gospels). Modern scholarship is **secular** in philosophy and does not assume that miracles happen. Secular scholars date the Gospels ***after*** the Jewish Revolt (which is why Jesus can "predict" the destruction of the Temple – it was actually in the past when the Gospels were written).

Mark's Gospel (68-70 CE, Rome?)

Most scholars now regard **Mark** as the earliest Gospel (this is the theory of **Markan Priority**, p187). Mark emphasises that Christians should expect persecution by Jewish leaders as well as *"governors and kings"* (**Mark 13: 9**) and this probably refers to the Christians being blamed by the Emperor Nero for the fire in Rome in 64 CE. There are several prophecies in Mark about the Temple being destroyed, but the author doesn't seem to know that this has actually happened (which would date Mark no later than 70 CE). Mark explains Jewish customs for his readers (e.g. **Mark 7: 3-4**) which suggests it was written for a church of Gentile converts to Christianity rather than Jewish Christians.

Matthew's Gospel (c.85 CE, Antioch?)

Early scholars used to suppose **Matthew** to be the earliest Gospel, which is why it comes first in the New Testament. This is because Matthew is a very 'Jewish' Gospel: it does not explain Jewish customs the way Mark does, it uses **proof-texts** from the Old Testament to support its view of Jesus as the **Messiah**, it shows a good knowledge of 1st century Palestine and a respect for the Jewish **Law** (e.g. **Matthew 5: 18-19**). Because Matthew refers to Jesus being famous *"throughout all Syria"* (**Matthew 4: 24**), scholars suggest that the Gospel was written for a group of Jewish Christians who escaped the destruction of the Jewish War and moved to Syria, probably to Antioch which had a large community of Jewish Christians.

The Gospel doesn't name its author but early tradition identifies the author as Matthew the Tax Collector from Capernaum who was recruited by Jesus to be one of his Twelve Disciples (**Matthew 9: 9-13**). However, the author does not identify himself as Matthew or write as if he is an eyewitness to the events in Jesus' life.

Luke's Gospel (c.85 CE, Greece?)

Luke is usually regarded as the last of the Synoptic Gospels to be written. It does not claim to be an eyewitness account but instead introduces itself as a report gathered from people who *were* eyewitnesses (**Luke 1: 1-4**). It is written in a good standard of Greek for an educated audience but it only has a hazy understanding of the geography of Palestine. Luke writes about some specific details of the Roman siege of Jerusalem in 70 CE, which dates it later than this event. Luke has a strong focus on the relevance of Christianity to Gentiles and on Jesus' moral teachings; it is sometimes called the 'Gospel of Compassion'. Luke tries to present Jesus as a philosopher-figure – someone the Roman Empire would find respectable and non-threatening.

John's Gospel (90-100 CE, Ephesus?)

John's Gospel has always been viewed as the last Gospel to be written. It describes Jesus' enemies as "*the Jews*" and seems to come from a time when Christians were ceasing to view themselves as Jewish; it also has a 'high Christology' and regards Jesus as the **Word of God made Flesh** (p81). It refers to Christians being expelled from Synagogues, which took place in the 80s-90s CE. John's Gospel is written in a 'backward-looking' style that refers to the events in Jesus' lifetime as having happened some time ago. However, it has a much more accurate knowledge of the geography of pre-70 CE Jerusalem than the other Gospels. This means some parts of John's Gospel might go back to original eyewitnesses.

All the dates above are speculations. If you read around you will find some Christian books and websites arguing for earlier dates. For example, some would date Luke to the early 60s because Luke doesn't seem to be aware of Paul and Peter dying in Rome during Nero's persecutions. These Christians regard descriptions of the Temple being destroyed as miraculous predictions of a <u>future</u> event rather than recollections of a <u>past</u> event. Your beliefs about miracles will influence how you date these Gospels.

Although John's Gospel is (probably) the latest in terms of composition, it's the earliest in terms of physical evidence. The oldest example of a Gospel yet discovered is the **Rylands Library Papyrus P52**. This fragment of papyrus (an ancient form of paper) was discovered in an Egyptian market in 1920.

It contains a fragment from **John 18** on the front and back: the scene where Pontius Pilate asks Jesus, "*Are you the King of the Jews?*" It has been dated to the early 2nd century CE.

THE NEW TESTAMENT CANON... AND THE REST

Matthew, **Mark**, **Luke** and **John** are the canonical Gospels. A 'canon' is an official list. There are non-canonical Gospels that aren't officially recognised and weren't included in the Bible. Sometimes they are called the APOCRYPHA (which is Greek for "hidden things").

These 'apocryphal' or 'non-canonical' Gospels were popular with some churches in the early Christian centuries, but came to be seen as deviant or inauthentic. We know about some of them because early Christian writers mention them (usually with hostility).

- **The Gospel of the Ebionites:** This group of Jewish Christians kept their own Gospel which presented Jesus as a vegetarian prophet; unfortunately, no copies have survived

Some of these Gospels were thought to be lost but copies have been discovered by archaeologists:

- **The Gospel of Thomas:** This is a 'sayings' Gospel the consists only of quotes from Jesus but no story; many of these sayings are very odd and it contains some unusual Parables (such as the whacky Parable of the Assassin)
- **The Gospel of Peter:** This Gospel is violently anti-Jewish, contains fantastical miracles and presents the Jewish king Herod Antipas, rather than the Roman governor Pontius Pilate, as ordering Jesus' execution
- **The Gospel of Judas:** Not written by Judas, but about him; this Gospel presents Judas positively, not as a betrayer but as being ordered by Jesus to hand him over to the authorities

The canonical set of four Gospels (**Matthew**, **Mark**, **Luke** and **John** – the *Tetramorph* or 'set of four' in Greek) are mentioned by **Irenaeus of Lyon** in 180 CE which shows they were informally accepted by Christian leaders early on. By about 400 CE, **Augustine of Hippo** regards the canon as accepted by everyone. So why did some Gospels not make it into the canon?

- Some Gospels offer unusual views of Jesus that don't fit with standard Christian beliefs – for example, Jesus arranging for his own betrayal in the **Gospel of Judas**
- Some belonged to minority Christian sects that faded from history – such as the **Ebionites** who tried to keep their Jewish roots
- Some were viewed as of late composition and not authentic – such as the **Gospel of Peter** which has lots of blatantly unhistorical events

However, some Gospels were forced 'underground'. The **Gospel of Thomas** seems to have been suppressed by the Bishop in Egypt in the 4th century CE. Its owners buried it in a sealed pot and it lay undiscovered for over 1500 years until it was accidentally dug up by Muslim farmers in 1945. These books are known as the **Nag Hammadi Library** (after the town where they were found).

Be cautious about what you read online about the Nag Hammadi Library. There's no evidence that the Gospel of Thomas was widely popular with Christians or dates back as early as the canonical Gospels. But it is interesting to read a different presentation of Jesus.

TOPIC 3.1 INTERPRETING THE TEXT

The Exam expects you to be familiar with the so-called **Synoptic Problem** and how scholars have interpreted the Gospels through different forms of 'criticism' ('criticism' here doesn't mean attacking the Gospels: it means analysing them in different ways).

Christianity After Jesus

None of the books in the New Testament is written by Jesus. As far as we know, Jesus never wrote down any of his teachings. The New Testament texts were written by Christian believers living in the decades after Jesus, people who passionately believed that Jesus had been raised from the dead and was no longer – or perhaps, had never been – an ordinary human being.

Some scholars refer to these people as the 'primitive' Christians – but 'primitive' in the sense of 'coming first' rather than being savage or basic. The primitive Christians experienced some influential events in the 1st century CE:

33 CE	Jesus is crucified in Jerusalem. In the weeks that follow, his Disciples report encountering him raised to life.
34 CE	One early Christian **Stephen** is stoned to death by a Jewish mob when he describes a vision of Jesus as the **Son of Man** enthroned in Heaven beside God (**Acts 6: 54-60**).
35-50 CE	The Christian movement spreads among Jews but also attracts Gentile converts. These Gentiles are largely recruited by **Paul**, a former **Pharisee** who once persecuted Christians himself but has now become one
50s-60s CE	The Gentile converts pose a problem: do they have to become Jews and follow the Jewish **Law** (including circumcision for the men)? or does the Law no longer apply to Christians? Opinions are divided with Paul arguing against the Law but many of Jesus' original Disciples (perhaps including **Peter**) wanting to continue following it.
64 CE	The Emperor Nero blames Christians for the fire in Rome and puts them to death in gruesome ways. Paul and Peter both die in this persecution.
67 CE	The Jewish Revolt throws off the **Roman occupation**. For a while the **Zealots** take control of Jerusalem and Christians became even more unwelcome, with many moving to Syria.
70 CE	The Romans invade Jerusalem and destroy the Temple, bringing an end to the **Sadducees** and **Essenes** too. Judaism is left without a leadership or a centre of worship.
70s-80s CE	Judaism reforms itself, with the **Pharisees** taking over leadership and the local Synagogues becoming the centre of worship and authority.
90 CE	The **Council of Jamnia** formally expels Christians from the Synagogues.
90s CE +	No longer considered to be Jewish by the Roman authorities, Christians are expected to worship the gods of Rome and the Roman Emperor himself. When they refuse, they are arrested and sometimes tortured and executed.

During this period, the Christians preserved memories of Jesus as part of an ORAL TRADITION – stories and teachings being passed on by word-of-mouth and shared when Christians gathered together in worship (the Jewish Christians at Synagogues at first, the Gentile Christians at each other's homes). Paul's **epistles** (letters) from the 50s CE give us some insight into this; we know the Christians gathered for a 'Love Feast' where bread and wine were shared (the **EUCHARIST**).

Dating of the Gospels

The traditional belief is that the Gospels were written in the late 50s or early 60s, before the persecutions by Nero and before the destruction of the Temple in 70 CE. The Gospels feature predictions that the Temple **will be** destroyed, but don't state that this has in fact happened. The **Book of Acts**, which is a sequel to Luke's Gospel, does not seem to be aware that Peter and Paul have been executed, which suggests it was written no later than the mid-60s CE.

If the Gospels were written this early, they really could be the work of the people they are traditionally linked to: **Matthew Levi** the tax-collector who joined Jesus' Disciples, **Mark** the secretary of Peter, **Luke** the companion of Paul and **John son of Zebedee** the Disciple of Jesus (p206). This would make the Gospels authentic eyewitness accounts of the things Jesus actually said and did.

There is a lot of disagreement between scholars over this. Many think that the Gospels were written **after** 70 CE, possibly right at the end of the 1st century CE. They were **not** written by eyewitnesses but by later Christians who had received an oral tradition about what Jesus said and did – an oral tradition that might have deviated pretty far from the historical facts in the intervening decades. This means there is a huge amount of interest in the 'oral period' when Christianity was taking shape: the decades after Jesus' lifetime but before the Gospels were written down.

- Did oral tradition faithfully preserve Jesus' historic behaviour, words and teachings? This is the view of many Catholic and conservative Protestant scholars.
- Did oral tradition massively distort Jesus' behaviour, words and teachings, possibly attributing to Jesus many beliefs that have no basis in fact? This is the claim of more liberal or modernist scholars.

There's a similar disagreement about Christology (beliefs about who Jesus is). Low Christology views Jesus as a human being EXALTED (raised up, promoted) by God to a supernatural state; high Christology views Jesus as a divine being who has been INCARNATED in human form.

- Did the low Christology emerge earlier in the oral period and the high Christology develop later?
- Does either type of Christology actually date back to Jesus' lifetime: are these beliefs Jesus had about himself and taught his followers or did they develop later?

The Quest for the Historical Jesus

19th and 20th century scholarship pursued what **Albert Schweitzer** called *"the quest for the historical Jesus"* (1906). Many scholars focus on the distinction between that **Martin Kahler** terms *"the Jesus of history and the Christ of faith"* (1892). The 'Historical Jesus' was a 1st century Jewish preacher who was executed by the Romans; the 'Christ of faith' is a cosmic being worshiped by millions and composed of ideas developed long after the historical Jesus died.

In fact, Kahler meant something different by his phrase, but the idea has stuck and someone has to get credit for it!

Jesus of History	Christ of Faith
Jesus of Nazareth was a genuine historical figure: a Palestinian Jew from 2000 years ago whose life, death and message profoundly influenced the people of his day. Even those who deny Jesus was the Son of God do not deny his existence. They may even approve of his life and message and find them worth studying, alongside other great religious leaders. These people are reflecting upon the historical Jesus.	Christians do not believe that Jesus became divine through his Resurrection; they believe that he was divine and one with God from the beginning of time. They believe that, in the person of Jesus, God became one of the human race in order to redeem us from our sin. When Christ was raised from the dead, he became our Lord and Saviour. For them, the Jesus of history is the same thing as the Christ of faith: Jesus was and is both human and divine.

The idea of the 'historical Jesus' first appears in the writings of **Hermann Reimarus** (1694-1768) whose posthumously published *Wolfenbüttel Fragments* put forward the idea that the historical Jesus was very different from the 'Christ' who was invented by his later followers.

Reimarus proposes that Jesus was a Jewish prophet who had no intention of founding a separate religion, but who got involved with a failed rebellion against the Romans and was executed for it. Jesus' followers stole his body to fake his resurrection from the dead.

*Reimarus' ideas are pretty hard-core even by the standards of Internet trolls. You will encounter his theory in more detail if you go on to **Topic 4 (Ways of Interpreting the Scriptures)***

Some scholars propose that the historical Jesus can be discussed, analysed and re-imagined quite separately from the Christ of faith – that the two have almost nothing to do with each other. For example, some scholars have proposed that Jesus was a Zealot or a Cynic philosopher or an unremarkable Jewish exorcist but they still worship Christ as a **symbol** of the love of God.

However, not everyone finds this idea easy to grasp and, for many, separating the historical Jesus from the Christ of faith leads to the *loss* of faith: if Jesus is nobody special in history, then Christ is just an idea his followers invented after he died, not someone who reveals God *"in Grace and Truth"* (p106).

The scholars who are prepared to re-interpret Jesus in fairly radical ways that make sense to modern readers are the MODERNISTS. The scholars who want to conserve the traditional idea of Jesus as a historical miracle-worker and Messiah are the CONSERVATIVES.

Sometimes the modernists are termed liberals and the conservatives are termed traditionalists.

This cartoon (from a traditionalist viewpoint) shows modernist Bible critics descending into darkness and atheism. The symbolism is straight out of John's Gospel!

In the 1980s, a group of 50 Bible scholars formed the **Jesus Seminar** to discuss, research and publish ideas about the historical Jesus. The Jesus Seminar codes Gospel passages in red that Jesus probably did say or do, in pink if its possible Jesus said or did them, grey if it's unlikely and black if Jesus almost certainly didn't really say or do these things. The Jesus Seminar is a modernist project and works on the assumption that miracles don't happen and that Jesus was an ordinary human and not a supernatural being.

This is the source of the conflict today between conservative/traditionalist and liberal/modernist Christian thinkers. For conservatives, the historical Jesus *is* the Christ of faith: he's a supernatural person who preformed miracles and predicted his own crucifixion and Resurrection. Liberals question these things and are prepared to admit that most of what we believe about Christ was invented decades or centuries after the death of Jesus.

THE SYNOPTIC PROBLEM

The Synoptic 'Problem' isn't really a problem in the same way that the **Problem of Evil** is a problem for believers. It's more of a puzzle that scholars have proposed different answers for over the years.

What is the Synoptic Problem?

Christians have always recognised a similarity between the three 'Synoptic' Gospels (**Matthew**, **Mark** and **Luke**). 'Synoptic' means 'seen together' and when passages from the Synoptic Gospels are placed side by side they can be seen to be remarkably similar. Sometimes they are word-for-word the same, but at other times they differ slightly, with one Gospel adding words or phrases or the other Gospel omitting them.

Here is an example: the miracle of the **Feeding of the 5000** (p147), which is described in all 3 Synoptic Gospels and in **John's Gospel**. This translation tries to capture the phrasing of the original Greek and the particular word used for 'fish' is noted:

SYNOPTIC GOSPELS			NON-SYNOPTIC
Matt 14:19-20	**Mark 6:41-42**	**Luke 9:16-17**	**John 6:11-12**
Taking the five loaves and the two fish (*ichthus*), looking up into heaven he blessed, and breaking, gave to the disciples the loaves, and the disciples to the crowds. And all ate and were satisfied.	And taking the five loaves and the two fish (*ichthus*), looking up into heaven, he blessed and he broke up the bread, and was giving to the disciples in order that they set before them, and the two fish he distributed to all. And all ate and were satisfied.	But taking the five loaves and the two fish (*ichthus*), looking up into heaven, he blessed them and he broke up, and was giving to the disciples to set before the crowd. And they ate and were satisfied.	Thus Jesus took the loaves, and giving thanks, he distributed to the ones reclining; similarly also, whatever they desired from the fish (*opsarion*). And when they are full, he says to this disciples, "Gather the remaining pieces in order that nothing be lost."

You can see how the Synoptics use the same phrasing and the same Greek word for fish (ichthus, meaning the actual animal 'fish') whereas John uses different phrasing and a different word for fish (opsarion, meaning fishy food, like a kipper)

Agreement in Wording

When **Matthew**, **Mark** and **Luke** describe the same episode, on average they share 50% of the same Greek words used to describe it (in contrast, they share 10% of the same words with **John**). Some passages are even more similar than that: when they introduce **John the Baptist**, Matthew and Mark share 90% of their Greek words, such as these rather precise terms:

> *John wore clothing made of camel's hair (trichon kamelou), with a leather belt (zonen dermatinen) round his waist [and] he ate locusts (akrides) and wild honey (meli agrion) –* **Mark 1: 6 and Matthew 3: 4**

> *Remember that Jesus and his disciples spoke Aramaic, not Greek. How likely is it that Matthew and Mark would use <u>exactly</u> the same words and phrases in Greek to translate the original Aramaic description of John the Baptist?*

Parenthetical Material

'Parenthesis' means 'brackets' – when a text adds a comment for the reader in brackets to make a point clearer (like this). All the Gospels contain parenthetical material; in fact, **John's Gospel** contains the most. However, the parenthetical material in the Synoptics is usually identical.

Parenthesis is something used in writing, not in speech, so this feature can't be due to the Gospel-writers being eyewitnesses to the same speeches or conversations.

Here's an example:

> *(Let the reader understand)* - **Mark 13:14 and Matthew 24: 15**

> *This parenthetical statement is deliberately addressed to a "reader" – not a 'listener' - so it's clearly been composed by the author, not some earlier eyewitness. What are the odds Matthew and Mark would use the <u>exact same phrase</u> to clarify the <u>exact same point</u> when they were writing their story?*

The use of identical parenthetical material is good evidence that one text has copied another rather than coming up with the same passage independently.

Luke's Prologue

Luke's Gospel begins by explicitly claiming to have taken material from earlier sources:

> *just as they were handed down to us by those who from the first were eyewitnesses –* **Luke 1: 2**

> *Luke is admitting right at the start that he's using material that was 'handed down' and not creating a Gospel "from scratch"*

Matthew 9: 9-13	Mark 2: 13-17	Luke 5: 27-32
	[13] Once again Jesus went out beside the lake. A large crowd came to him, and he began to teach them.	[27] After this, Jesus went out
[9] As Jesus went on from there,	[14] As he walked along,	
he saw a man named Matthew sitting at the tax collector's booth. 'Follow me,' he told him, and Matthew got up and followed him.	he saw Levi son of Alphaeus sitting at the tax collector's booth. 'Follow me,' Jesus told him, and Levi got up and followed him.	and saw a tax collector by the name of Levi sitting at his tax booth. 'Follow me,' Jesus said to him, [28] and Levi got up, left everything and followed him.
[10] While Jesus was having dinner at Matthew's house, many tax collectors and sinners came and ate with him and his disciples.	[15] While Jesus was having dinner at Levi's house, many tax collectors and sinners were eating with him and his disciples, for there were many who followed him.	[29] Then Levi held a great banquet for Jesus at his house, and a large crowd of tax collectors and others were eating with them.
[11] When the Pharisees saw this,	[16] When the teachers of the law who were Pharisees saw him eating with the sinners and tax collectors,	[30] But the Pharisees and the teachers of the law who belonged to their sect
they asked his disciples, 'Why does your teacher eat with tax collectors and sinners?'	they asked his disciples: 'Why does he eat with tax collectors and sinners?'	complained to his disciples, 'Why do you eat and drink with tax collectors and sinners?'
[12] On hearing this,	[17] On hearing this,	
Jesus said, 'It is not the healthy who need a doctor, but those who are ill.	Jesus said to them, 'It is not the healthy who need a doctor, but those who are ill.	[31] Jesus answered them, 'It is not the healthy who need a doctor, but those who are ill.
[13] But go and learn what this means: "I desire mercy, not sacrifice."		
For I have not come to call the righteous, but sinners.'	I have not come to call the righteous, but sinners.	[32] I have not come to call the righteous, but sinners to repentance.'

This episode, describing Jesus calling Matthew (also called Levi) to be his disciple, shows how similar the Synoptic Gospels can be.

Implications: independent versions of the same story?

Some Christians argue that **Matthew**, **Mark** and **Luke** all independently came up with their Gospels, either as eyewitnesses or reporting an 'oral tradition' (story passed on by word-of-mouth) that had been handed down to them. They explain the Synoptic similarities like this:

- The Gospel-writers were all describing the same historical events so obviously they describe them in the same ways
- The Gospel-writers were all inspired by the Holy Spirit to write in the same way

The first solution is **historically naïve**. Even though the Gospel-writers describe some things in the same way, they describe other things in different ways. Why would they do that? **John's Gospel** doesn't match the wording of the Synoptics (John's wording is 92% unique). Does this mean that John's Gospel describes completely different events?

> *This argument would imply that Jesus was crucified twice: once the way the Synoptic Gospels describe it and once the way John's Gospel describes it. But that's absurd. Clearly, they're describing the <u>same</u> crucifixion, so we need a different explanation for the similarity in the way the Synoptics describe things.*

The idea of **divine inspiration** faces the same problem: why would the Holy Spirit inspire the Gospel-writers to use the same language and describe the same details some times – but not others? Why would the Holy Spirit inspire John's Gospel to describe things differently – or is John's Gospel not inspired by the Holy Spirit in the way that the Synoptics are?

The idea of the Gospels as **inspired** by God is explored in Topic **4 (Ways of Interpreting the Scripture)**.

Implications: interdependence or a proto-Gospel?

A popular solution is that the Synoptic Gospels are **interdependent**: they have all copied from each other. Church tradition states that **Matthew** was the first Gospel to be written and that **Mark** and **Luke** copied passages from Matthew (with Mark cutting out details and Luke adding more in). This is the theory of MATTHEAN PRIORITY.

A different solution to the Synoptic Problem would be the existence of another **Proto-Gospel** (p183). This is an early original Gospel that the Synoptics are copying passages from. If they are all using the same proto-Gospel, that would explain their similarities. If **John's Gospel** does not make use of the proto-Gospel for its material, that would explain John's differences in language and style.

The problem is that no trace of a proto-Gospel has been discovered by archaeologists and there is no mention of a proto-Gospel by any of the ancient Christian writers like **Irenaeus**, **Jerome** and **Augustine**, who all describe Matthew, Mark and Luke as the earliest Gospels known. The concept of proto-Gospels is described in more detail next.

Is the Synoptic Problem really a problem for believing in the Bible?

YES	NO
Christians claim the Gospels are "*inspired*" texts – they are revelation from God. The Synoptic Problem suggests they have a more straightforward origin: they are copied from a lost **Proto-Gospel**.	The Gospels are still "*inspired*" even if parts are copied. Luke's Gospel clearly states it has used sources in its prologue. The Synoptic Gospels probably copied from each other or Mark and Luke copied Matthew**.**
If there was a lost Proto-Gospel, then it was closer to the historical Jesus than the Gospels we now have. That makes the Bible unreliable. It shows that books of the New Testament are ordinary literary texts, products of human error and human judgment.	If the New Testament writers were inspired by the Holy Spirit, then you would expect coherence and unity in their writings and this is what you find. There's no evidence for any 'proto-Gospel'; it's more likely the Synoptic Gospels products of are different eyewitnesses.

Proto-Gospels

One solution to the **Synoptic Problem** would be the existence of a lost Gospel – a **proto-Gospel** ('earliest Gospel') that the Synoptic Gospels all copy from. Some scholars use the term *ur-Gospel* instead of proto-Gospel.

> *If you type 'proto-Gospel' into a search engine, you will find a lot of links to a text called the* **Protoevangelion of James.** *This is a late-2nd century birth narrative based on* **Matthew** *in which Mary and Jesus hide from Herod's soldiers. It's* not *a proto-Gospel and it's got* nothing *to do with this topic so please ignore it.*

A proto-Gospel would be an early written version of the Gospels (like a PROTOTYPE or 'first attempt') that the Synoptic Gospels copy from. The idea is that **Matthew**, **Mark** and **Luke** all had this proto-Gospel in front of them when they wrote their Gospel accounts; they copied some of it but they made changes, adding details in or ignoring passages that didn't suit them.

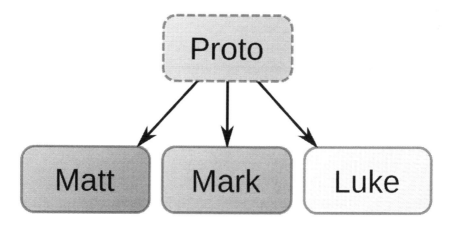

- The proto-Gospel would have been written in Aramaic (the language spoken by Jesus and his Disciples), but the Gospel-writers perhaps had a Greek translation
- The proto-Gospel probably included just the sayings (*logia*) of Jesus and the Gospel-writers added in situations and settings
- The proto-Gospel represented the original preaching (*kerygma*) of Jesus and his Disciples before it was altered by later generations of Christians

The strongest evidence for a proto-Gospel is that Luke's Prologue (**Luke 1: 1-4**) clearly states that people before him have "*drawn up an account*" of Jesus' ministry and that these people were "*eyewitnesses*" but that he is merely "*writing an orderly account*" of this source.

The biggest problem is that there is no reference to this proto-Gospel in any of the earliest Christian writers. Around 130 CE, **Marcion of Sinope** lists his personal 'canon' of New Testament scripture, but doesn't mention the proto-Gospel (he prefers Luke). **Irenaeus of Lyon** refers to the canonical four Gospels (the *Tetramorph*) in 180 CE, again with no mention of any proto-Gospel.

Early writers mention several Christian texts that are lost to us now (such as the Gospel of the Ebionites) and some that were lost for centuries but have been discovered by archaeologists (such as the Gospel of Thomas) but they never mention the proto-Gospel or anything that sounds like it.

The Gospel of Thomas: a proto-Gospel?

The long-lost **Gospel of Thomas** was discovered at **Nag Hammadi** in 1945. Scholars suggested that it could be the missing proto-Gospel. In its favour, Thomas does consist entirely of *logia* (sayings of Jesus) with no narrative or story to give them context. About half of these *logia* appear in the Synoptic Gospels too.

Thomas might have inspired John's Gospel more indirectly. **Elaine Pagels** points out that John's Gospel seems to have passages that specifically contradict *logia* in Thomas, as if John's Gospel was written to prove Thomas wrong. For example, a *logion* in Thomas says that the light of God is born from within, but John says that the world does not recognise the **Light** (p90). Thomas himself appears as a character in John's Gospel: he doubts Jesus' Resurrection and is proved wrong. This suggests Thomas was around before John.

On the other hand, the Gospel of Thomas doesn't seem to be early enough to be a proto-Gospel. The copy discovered at Nag Hammadi dates from the 4th century CE and is translated from an original from the 2nd century CE – but a proto-Gospel would have to be from the first half of the 1st century CE, probably from the 50s or 60s CE.

Could Matthew be the proto-Gospel?

The early church writers believed **Matthew** to be the first Gospel written, with Mark and Luke copying passages from Matthew. The theory that Matthew is the proto-Gospel is called **MATTHEAN PRIORITY**. This is also known as the **AUGUSTINIAN HYPOTHESIS** because it was proposed by **Augustine of Hippo**.

According to this view, Matthew was one of Jesus' Twelve Disciples and wrote his Gospel in Aramaic or Hebrew. It was translated into Greek and this was the version used by **Mark** and **Luke** to write their Gospels, with Mark abbreviating Matthew to create a shorter Gospel (but adding in some material based on the preaching of Peter) and Luke using Matthew and Mark to create an expanded Gospel.

This theory makes sense and explains why the earliest Christian writers regard Matthew as the earliest Gospel and why there's no mention of an earlier proto-Gospel. This is sill the view taken by the Catholic Church.

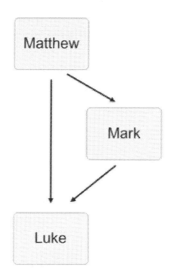

Augustinian hypothesis

The main problem with this theory is that Mark misses out so much material from Matthew: for example

- the Virgin Birth
- the Lord's Prayer
- the Sermon on the Mount

These are such important passages, it's hard to see why Mark would not include this material if he knew about it from Matthew. The earliest versions of Mark do not even contain descriptions of the Resurrection: why would Mark not copy *that* from Matthew? This has led to the alternative theory of **Markan Priority** (p187) in which Mark is the proto-Gospel instead.

Implications

If there is a lost **proto-Gospel** out there (or if Thomas is that proto-Gospel), then the New Testament is fundamentally unreliable. This is because the proto-Gospel represents a much more authentic version of Jesus' real sayings and teachings, which have been added to and perhaps distorted by the Synoptic Gospels.

For example, there is no **APOCALYPTIC** element in Thomas – no teachings about the imminent end of the world. The apocalyptic element is certainly present in the Synoptic Gospels. There's also no Crucifixion in Thomas. If Thomas is the proto-Gospel, then Jesus never taught that the world was going to end or predicted that he was going to be crucified. Instead, his followers added these teaching to their Gospels after Jesus' crucifixion, creating a religion very different from the one Jesus taught.

However, the development of Christian ideas seems to be the opposite way round. **Bart Ehrman** points out that , as time passes, Christian writing becomes less and less apocalyptic and more reconciled to the fact that the world is not going to end and Christ is not coming back straight away. If there is a proto-Gospel, it's more likely that it would be apocalyptic, rather than the Gospel-writers adding apocalyptic fantasies to a proto-Gospel that didn't have this theme.

The existence of proto-Gospels is important for the **4-Source Solution** (p193) to the **Synoptic Problem**.

Does the theory of a proto-Gospel solve the Synoptic Problem?

YES	NO
The Synoptic Gospels must have gotten their testimony about Jesus from somewhere and the similarities between them suggest that they didn't all come up with it independently. A lost proto-Gospel would explain the similarity in language and structure between the Synoptic Gospels.	No proto-Gospel that matches the Synoptics has been discovered: it's pure theory. The *Gospel of Thomas* doesn't fit the bill (lack of apocalyptic themes or crucifixion) and Matthew can't be the proto-Gospel that Mark uses because too much stuff is missed out.
A proto-Gospel is a 'stepping stone' between the word-of-mouth preaching of Jesus and his Disciples (called the *kerygma*) and the eventual composition of the Synoptic Gospels. Since the Gospels were written decades after Jesus' time, the authors would need a 'source' to base their stories on.	Liberal scholars date the Gospels late in the 1st century CE but traditionalists date them much earlier. If the Synoptics are independent eyewitness accounts of the events of Jesus' life, they don't require an intermediate 'source'. There was no need for proto-Gospels because actual Gospels were written straight away.

The Priority of Mark

For centuries, **Matthew** was regarded as the earliest Gospel. This was the view of **Irenaeus of Lyon** and **Clement of Alexandria** in the 2nd century CE and it was supported by detailed argument by **Augustine of Hippo** (the Augustinian Hypothesis). However, since the 18th century, the majority of Bible scholars have come round to the view that **Mark**, not Matthew, is the earliest Gospel. This is the theory of **Markan Priority** (with 'priority' meaning 'coming first').

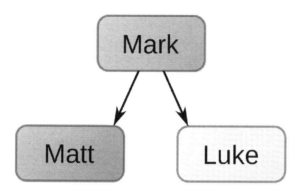

There are several problems with the Augustinian Hypothesis (that **Mark** is an abridged or shortened version of **Matthew**):

1. Mark does not feature several passages that are very important to Christians: the Virgin Birth, the Lord's Prayer, the Sermon on the Mount and (in its earliest versions) appearances by the Risen Christ after the Resurrection. Since these passages are present in Matthew, it's hard to explain why Mark would leave them out if Mark was copying Matthew.
2. Mark has very poor Greek grammar and uses a lot of slang words, whereas Matthew and Luke are written in quite correct Greek. It's hard to explain why Mark would take Matthew's good Greek and deliberately mess it up
3. Similarly, Mark contains a number of Aramaic words and expressions that aren't in Matthew. For example, **Mark 7: 11** uses the Aramaic word "*corban*" to mean a ritual dedicated to God. Why would Mark deliberately add Aramaic expressions into Matthew's narrative (then explain them in Greek)?

However, if Mark is the first Gospel and was copied by Matthew and Luke, these puzzles disappear:

1. Mark missed out these passages because he didn't know about them; Matthew and Luke add them in to 'fill out' the story Mark tells
2. It makes sense that Matthew and Luke would correct Mark's bad Greek
3. Mark uses Aramaic expressions because he's translating from the original Aramaic that Jesus and his Disciples spoke; Matthew and Luke are writing for a Greek-speaking audience that wouldn't understand these expressions, so they take them out

One of the most powerful arguments for Markan Priority is the presence of HARD READINGS in Mark. These are passages which describe Jesus in unflattering ways or which seem to go against later Christian beliefs about Jesus. In every case, Matthew and Luke cut out or tone down these passages, making them less difficult for Christians to accept.

> *[Jesus] looked around at them in anger* – **Mark 3: 5**

This suggests Jesus had a temper. Matthew completely misses out this verse, but Luke changes it to something less problematic:

> *[Jesus] looked around at them all* – **Luke 6: 10**

> *Jesus getting angry goes against the Christian image of of "gentle Jesus, meek and mild". Mark was writing when there was still a memory of the historical Jesus who did get angry sometimes; Matthew and Luke describe a less historical but more perfect person who never loses his cool*

A similar argument is based on CHRISTOLOGY (beliefs about Jesus' relationship to God). Mark seems to have a 'low Christology' or what **Bart Ehrman** calls an 'Exaltation Christology'. This is the belief that Jesus is human being who is EXALTED (raised up, promoted) by God. Mark begins his story with Jesus being baptized by John the Baptist (**Mark 1: 9-11**) and suggests that this is the moment when Jesus becomes **God's Son**.

Whereas Matthew and Luke present Jesus as being the **Son of God** from the moment of his conception. Most scholars think a low Christology comes earlier in Christian tradition than a high Christology (**John**, which has the highest Christology of all – an INCARNATION CHRISTOLOGY – is the latest Gospel).

Implications

If these arguments are correct (and the majority of Bible scholars think they are), then Mark is the earliest Gospel – perhaps the **proto-Gospel** – and Matthew and Luke both had copies of Mark in front of them when they wrote their Gospels. Matthew kept a lot of Mark's text (90% of it) and Luke kept rather less (about 50%).

This also makes sense of Luke's Prologue, which claims to "*write an orderly account*", from an earlier source:

> *Many have undertaken to draw up an account of the things that have been fulfilled among us* – **Luke 1: 1**

This passage could refer to Mark and perhaps the **Q-Source** (p190) and **Special Luke** (p193).

Does the theory of Markan Priority make the Bible more trustworthy?

YES	NO
Mark was the secretary/translator of **Peter**, the leader of Jesus' Twelve Disciples. Therefore, his Gospel is based on the best possible eyewitness. That's why Mark uses Aramaic expressions and preserves some 'hard readings' – it's authentic history.	By presenting Matthew and Luke as simply copying chunks of Mark and making their own changes, this theory presents the Bible as a creation of flawed humans rather than a set of independent eyewitnesses inspired by the Holy Spirit.
Markan Priority is essential for the **2-Source** and **4-Source** solutions to the **Synoptic Problem**. It explains the similarity between the Gospels and (if we take the **Q-Source** into account) the differences as well.	These solutions break up the unity and coherence of the Gospels by presenting them as 'jigsaws' or 'collages' made up of different sources stitched together, rather than independent eyewitnesses.

The Q-Source

If we accept the theory of **Markan Priority** (p187), the **Synoptic Problem** does not completely go away. There is still a lot of material shared by **Matthew** and **Luke** which isn't in **Mark**. This is explained by the theory of the **Q-Source**.

There are 230 passages where Matthew and Luke share close (almost word-for-word) texts, but which aren't in Mark. These include:

- **Jesus being tempted by the Devil:** Matthew 4: 1-11 and Luke 4: 1-13
- **The Beatitudes (Sermon on the Mount):** Matthew 5: 3-12 and Luke 6: 20-23
- **The Lord's Prayer:** Matthew 6: 9-13 and Luke 11: 1-4
- **Many Parables, such as the Lost Sheep:** Matthew 18: 12-14 and Luke 15: 1-7

A theory to explain this is that Matthew and Luke both had access to the same source – a sort of **proto-Gospel** (p183) that originally contained these passages. In the 20th century, this mysterious source was termed *Q* (short for *Quelle*, which is German for 'source').

> So the 'Q-source' is really the 'source-source'.
> And while we're at it, it's S-O-U-R-C-E, not SAUCE.
>
> It's not something you put on a burger.

Q would have been a collection of sayings (*logia*) of Jesus – although the story of Jesus' temptation and the healing of the Centurion's Servant seem to be from *Q* too, so perhaps it had narratives in it as well as sayings. There's a lot of debate about whether *Q* was originally written down or whether it was a memorised list of *logia* that was recited in churches. Luke seems to preserve more of the original order of *Q* than Matthew, who spreads the various *logia* throughout his Gospel.

No copy of *Q* has ever been discovered. More baffling, there's no mention of *Q* existing by any of the early church writers who discuss the background of the Gospels. However, there is this tantalizing quote from **Papias of Hieropolis** (125 CE):

> *Matthew compiled the* logia *of the Lord in a Hebrew manner of speech, and everyone translated them as well he could* – **Papias of Hieropolis**

This used to confuse scholars because Matthew's Gospel was originally written in Greek, not Hebrew or Aramaic. But perhaps this is a reference to the ***original*** person called Matthew (maybe Jesus' disciple) creating *Q* in Aramaic, which the Gospel-writers Matthew and Luke (we don't know their real names) *'translated as well as they could'* into Greek.

This would make sense of Luke's Prologue where he describes how:

> *Many have undertaken to draw up an account of the things that have been fulfilled among us* – **Luke 1: 1**

Luke admits to basing his Gospel on previous sources, so *Q* could be what he is referring to here.

Implications

The **Q-Source Hypothesis** is accepted by the majority of Bible scholars, but not by everyone. The lack of any clear reference to **Q** in ancient Christian writings is puzzling, because a book containing the authentic *logia* (sayings) of Jesus would have been a treasured possession of early Christians. However, maybe once **Q** was incorporated into Matthew and Luke's Gospels, Christian readers preferred them to a dry list of sayings (because the Gospels give the sayings a context and dramatize them) and the original collection was forgotten about.

> *The* **Q***-hypothesis has been developed into the* **2-Source** *and* **4-Source** *solutions to the* **Synoptic Problem***.*

Some fundamentalist Christians object to the **Q**-hypothesis. They believe that the Gospels are eyewitness accounts written by the original **Matthew** (a Disciple), **Mark** (Peter's secretary) and **Luke** (Paul's traveling companion). The **Q**-hypothesis suggests that Luke and Matthew's Gospels were actually written by people who had no personal link to Jesus or his Disciples. Instead, they cobbled their Gospels together from a list of old sayings, perhaps inventing situations to give these sayings a context. Some Christians are suspicious that the **Q**-hypothesis is just another attempt by atheists to make the Bible look like a flawed human document rather than Scripture **inspired** by God.

Does the Q-hypothesis make the Bible more trustworthy?

YES	NO
The theory of the **Q**-Source provides a link from Gospels written in the 80s CE back to the events of Jesus' lifetime. Matthew and Luke are written **after** the destruction of the Temple in the Jewish Revolt but draw upon materials like **Q** from **before** that important event.	There is no evidence for **Q** – either physical evidence (no copies exist) or literary evidence (no ancient writers ever refer to it; instead they refer to the four canonical Gospels being the earliest accounts). **Q** is a theory that supports a late dating of the Gospels preferred by atheists.
No copies of **Q** are known - but then no copies of the *Gospel of Thomas* were known until the Nag Hammadi Library was discovered in 1945. Thomas is another 'sayings Gospel' – a collection of *logia*. This makes the existence of **Q** more plausible, as do references by Papias and in Luke's Prologue.	If the canonical Gospels are what they have always been claimed to be – independent eyewitness accounts of Jesus' ministry, crucifixion and Resurrection – then there's no need for **Q**. If the Gospels were written in the 60s CE then there's no need for a 'sayings Gospel' since this is within the lifetime of the historical Matthew, Mark and Luke.

SOLUTIONS TO THE SYNOPTIC PROBLEM

The ideas of **Markan Priority** (p187) and the **Q-source** (p190) have been widely accepted, among liberal scholars at least. This has led to two popular solutions to the **Synoptic Problem**.

The 2-Source Solution

This solution was proposed in the 19th century. It states that **Matthew** and **Luke** both used **Mark** and the **Q-source** to write their Gospels, with Matthew relying more heavily on Mark and Luke relying more on **Q**.

Matthew and Luke then improve upon this material (e.g. improving on Mark's Greek and removing Aramaic phrases) and they both add context and background to the material from **Q** (which many scholars think was just a collection of *logia* or sayings).

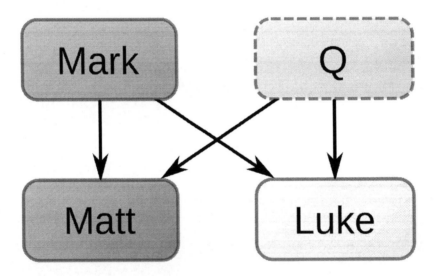

We can see Matthew and Luke improving on Mark in their use of terminology. Mark refers to **Herod Antipas,** the ruler of Galilee, as a "king" (*basileus*), which isn't strictly correct. Luke changes this to Antipas' correct title of "*tetrarch*".

However, Matthew seems to get tired of correcting Mark on this and, after starting off calling Herod Antipas a *tetrarch*, he lapses back into Mark's incorrect title of *basileus*. This reveals Mark's incorrect material 'showing through' Matthew's attempt to produce a corrected Gospel. This sort of evidence makes the 2SS persuasive.

The 4-Source Solution

Burnett Streeter (1924) suggested this improvement on the 2-Source Solution. Streeter suggests that, as well as drawing upon Mark and **Q** (p190), Matthew and Luke made use of two **proto-Gospels** (p183), referred to as **Special Matthew** (or **M**, Matthew's unique source, which Streeter thinks comes from Jerusalem) and **Special Luke** (or **L**, Luke's unique material, which Streeter thinks comes from Antioch in Syria).

This means there are a total of 4 sources being used: Mark, **Q**, **M** and **L**. Matthew did not have access to **L** and Luke did not have access to **M** but both used Mark and **Q**.

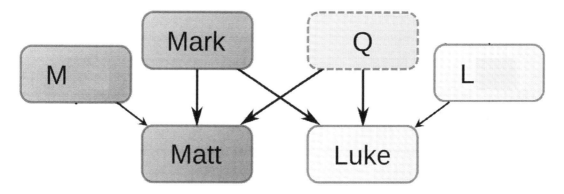

The 4SS is very popular among scholars who date Matthew and Luke to the 80s CE and propose that they were **not** written by actual Disciples of Jesus or Paul. The 4SS explains how people living far away from Jerusalem and Galilee and long after the crucifixion of Jesus could get their information about what happened.

For this reason, the 4SS is unpopular with fundamentalist Christians because they argue that Matthew and Luke were written at the same time as Mark, in the 60s CE, by actual Disciples who were eyewitnesses and therefore didn't need 'sources'.

Implications

These solutions depend on the existence of **Q** and we have no physical evidence for this text and no direct reference to it in early Christian writings. Fundamentalist Christians often attack these solutions by denying the existence of **Q** and claiming instead that Matthew and Luke are eyewitnesses who don't needed sources.

The 2SS and 4SS also depend on **Markan Priority** (p187), which is widely accepted but some scholars (especially Catholics) continue to propose versions of the Augustinian Hypothesis that Matthew is the earliest Gospel, copied by Mark and Luke.

Both 2SS and 4SS have a problem with MINOR AGREEMENTS between Matthew and Luke. Matthew and Luke are supposed to have been written independently, without knowing each other and without access to each other's Special Sources (**M** and **L**).

However, there are passages where they use the same words to describe events that aren't in Mark or *Q*. A famous example is the scene where the Roman soldiers mock Jesus. They blindfold him, hit him and then say:

"Prophesy! Who hit you?" - **Matthew 26: 68 and Luke 22: 64**

*Some scholars explain this by saying that Luke **did** have access to Matthew (this would be the 3-source solution or 3SS). Others suggest that this passage could be in a different version of Mark from the one we have today (but there's no evidence for that).*

Despite this, the 2SS and 4SS are the most popular solutions to the **Synoptic Problem** at the moment. There are even fundamentalist Christians who are prepared to accept the 2SS, because it explains the material shared between Mark, Matthew and Luke so well. The 4SS is more controversial, because it presents Matthew and Luke as 'copying and pasting' different documents together rather than writing accounts of what they themselves experienced.

An important factor in the popularity of the 4SS is disbelief in miracles and prophecy: many modern scholars think Matthew and Luke must have been written *after* the destruction of the Temple in 70 CE because they describe Jesus predicting it... however, fundamentalist Christians argue that Jesus *really did* predict this through the power of prophecy, so the Gospels date from *before* 70 CE. The persuasiveness of these solutions depends to a large extent on your own beliefs about **miracles** and the **Person of Jesus**.

Do the 2- and 4- Source Solutions really solve the Synoptic Problem?

YES	NO
The 2SS and 4SS are both elegant solutions: they don't involve bringing in extra complications; in philosophical terminology, they are PARSIMONIOUS. They also have real explanatory power (they show exactly *how* the Gospels were put together).	These solutions depend on unproven theories. For example, the existence of the *Q-source* is essential to both of them, but *Q* has never been discovered and is not mentioned by early writers. **Markan Priority** also goes against early tradition which is that Matthew is the first Gospel.
The 4SS has a particular benefit of explaining how the Gospel writers late in the 1st century CE could have access to information from the time of Jesus' ministry in the 20s and 30s CE: they made use of **proto-Gospels** (Special Matthew and Special Luke).	This is only an advantage if you refuse to accept that Jesus could have miraculously predicted the destruction of Jerusalem in 70 CE. But if Jesus was the **Son of God** then he **COULD** prophesy and so the Gospels are from the 50s or 60s CE, written by eyewitnesses who don't need 'sources'.

THEORIES OF BIBLICAL CRITICISM

Source Criticism

If you've studied the pages on the **Synoptic Problem** (p178) and its **2- or 4-Source Solutions** (p192), then you will have seen Source Criticism in action.

Source Criticism is an approach to New Testament Studies that tries to determine the sources used to develop the final form of the Biblical text. A Source Critics asks, **"Where did the author get this information? What previous documents or word-of-mouth traditions contributed to this?"**

This type of criticism treats Bible texts as human documents that have been created in the same way as other biographies, histories or legends. It ignores the role of **revelation** or the Holy Spirit *'inspiring'* writers. Source Criticism does not treat the Bible as inerrant (without mistakes) – on the contrary, it looks for mistakes or contradictions as indications that material from two different sources may be present. For example, Mark incorrectly refers to Herod Antipas as a "king" but Luke and Matthew correct this to "*tetrarch*"; on occasions when Matthew refers to Antipas as "king" that's an indication he is using Mark as a source.

Source Criticism was originally applied to non-religious texts, for example the classical literature of Ancient Greece. In the 18th century, **Jean Astruc** took the techniques that Source Critics had used on Homer's *Iliad* and applied it to the Old Testament, demonstrating that several different sources had been used to create the **Book of Genesis**.

Since then, Source Criticism has identified the **Synoptic Problem** as involving different sources being used by Mathew, Mark and Luke. Source Critics propose **solutions** involving **proto-Gospels** (p183), **Markan Priority** (p187) and the *Q-source* (p190).

In a nutshell: Source Criticism looks at texts as jigsaw puzzles or collages made up of various 'bits' that originally came from somewhere else; it tries to identify the components of a text and trace their origin back to earlier sources.

Implications

Source Criticism has secular (non-religious) assumptions:

- The Bible is a collection of human documents, not divinely inspired ones
- The Bible contains errors and contradictions
- The Bible's books were assembled through copying and editing earlier sources rather than being eyewitness testimonies

New Testament Source Criticism is also linked to the theory of the late dating of the Gospels. Traditionalists who believe the Gospels are eyewitness accounts date them to the 50s or 60s CE and treat the predictions about the destruction of Jerusalem in 70 CE as a miraculous prophecy; Source Critics treat these prophecies as "wisdom with hindsight" being written after 70 CE, making it *look* like Jesus predicted things that he didn't. Source Criticism explains how people living long after Jesus' time could use earlier sources to write Gospels that seem (on the face of it) to read like eyewitness accounts but aren't really.

Traditionalists reject these assumptions: for them, the Bible is divinely **inspired**, inerrant (without mistakes) and the product of eyewitnesses who saw Jesus' miracles with their own eyes. They often view Source Critics as trying to undermine religious faith with their theories about the Gospels being 'second hand' accounts.

Is Source Criticism helpful for interpreting the New Testament?

YES

Source Criticism is elegant (leaving few remaining questions) and has great explanatory power. It offers a view of how the Gospels were composed that doesn't involve guidance by the Holy Spirit, amazing coincidence in wording or miraculous prophecies.

Source Criticism explains the similar material in the Synoptic Gospels by proposing these writers shared the same sources. The alternatives are much harder to believe: that the Gospel-writers were mystically controlled by the Holy Spirit or just coincidentally used the same words to describe things. **Occam's Razor** tells us to prefer the simpler explanation.

NO

Source Criticism is a bunch of wild theories that cannot be backed up. None of the 'sources' has been discovered – we have no records of *Q* or any of the so-called proto-Gospels and they are never mentioned by early Christian authors either.

Source Criticism often has an agenda: to undermine Christian faith by presenting the Bible as a flawed, human document and break up its unity and coherence into a set of contradictory 'sources' that disagree with each other. Instead of helping, this makes it impossible to interpret the New Testament as relevant to living today; it just becomes another old book.

Form Criticism

Source Criticism (p195) has been around for hundreds of years but **Form Criticism** only developed in the 20th century in the works of a group of German Bible scholars. As with Source Criticism, this new type of criticism was first applied to the Old Testament then moved on to the New Testament later.

Form Criticism tries to go back further than identifying sources. It assumes that the Gospels are made up of **"units"** of text (for example, Parables or miracle stories) and that these 'units' were passed down as part of an **oral (word-of-mouth) tradition** before they were written down in the Gospels. Form Critics try to identify these 'units' within the text, compare them to each other and work out what they *originally* meant before they ended up in the Gospel. These 'units' are called **PERICOPAE** by Form Critics.

The founder of Form Criticism was **Hermann Gunkel** (1918) who used a key phrase to explain how it works: "*Sitz im Leben*", which means "setting in life". This refers to the social context that a 'unit' of text was created in and what it meant to the Christian group that first used it.

Form Critics argue that before the Gospels were written down, there was an **'oral period'** where stories about Jesus and sayings (*logia*) attributed to him were passed around by believers. **Martin Dibelius** (1919) suggests there are at least five FORMS of text in the Gospels:

- **Paradigms** (brief stories presenting Jesus as a role model which may be based on Jesus' IPSISSIMA VERBA or "true words")
- **Tales** (longer miracle stories that are meant to entertain)
- **Myths** (stories which explore a truth but which aren't historical)
- **Legends** (stories which seem to be historical but which present the hero as stereotypically heroic)
- **Exhortations** (wise sayings and teachings)

Form Critics argue that the Gospel-writers pulled together these *pericopae* into an overall story, but often didn't understand the *Sitz im Leben* of the group that had originally told them. This means that some stories get misinterpreted.

Rudolph Bultmann is a famous Form Critic of the 20th century who argues that stories about Jesus were almost entirely misunderstood by the Gospel-writers and need to be **DE-MYTHOLOGIZED** (stripped of their supernatural details) to get back to their original meaning.

In a nutshell: The Gospels are made up of lots of different units of text all strung together: miracle stories and Parables and wise sayings and memorable stories. These units were all separate *pericopae* back in the oral period before the Gospels were written down, then they got 'fixed in place' in the finished Gospel. Form Criticism tries to unpick these *pericopae* and reconstruct what they originally meant.

Examples of Form Criticism

PARADIGM: In **Mark 2: 18-22**, Jesus is questioned about why his Disciples aren't fasting and Jesus answers with famous images of a wedding and wine being poured into new wineskins. This is a **paradigm**: it's brief and memorable and it emphasizes Jesus' special teachings. **Dibelius** thinks it may preserve an actual thing Jesus said: his *ipsissima verba*. However, the *Sitz im Leben* is that early Christians were trying to workout whether or not they had to follow the **Jewish Law** (p102). This text (which suggests Christians *don't* have to follow the Law) may have been changed or even invented to support an argument going on in the early years of Christianity.

> *Form critics are very interested in pinning down speeches and actions that might go back to the historical Jesus – but they don't think there are many*

TALE: In **Mark 6: 42-45**, Jesus walks on water. **Dibelius** thinks that the *Sitz im Leben* may have originally been a religious experience for some of Jesus' Disciples but it has been expanded into a miraculous story. Form Critics like Dibelius and (especially) **Bultmann** don't believe in miracles, so they see these tales as exaggerations or fantasies which sometimes get in the way of a moral message that was the original point. For example, Bultmann thinks the **Sign of Feeding the 5000** (p147) was originally a message of sharing that got overshadowed by a miracle story.

> *Form criticism does think there are important messages in the Bible – just not the ones traditional Christians find there*

MYTH: In **Matthew 4: 1-11**, Jesus fasts in the desert and is tempted by the Devil. This story contains many deep issues about faith, moral choices and evil. Many Christian artists have described it, painted it and dramatised it; **Fyodor Dostoevsky** devotes a wonderful chapter of *The Brothers Karamazov* (1880) to exploring it.

But according to **Dibelius** and **Bultmann**, it didn't happen and is fiction. Bultmann suggests a *Sitz im Leben*, that a criticism of the early Christians was that Jesus was just a magician, so they composed this myth to reject that criticism (because it shows Jesus refusing to perform miracles for popularity).

Another *Sitz im Leben* could be that early Christians were encouraged to join the **Zealot** (p68) movement but this myth was created to reject that course of action (because Jesus refuses worldly power offered by the Devil).

LEGENDS: Matthew's birth-narrative shows Jesus having a supernatural birth and surviving murder attempts by a jealous rival. Alexander the Great was supposedly conceived when a thunderbolt fell from heaven and made his mother pregnant; Plato was said to be the son of the god Apollo. Hercules was the son of Zeus and a mortal woman and the jealous goddess Hera sent two snakes to kill him in the crib.

From a Form Criticism perspective, Matthew is providing Jesus with the sort of birth-narrative that all the great heroes of Greek and Roman history and mythology have. Dibelius calls this the Law of Biographical Analogy (which means, your hero must have a biography similar to the existing heroes in your world). **Bultmann** (of course) goes even further, arguing that Jesus' Resurrection is a Legend too, because lots of heroes in pagan mythology die and come back to life (notably Adonis, Dionysus and Osiris).

> *Form criticism treats Christianity as "just another myth"*

EXHORTATIONS: These are wise proverbs, often fairly general in character, that don't have any particular context. Some may not even be Jesus' own teachings. For example, the Jewish teacher **Hillel the Elder** (died 10 CE) summarised the Jewish **Law** (p102) with this phrase:

> *What is hateful to you, do not do to your fellow: this is the whole Torah* – **Hillel the Elder**

This is known as the **GOLDEN RULE** in Ethics and Jesus repeats it:

> *Do to others what you would have them do to you, for this sums up the Law and the Prophets* – **Matthew 7: 12**

Form Critics suggest that this *pericope* might originally have been a Jewish exhortation that got added to Jesus' teachings during the 'oral period' then found its way into the Bible. The *Sitz im Leben* would be a community of Jewish Christians familiar with Hillel's teaching who wanted to present Jesus as being just as wise as Hillel.

> *Notice how form critics often deny Jesus' originality or special-ness by focusing on what he shares with (or borrows from) others. Christians point out that Jesus' version of the Golden Rule goes further than Hillel's: Hillel tells you what **not** to do but Jesus tells us what **to** do*

Implications

Source Criticism has some implications that traditional Christians are uncomfortable with, but Form Criticism is **much** more hostile to traditional beliefs about Jesus and the New Testament – especially **Rudolph Bultmann**'s version of Form Criticism.

Form Criticism presents most passages in the Gospels as fictional or at least wildly exaggerated – and sometimes as originally referring to someone other than Jesus! Form Criticism casts a lot of doubt on whether it is possible to reconstruct a 'historical Jesus' from the Gospels. It presents most of the beliefs about Jesus as taking shape **after** Jesus' lifetime among Christian communities who were developing myths and legends about their founder.

It also suggests that the Gospel-writers threw these *pericopae* together without understanding the point and purpose of them. Form Critics see it as their job to "get behind" the Bible and reconstruct the original stories about Jesus, which might have been rather different from the versions that appear in the Gospels. The sort of scholars who argue that Jesus was really a **repentant Zealot** (R.F. Brandon) or a **wandering Cynic philosopher** (John Dominic Crossan) are coming from a background of Form Criticism; so too are the scholars (and lazy websites) who argue that Christianity has 'stolen' myths and stories that originally applied to pagan gods like Adonis or Mithras.

Obviously, traditionalist Christians are completely opposed to these interpretations. They argue that Form Criticism is subjective and imaginative; since we have no records of these *pericopae* as they were before the Gospels recorded them, Form Critics are free to imagine anything they like and most of them like to imagine things that diminish the importance of Jesus and undermine Christian faith.

On the other hand, Christians do appreciate *some* insights from Form Criticism, such as the idea that the **Prologue in John** is a hymn that was originally sung when Christians worshiped together. There are different genres in the Gospels and there have been confusions in the past when readers failed to recognise that a passage like this is really a poem.

Does Form Criticism help us to interpret the New Testament?

YES	NO
Form Criticism recognises that the Gospels are made up of units with different genres: there are myths and legends as well as memories of the actual words of Jesus. Form Criticism helps separate the *IPSISSIMA VERBA* (true words) of the Historical Jesus from the fictional stuff.	Form Criticism goes even further than **Source Criticism** in breaking up the unity and coherence of the Gospels, carving them up into stand-alone units that only meant something to a particular group in the past. This gives the Bible little relevance to today.
The Gospels can be relevant to today, but first they have to be DE-MYTHOLOGIZED. The Gospel-writers misunderstood a lot of the material they used and took supernatural events at face value. When stripped of these supernatural elements, the original preaching (*kerygma*) of Jesus can be found. For example, the **Feeding of the 5000** is really a message about the importance of sharing.	The interpretations Form Critics offer are utterly subjective and reflect their own atheist assumptions and prejudices. They assume that miracles don't happen and that Jesus was just an ordinary moral philosopher, then 'discover' that anything striking about Jesus' teaching or life is really just a commonplace bit of ethical advice. This makes the Bible less interesting and influential, not more.

Redaction Criticism

In some ways, Redaction Criticism is the oldest type of Biblical Criticism because it focuses on what distinctive beliefs and perspectives different Biblical authors bring to their material. For example, it has long been recognised that **Matthew** presents a very Jewish view of Jesus who **fulfils** Old Testament prophecy; **Luke** presents a compassionate Jesus who is the Saviour of the world; and **John** presents Jesus as the **Word made Flesh** (p81).

However, Redaction Criticism has become very influential since the 20th century. It has built on (and largely replaced) **Form Criticism** (p197) as a popular way of interpreting the New Testament.

Like **Source Criticism** (p195), Redaction Criticism regards the Gospels as being composed from various sources available to the Gospel-writer (**Mark, Q, proto-Gospels**). Like **Form Criticism**, Redaction Criticism also acknowledges these sources are composed from 'units' (*pericopae*) that grew out of an oral tradition before they came to be written down. However, the big difference is the importance of the Gospel-writers themselves – this person is an editor or **REDACTOR** of the material they use.

Form Critics like **Rudolph Bultmann** [*left*] tend to present the Gospel-writers as ignorant about the true meaning of the texts they draw upon; Redaction Critics focus on how the Gospel-writers **choose, edit and alter the texts** to suit their own purposes and express their distinctive agenda.

For example, **John's Gospel** uses the phrase "*the Jews*" to describe Jesus' enemies (e.g. in the **Sign of Raising Lazarus**, p159) and this reveals the Gospel-writers own anti-Semitic agenda.

- Redaction Critics look for recurring **MOTIFS** in a text that indicate the writer's priorities. For example, in **Matthew** the proof-texts show his focus on Jesus fulfilling Old Testament prophecy; in **John** the **"I Am" Statements** reveal John's high Christology.
- Redaction Critics compare two different accounts of the same event (eg in the Synoptic Gospels, or comparing **John** with the Synoptics) and focus on what one writer leaves in or takes out (for example, **John** never names Jesus' mother and downplays John the Baptist's role)
- Redaction Critics identify the distinctive vocabulary and style of an author (for example, **Luke** referring to Jesus as "*Lord*" or **John** referring to "*Eternal Life*") and what this reveals about the writer's beliefs

When you consider all these examples from earlier in the course, you'll see that you've been 'doing' Redaction Criticism all along

Redaction Critics tend to use three techniques developed by Form Criticism to explore how the Gospel-writes redact (edit) their texts:

- **Criterion of Multiple Attestation:** If a passage or event appears independently (not copied from the same source), then it's more likely to be historical. For example, all the Gospels describe the crucifixion of Jesus independently of each other.
- **Criterion of Embarrassment:** The Gospel-writers try to remove details that are embarrassing for their beliefs (for example, details that show Jesus to be flawed) but if these details are included it suggests they are historical
- **Criterion of Dissimilarity:** The Gospel-writers often describe Jesus as imitating Jewish themes in the Old Testament or else 'project back' their own Christian practices onto Jesus. If a passage has Jesus behaving in a way that is unlike Jewish practices and also unlike later Christian practices, this 'double dissimilarity' suggests it is historical. A good example would be Jesus forgiving the woman caught in adultery (the *Pericope De Adultera*, **John 8: 1-11**): Jews did not forgive adultery and neither did the early Christians, so this passage is unlikely to be copied from an earlier Jewish source or invented by a later Christian one.

In a nutshell: Redaction Criticism regards the Gospel-writers as careful editors (**redactors**) whose choices of what to leave in, what to leave out and what to change reveal their distinctive beliefs and concerns.

Examples of Redaction Criticism

THE MESSIANIC SECRET: Wilhelm Wrede is a Redaction Critic that you studied in **Topic 1** (p26). He presents **Mark** as a redactor who adds in passages to his Gospel where Jesus demands people keep his Messiah-ship a **secret**. Wrede thinks this reveals Mark's agenda which is to present Jesus as the **Messiah** even though Jesus did not claim to be the Messiah in his lifetime.

*Wrede's theory is largely discredited (for example, by **Morna Hooker**) but it is a good example of Redaction Criticism at work*

JOHN THE BAPTIST: John the Baptist is an important figure in the Gospels. He lives in the desert, wearing animal skins and fasting. He has a huge following and he preaches that Jews should repent their sins; as a sign of this repentance, he baptizes people in the River Jordan. He is executed by Herod Antipas at the time when Jesus began his ministry (perhaps 30-32 CE).

- In **Mark's Gospel**, Jesus comes to be baptized by John at the very start of his ministry. This is when the Holy Spirit descends on Jesus and God's voice declares that Jesus is his Son (**Mark 1: 1-11**).
- In **Matthew**'s version, John also condemns the Pharisees as a "*brood of vipers*". When Jesus comes to be baptized, John is unwilling to baptize him because he recognises that Jesus is greater than him; however, Jesus insists and John obeys (**Matthew 3: 1-20**)

- In **Luke**'s version, John is revealed to be related to Jesus (they are cousins); not only does John condemn the Pharisees but he baptizes publicans and soldiers too; he explicitly tells people he is not the **Messiah (Luke 3: 1-22)**
- In **John's Gospel**, John the Baptist appears in the Prologue: there is no mention of him baptizing Jesus; instead he explains at length that he is not the Messiah; John identifies Jesus as the "*Lamb of God*" who will provide a TRUE baptism with the Holy Spirit and some of his followers leave to follow Jesus instead (**John 1: 1-37**)

This passes the **criterion of multiple attestation**: it's in all the Gospels and **Flavius Josephus** describes John baptizing people in his *Jewish Antiquities* (94 CE). The **criterion of embarrassment** makes it likely John really did baptize Jesus (it's embarrassing for the early Christians to admit so they wouldn't make it up) and the **criterion of dissimilarity** adds to idea that this is a historical event.

Redaction criticism can explain the different descriptions in the Gospels:

- **Mark** presents Jesus as a **secret Messiah** (p26), so John the Baptist does not recognise him as anyone special. Mark also has a 'low Christology' and views Jesus as human so he doesn't see a problem with Jesus needing to be baptized.
- **Matthew** has a higher Christology and does see a problem with Jesus being baptized by John – it implies that John is Jesus' superior. Matthew adds in the exchange between them to make clear that the baptism is just 'for appearances'. He also makes John agree with his own agenda: he represents John as attacking the Pharisees too
- **Luke** has a more universal message and presents John as baptizing the same outsiders that Jesus preaches to. Luke clarifies that John is not the Messiah, which

suggests that there were followers of John who thought he *was* the Messiah.
- **John** goes out of his way to make John the Baptist inferior to Jesus: there is no baptizing scene and John the Baptist deliberately explains that he's *not* the Messiah and that Jesus *is*. The fact that John's followers join Jesus shows that Jesus replaces John.

Redaction Criticism shows how, as time goes by, the Gospel-writers inflate the status of Jesus and diminish the status of John the Baptist. If there were a rival sect devoted to John the Baptist in the 1st century (perhaps believing that John had been the Messiah, not Jesus), then these passages are Christian propaganda to prove their rivals wrong. The embarrassing detail about Jesus being baptized by John is sidelined then deleted. John is turned into someone who 'prepares the way' for Jesus, not an important religious leader in his own right.

A more controversial theory is that Jesus was actually a **FOLLOWER** of John the Baptist who broke away to form his own group (taking some of John's followers with him). This would definitely be a detail that the Gospel-writers would delete, but if it was so well-known then Mark, Matthew and Luke could not avoid mentioning the baptism of Jesus; John, writing much later in the 1st century, *could* avoid mentioning it because all the people who knew the historical Jesus were by then dead.

Implications

Redaction Criticism emphasizes the creative role of the Gospel-writers and encourages readers to consider what the writer is trying to convey by including details or leaving them out. This encourages careful reading of the Gospels, which is a good thing. Unlike **Form Criticism** (p197), it doesn't present the Gospels as a mess of conflicting 'units' or the historical Jesus as irrecoverable. However, it does borrow from Form Criticism a sense of the importance of the social setting (*Sitz im Leben)* that the early Christians operated in. The Gospel-writers are trying to correct or reinforce some issue in their own community in the 1st century and this keeps the historical context in focus.

There are objections to Redaction Criticism. It represents the Gospel-writers as being creative to the point of deception: they delete material that they know is true or else twist it in misleading ways to serve their agenda. This turns the Gospels into propaganda writing rather than truthful accounts. There's no sense that the Gospels are "*inspired*" and they are certainly not eyewitnesses: they are more like pieces of modern journalism with lots of bias.

Traditional Christians will reject this view of the Gospel-writers as untruthful and biased. They regard scripture as being "*inspired by God*".

> *Prophets, though human, spoke from God as they were carried along by the Holy Spirit –* **2 Peter 1: 21**

However, Christians do appreciate *some* aspects of Redaction Criticism, such as focusing on the different concerns that characterise each of the Gospels and explaining why there are differences between John and the Synoptics or between the way Matthew and Luke both use the same passage from **Mark** or **Q** (p190).

For example, Luke reports Jesus saying "*blessed are the poor*" (**Luke 6: 20**, from the **Q-Source**); Matthew reports this too but alters it slightly to "*blessed are the poor in spirit*" (**Matthew 5: 3**). Both writers interpret Jesus differently: Luke is focused on literal poverty, Matthew on spiritual poverty. This sort of Redaction Criticism gives a fuller picture of the Gospels and most Christians do not object to it.

Does Redaction Criticism help us to interpret the New Testament?

YES   **NO**

If we accept that Matthew and Luke adapt **Mark**, **Q** and their own **special sources**, then Redaction Criticism helps us understand why they leave some things in, take other things out and make the changes they do. It credits the Gospel-writers with being artists with a message rather than just regurgitating sources and oral traditions.

There are many puzzling gaps in the Gospels or passages that don't make obvious sense. Redaction Criticism clarifies these passages by looking at the historical context in which the Gospels were written and who their audiences were. It provides the best way of getting back to the 'historical Jesus' behind the 'Christ of faith'.

Many Christians reject the idea of the **Q-Source** or **Proto-Gospels**, arguing there's no evidence for these documents existing. Traditionalists view the Gospels as eyewitness accounts of Jesus' life and Resurrection, not the work of editors imposing their own 'slant' on events they never personally saw

The puzzling passages in the Gospels should be approached with prayer and humility, not by assuming the Gospel-writers are liars. Most of the historical context Redaction Critics write about is pure speculation and there is a strong atheist agenda in a lot of Redaction Criticism to portray Jesus as an ordinary 'man of his time' rather than the Risen Son of God.

TOPIC 3.2 PURPOSE & AUTHORSHIP OF THE FOURTH GOSPEL

The Exam expects you to be familiar with the so-called Fourth Gospel (**John's Gospel**) and the different theories about who wrote it and why.

John son of Zebedee

This is the traditional author of the Fourth Gospel, one of Jesus' Twelve Disciples. He is the youngest of the Disciples and his older brother James is also one of the Twelve. The two brothers were Galilean fishermen who became followers of **John the Baptist**, then left to follow Jesus.

According to tradition, John's brother James was the first of the Disciples to be martyred, but John lived to a ripe old age in Ephesus (in modern Turkey) and died in 98 CE. This would make him in the right place and time to write the Fourth Gospel which is named after him (although the Gospel never claims to be written by 'John').

There are three **epistles** (letters) in the New Testament that claim to be written by John. These certainly have similar themes and concerns to the Fourth Gospel and could be written by the same person, but Christian critics have always been rather divided on whether they were written by John son of Zebedee or another Christian named 'John' (it was a very common name).

There is also the **Book of Revelation** which is written by someone called 'John' and is addressed to the Christian churches in Turkey. Tradition says this is the same John, who was sent into exile on the island of Patmos (near Ephesus) by the Romans. However, the language and tone of Revelation is very different from the Fourth Gospel, so scholars doubt it really is the same writer.

Argument for Authorship

19th century scholars used to think the Fourth Gospel was very late (e.g. 2nd century) – far too late for John son of Zebedee to be the author. However, many modern scholars place the date of the Fourth Gospel in the 90s or 100s CE, so possibly within the lifetime of John.

The discovery of **Rylands Library Papyrus P52** confirms this: this ancient manuscript is a fragment of the Fourth Gospel which has been carbon dated to the early 2nd century, proving that the Gospel is not as late as people used to think.

Bishop John Robinson, in *The Priority of John* (1984), goes further, arguing that the Fourth Gospel dates from as early as the 60s CE.

This is because it never mentions the destruction of the Temple and shows detailed knowledge of Judea before the Jewish Revolt. Robinson argues that John son of Zebedee is the Gospel-writer and is in fact the 'other disciple' known to the High Priest who was an eyewitness at Jesus' trial (**John 18: 15-16**).

> *Robinson's theory is considered a bit 'whacky' by other Bible critics but it's worth remembering that the popular view of the Fourth Gospel being 'late' can be questioned.*

The main argument against this authorship is that John son of Zebedee was a Galilean peasant fisherman, whereas the Fourth Gospel is written in a good standard of Greek with a knowledge of **Hellenic** (Greek) philosophy (p48). It doesn't seem likely that someone from John's background would write like this. However, in his long life it is possible John could have received a good education and mastered Greek philosophy.

The Beloved Disciple

A mysterious figure appears in the final chapters of the Fourth Gospel, referred to as "*the disciple whom Jesus loved*" or "*the beloved disciple of Jesus*". This person appears 5 times: at Jesus' farewell Discourse, at the foot of the Cross, at the Empty Tomb and 2 times when the Risen Christ appears to the other Disciples; the Fourth Gospel ends claiming that the Beloved Disciple wrote the Gospel down:

> *This is the disciple who testifies to these things and who wrote them down. We know that his testimony is true* – **John 21: 24**

> *Notice, though, that the author isn't claiming to be the Beloved Disciple: this passage suggests that the Beloved Disciple has died and his followers have written the Fourth Gospel based on the Beloved Disciple's testimony.*

So, who is the Beloved Disciple? There are several theories:

- **John son of Zebedee:** This was the view of several early Christian writers. **Polycrates of Ephesus** (d.196 CE) claimed that John was the Beloved Disciple. John son of Zebedee is never mentioned in the Fourth Gospel, so the Beloved Disciple must be him, by a process of elimination. However, the Beloved Disciple only appears in **John 13**, whereas John son of Zebedee was a Disciple right from the beginning.
- **Lazarus:** The Beloved Disciple only makes an appearance after **Lazarus has been raised from the dead** (p159). Lazarus is three times described as the person Jesus "*loved*". This also explains the odd tradition in **John 21: 22-23**, that the Beloved Disciple cannot die until the Second Coming of Christ – if Lazarus really was raised from the dead, people might have thought he was immortal.
- **It's symbolic:** The Beloved Disciple might not be a single person at all, but instead represents believing Christians generally – or the reader in particular. Perhaps YOU, the reader of the Fourth Gospel, are supposed to identify with the Beloved Disciple and "*testify to these things*" yourself by believing in Jesus

The Johannine Community

Raymond E. Brown proposes that the Fourth Gospel wasn't written by a single person: it was a community effort, written in stages, beginning in the 60s CE and not complete until 100 CE. Brown thinks the **Johannine Community** were originally followers of John the Baptist who stayed as part of the Jewish religion right through to the 80s CE. They believed Jesus to be their Messiah.

After the destruction of the Jerusalem Temple, Judaism reorganised itself. In 90 CE, the **Council of Jamnia** set out new rules for Jewish worship and expelling the *minim* (heretics, which included Christians). The Johannnine Christians found themselves friendless and despised. They were in danger, because if they refused to worship the Roman gods (and the Emperor) they could be arrested since they were no longer exempted for being Jews. Brown thinks some of them were executed and this produced bitter feelings towards their former Jewish friends.

The Johannine Community had an influx of new members who were converted Samarians (a group that was disliked by the Jews and disliked the Jews in return). This intensified the Community's us-versus-them view of the world. It also helped them survive persecution and develop a very high Christology – a view of Jesus as the **incarnation of God's Word** (p81).

Brown argues that the Fourth Gospel doesn't just report the life and Resurrection of Jesus: it's also an **allegory** for the experiences of the Johannine Community itself:

- The Gospel starts with John the Baptist, because the Community started as followers of John the Baptist; John is presented positively (he recognises that Jesus is the *Light of the World* and the *Lamb of God*) but diminished in status (he does not baptize Jesus, he is not the Messiah)
- Jesus starts his Ministry by cleansing the Temple of money-changers; this comes at the *end* of Jesus' ministry in the Synoptic Gospels but the Fourth Gospel establishes the theme of conflict with the Jews early on
- Jesus visits Samaria and makes converts there (**John 4: 39-42**), representing the ethnic makeup of the Johannine Community containing of Samaritans and former-Jews
- Jesus' **Signs** (p135) establish that he is creating a new religion that will separate from Judaism, as with new wine from water, healing the blind man or raising Lazarus; a key breaking point with Judaism is over observing the Sabbath rules, which Jesus ignores.
- The other Christian churches founded by the Apostles are represented by Peter and the Twelve Disciples. The Beloved Disciple is always shown to be closer to Christ than they are: he sits with Jesus at supper, he is at the foot of the Cross, he outruns Peter to get to the Empty Tomb. This represents the Johannine Community being 'ahead' of other Christians at the time with its high Christology.

By viewing the Fourth Gospel in terms of the **Sitz im Leben** *of the Johannine Community in the 80s and 90s CE, Brown is drawing from* **Form Criticism**; *by looking at how the editor (redactor) of the Gospel uses the material to push his own group's agenda, Brown is drawing from* **Redaction Criticism**.

The Structure of the Fourth Gospel

Raymond E. Brown sets out this plan of the Fourth Gospel:

The Prologue (John 1: 1-18)

This is a hymn worshiping the **Logos** (p81) that establishes Christ's pre-existence (he existed before the human life of Jesus); it is interspersed with passages where John the Baptist comments on Jesus being the **Word of God**.

The Book of Signs (John 1: 19 - John 12: 50)

A series of Signs, Discourses and encounters where the Word of God reveals himself to the world but his own people will not accept him. There are **7 Signs** (p135) and 7 **"I Am" statements** (p119) that explore this meaning. In addition, there is the important meeting between Jesus and Nicodemus where being 'Born Again' is discussed. This section concludes with the final Sign which is the **raising of Lazarus from the dead** (p159) and the decision of the Jewish High Priest to execute Jesus.

The Book of Glory (John 13:1 - John 20: 31)

The Word of God reveals his Glory by dying on the Cross and returning to God, through the Resurrection and his Ascension to a fully glorified **Eternal Life** (p87) that he shares with **believers** (p93). This is the section where the Beloved Disciple appears. If the sections of the Gospel were originally distinct sources, then this might be the source that comes from the Beloved Disciple's eyewitness testimony.

Epilogue (John 21: 1-25)

A series of Resurrection appearances in Galilee and the concluding testimony of the Beloved Disciple. Since the Book of Glory has already come to a very final conclusion, scholars suggest this section was added later (probably after the Beloved Disciple's death).

Brown believes that these sections may have begun as separate **sources** (p195) but that the final author of the Gospel **redacted** (p201) them together to form a single book.

> This is a good example of the way *Source Criticism* identifies different sources within a text and *Redaction Criticism* explores how they have been put together by the redactor (editor). The identification of the opening prologue as a 'hymn' is an example of *Form Criticism*. Brown is a Catholic priest, but some Christians would object to breaking the Gospel up like this and insist it should be read as a consistent unity.

JESUS AS CHRIST

In **John's Gospel**, the 'Book of Signs' concludes with this appeal:

> But these are written that you may believe that Jesus is the Christ, the Son of God, and that by believing you may have life in his name – **John 20: 31**

Christos is the Greek word for '**Messiah**' (p12) and it is used extensively in John's Gospel, but in ways rather different from the Synoptic Gospels. For example, in the Synoptic Gospels, Jesus is secretive about being the Messiah, but in John's Gospel he announces it openly (e.g. **John 4: 26**).

What does it mean to call Jesus 'Christ'?

At the start of John's Gospel, **Andrew** tells his brother Peter that:

> We have found the Messiah – **John 1: 41**

The Fourth Gospel uses the Aramaic word ("*Messian*") for Messiah but the Gospel-writer immediately translates this as "(*that is, the Christ*)" for the benefit of readers unfamiliar with Jewish terms. The fact that the Gospel-writer uses both terms (*Messiah/Christ*) is a clue that the Fourth Gospel will develop its own interpretation of what these words mean that's rooted in Jewish beliefs but isn't entirely the same as them.

> *What you've just read is a good example of **Redaction Criticism**: looking at the choice of words the redactor of John's Gospel makes*

The first chapter of John's Gospel contains several other Messianic titles: "*the one Moses wrote about in the Law, and about whom the Prophets also wrote*", "*Son of God*", "*Son of Man*" and "*King of Israel*". By starting the Gospel this way, John highlights the importance of 'Christ' for understanding who Jesus is.

'Christ' as King

C.H. Dodd argues that, in the Fourth Gospel, the most important meaning of 'Christ' is a **King**. This is why Nathanael calls Jesus the "*King of Israel*" at the start of the Gospel while, at the end of it, Pontius Pilate puts a mocking sign on Jesus' cross calling him "*Jesus of Nazareth, King of the Jews*". However, the Fourth Gospel never mentions the **line of David** (p15) and is not interested in the conventional idea of the **Kingly Messiah**.

- In the middle of the Gospel, straight after the **Feeding of the 5000** (p147), the Galileans try to crown Jesus king, but he escapes them
- When Jesus enters Jerusalem, the crowds greet him singing: "*Blessed is the King of Israel!*" (**John 12: 13**)
- However, days later the crowd demands Jesus is crucified by saying: "*We have no king but Caesar!*" (**John 19: 15**)

- At Jesus' trial, Pilate asks Jesus if he is a king, Jesus replies:

My kingdom is not of this world – **John 18: 36**

The crowds do not see who Jesus truly is: they are expecting the Christ to be a worldly king and they turn on Jesus in anger when he disappoints them. John's Gospel teaches a different sort of meaning of 'Christ'. For John's Gospel, the Christ is a spiritual King who rules over humans' souls, not an earthly king who rules over territory on maps.

This links to the instruction in John's Gospel that believers must be **Born Again**. As physical beings, Christians are the subjects of worldly kings, like the Roman Emperor or Herod; but as creatures who have been spiritually re-born, they have one spiritual King: Christ.

Christ as 'Lamb of God'

C.H. Dodd also argues that 'Christ' can be understood as the **'Lamb of God'**. This is what John the Baptist recognises Jesus as:

the Lamb of God, who takes away the sin of the world! – **John 1: 29**

This phrase is unique to the Fourth Gospel; it doesn't appear in the Synoptics and Jews did not describe the Messiah as being like a Lamb. **Dodd** and **Raymond E. Brown** conclude that the phrase is not something John the Baptist actually said.

> *It fails the **Criterion of Multiple Attestation**, since John the Baptist appears in the Synoptics too but he never uses this phrase there*

The Fourth Gospel clearly links the *Lamb of God* to the Christ because, as soon as John the Baptist calls Jesus the *Lamb of God*, Andrew goes to Peter to announce that they have found the **Messiah** (p12).

The comparison here is with the **Paschal Lamb**. This is the animal sacrificed by the High Priest every Passover Festival in the Jerusalem Temple. This sacrifice commemorates the events in **Exodus 12: 1-28** when the first Paschal Lambs were killed and the blood sprinkled on the door of every Israelite in Egypt so that the Angel of Death would 'pass over' their houses. The Lamb of God is therefore a SACRIFICIAL VICTIM: someone who will die so that others can live. Jesus is the Lamb of God because his death will give believers **Eternal Life** (p87). Just like the Paschal Lamb, Jesus is "*without blemish*" (i.e. sinless).

The Fourth Gospel changes the dating of Jesus' crucifixion to continue this symbolism. In the Synoptic Gospels, Jesus is crucified on the day of Passover (a Friday), but in the Fourth Gospel, Jesus is crucified the day ***before*** Passover (Thursday). This is because the day before Passover is the day the Paschal Lamb is sacrificed: the Gospel presents Jesus dying on the Cross at the same time as the Paschal Lamb dies in the Temple. However, Jesus is the TRUE Lamb of God; the poor animal being killed in the Temple is the substitute.

This is a different understanding of 'Christ' from the idea of a King and different also from the way the Messiah is viewed in Judaism. It is a distinctively Johannine view of Jesus as the Christ.

Is the purpose of the Fourth Gospel to present Jesus as the Christ?

YES	NO

The Book of Signs begins with Andrew announcing that Jesus is the Messiah and the Book of Glory ends with the promise that readers will have **Eternal Life** if they believe Jesus is the Christ.

The Fourth Gospel presents Jesus as a different sort of Christ from what is expected: a King, but a spiritual king with a spiritual kingdom. The Gospel is trying to change our understanding of what 'Christ' means.

Andrew's announcement follows straight on from John the Baptist's declaration that Jesus is the Lamb of God. This presents Jesus as a sacrificial victim who will die for humanity's sins. This is the true meaning of 'Christ' in Christianity.

This is a very unusual interpretation of Christ. It's not found in the Synoptic Gospels (which link Jesus' suffering instead to the **Suffering Servant in Isaiah 53**). All Christians believe Jesus dies an atoning death, but the idea of Jesus as the Paschal Lamb is unique to the Fourth Gospel.

JESUS AS SON OF GOD

In **John's Gospel**, the 'Book of Signs' concludes with this appeal:

> *But these are written that you may believe that Jesus is the Messiah, the Son of God, and that by believing you may have life in his name* – **John 20: 31**

Moreover, back at the beginning of the Book of Signs, Nathanael declares that Jesus is the "*Son of God*" (**John 1: 49**) so this claim 'bookends' the Fourth Gospel. *Huios Theos* is the Greek phrase for **'Son of God'** (p112) which is used in all four Gospels. However, John's Gospel uses this phrase 29 times and speaks of God as 'Father' over 100 times.

What does it mean to call Jesus the 'Son of God'?

In the Old Testament, the phrase *Son of God* can apply to the whole Jewish nation or to a king of Israel. It is a symbolic expression, meaning that the Jewish people are loved by God ***as if*** they were his children or that a king of Israel ***represents*** God on Earth by protecting and leading the Jewish people. This is the sense in which Jews expect the **Messiah** to be the *Son of God* - the Messiah will be chosen by God, sent by God to do his work and entrusted with power and responsibility by God, ***as if*** he were a son, all the while ***representing*** God to the people on Earth.

The Synoptic Gospels present Jesus as the *Son of God* in a similar way to this Jewish view. In **Mark's Gospel**, Jesus is 'adopted' as God's Son when he is baptized and God's voice announces "*This is my beloved Son*!" However, **Matthew** and **Luke** go further with their birth-narratives: Jesus is announced to be God's Son as soon as he is conceived.

The Fourth Gospel goes furthest of all: Jesus is God's Son since the creation of the universe!

> *This is one of the reasons why the Fourth Gospel doesn't bother with a birth-narrative. Christ existed in the heavenly realm <u>before</u> he appeared on earth. There's no baptism scene because Christ has <u>always</u> been the 'beloved son' of God*

In the Fourth Gospel, Jesus is an eternal being who is present on Earth. He remembers his pre-Earthly existence.

> *I know where I came from and where I am going. But you have no idea where I come from or where I am going* – **John 8: 14**

This Gospel includes ironic jokes about people who do not realise Jesus is the Son of God because they only see a 30 year-old man. When Jesus claims that the ancient patriarch Abraham is delighted with him, the Jewish leaders sneer that Abraham lived centuries ago but Jesus is "*not yet fifty years old*" (**John 8: 57**). Jesus replies with the famous claim:

> *Before Abraham was born, I am!* – **John 8: 58**

> *Yes, this is one of those **"I Am" statements** the Johannine Jesus is always making.*

Jesus is not just claiming to be very very old (Abraham lived 1500 years previously). Jesus is claiming he comes from outside time altogether: he is eternal. As **C.H. Dodd** says, Jesus belongs *"to a different order of being... outside the range of temporal relations."*

This is a much more unusual idea than being someone God treats *as if* they were a son. **C.H. Dodd** argues that Jesus is on a journey from God to Earth, then from Earth back to God again - and he is taking the people of Earth with him (or at least, all of those who **believe in him**, p93). Those who are united with Christ are 'drawn' by him into his spiritual world of **Eternal Life** (p87).

> *The Johannine Jesus is a divine being on a rescue mission - to rescue humanity!*

Jesus' miraculous **Signs** (p135) can be seen as a proof of his heavenly origin. However, the Fourth Gospel places much more emphasis on the idea that Jesus' heavenly origin gives him **insight** into the nature of God. Jesus' whole life reflects what God is like, because Jesus is sent from God.

> *The one who sent me is with me; he has not left me alone, for I always do what pleases him* – **John 8: 29**

Implications

This is a very 'high Christology'. For many traditional Christians, the Fourth Gospel is the one that 'makes sense' of the other Synoptic Gospels. The **revelation** that 'Son of God' means a divine being from outside of time caught on with the wider Christian churches and, by the 2nd century CE, most Christians hold this 'high Christological' view of Jesus as God incarnate.

> *Redaction Critics often point out that the Fourth Gospel has altered the person of Jesus into something pretty far removed from the historical Jesus: that this is not what the original Jesus taught or his disciples believed. However, if the Fourth Gospel really was written by* **John son of Zebedee**, *maybe this idea does go back to the original Jesus of Nazareth.*

This sort of belief in 'Son of God' marks a clear break with Judaism, which utterly denies that God can be a human being or a human being can be God. Today there are Unitarian Christians who still reject this sort of interpretation of 'Son of God': they believe that Jesus was inspired by God but they do *not* believe Jesus is God incarnate.

The appeal of the 'high Christological' view is that Jesus is not just a teacher or saviour who lived two thousand years ago; as an eternal being united with God, Jesus is present in your life right now. This means 'believing in Jesus' isn't about holding an opinion concerning a long-dead prophet; it's about forming a relationship with a divine person who is still alive today.

Is the purpose of the Fourth Gospel to present Jesus as the Son of God?

YES	NO
Unlike the Synoptic Gospels, Jesus is openly declared to be the Son of God in John's Gospel: Nathanael says it when he joins Jesus' Disciples and Martha says it before Jesus **raises Lazarus from the dead**.	'Son of God' doesn't mean the same thing in the Fourth Gospel as it (perhaps) means in the Synoptics. The Johannine Jesus is the incarnated Son of God, which is a surprising new idea.
In all the Gospels, Jesus is recognised as the Son of God by some people (such as Peter) – it just happens more often in John's Gospel. In all the Gospels, Jesus represents the ways of God to humanity and forgives sins on behalf of God. In John's Gospel with its **"I Am" statements**, Jesus is just more dramatic about this.	The Synoptic Gospels to varying degrees have an Exaltation Christology, viewing Jesus as a human exalted or adopted to be God's Son. In the Fourth Gospel, Jesus is an eternal being who is present on Earth. He does more than forgive sins: he offers his own **Eternal Life** to people who believe in him (and Christians believe he still does!)

LIFE IN HIS NAME

In **John's Gospel**, the 'Book of Signs' concludes with this appeal:

> *But these are written that you may believe that Jesus is the Messiah, the Son of God, and that by believing you may have life in his name* – **John 20: 31**

This echoes a promise made in the **Prologue** (p77):

> *to those who believed in his name, he gave the right to become children of God* – **John 1: 12**

The Gospel is offering a new **Life** (p87) to readers who believe in Jesus, but what do they have to do to become **Children of God** (p96)? The answer is contained in the phrase "*in His Name*".

How do Christians get Life in His Name?

The Greek language has three words for "**Life**":

- *Bios*, which is physical or biological life
- *Psyche*, which is mental life or consciousness
- *Zoë* , which is spiritual life

Bios-life is temporary and always runs out in the end. When Jesus **raises Lazarus from the dead** (p159), he restores Lazarus to *Bios*-life, but Lazarus will get sick again and die sooner or later. *Psyche*-life depends on *Bios*-life: we can't think or feel when our bodies are destroyed or badly damaged. Neither of these types of Life is what the Gospel is referring to.

Zoë life is different: it is eternal life not just in the sense of being EVERLASTING (it goes on forever) but in the sense of being TIMELESS. The closest we come to *Zoë*-life in ordinary experience is when we are "in the moment" and experience some pleasure deeply and completely in a very fulfilling way. A *Zoë*-life would be like this all the time: deeply fulfilled and engaged with living, appreciative and grateful for everything that comes along, concerned and caring for everyone around you.

> *Traditional Christians regard Zoë-life as both everlasting and timeless- it is a deeply fulfilling way of living and it won't end with death. However, some liberal Christians focus more on the 'timeless' aspect of Zoë-life, perhaps because they don't believe in life after death; some traditional Christians focus more on the 'everlasting' side of things, perhaps because they think earthly life is supposed to be sad and difficult.*

This new type of life can be gained by **believing in Jesus** (p93). This isn't just a matter of agreeing to a bunch of factual statements about Jesus (that he's the Son of God, that he rose from the dead, that he's your Saviour). It's more to do with forming a loving and trusting relationship with Jesus Christ – it's a personal commitment to Jesus.

This is where "*in His Name*" comes into it. Names were very important in Hebrew: they carried power. The holy Name of God was too sacred to pronounce or even write. The Hebrew word for name is *SHEM*, which is linked to the verb meaning "to place". *SHEM* is not just the name that identifies you: it's also your place in the world, your rank or position in the scheme of things.

Because Jesus is the **Son of God** (p112, 213), his name counts as if it was God's Name. This means Jesus has God's authority and power. The Bible connects the exaltation of Jesus' Name to his Resurrection:

> *God exalted him to the highest place and gave him the name that is above every name –* **Philippians 2: 9**

> *Jesus has the most exalted name in the universe - the most status, the highest rank*

Names can also be "loaned out". For example, a herald might deliver a message 'in the name of the king' and this means that, while he's delivering the message, the herald is in the king's place and has the king's authority and you have to listen respectfully as if it was the king himself speaking. If you tell someone to do something 'in your name', you're telling them you will take responsibility for it: in effect, it counts as if you were doing it, as if they were really you.

So if you act on Jesus' Name, you receive Jesus' status – and his *Zoë*-life that goes with it. But acting on Jesus' Name means acting like Jesus: living your life the way he lived his, which is a life of selflessness, compassionate love and sacrifice for others.

"*Life in His Name*" therefore means a gift of everlasting and/or timeless life, so long as you embody Jesus' Name in your own life, in the things you say and do.

That sounds difficult to do, but fortunately there's help. When you act in the Name of a more powerful person, you get that person's assets added to yours. If you act in a billionaire's name, you get access to his money, so long as you use it for the things he wants. Living in Jesus' Name gives you access to Jesus' spiritual strength. In the Fourth Gospel, Jesus talks about the 'Helper' or 'Comforter' who strengthens believers who do things in his Name: the Greek word is ***PARACLETE***.

> *If you love me, keep my commands, I will ask the Father, and he will give you another Paraclete to help you and be with you for ever –* **John 14: 15-16**

> *In this passage,* Paraclete *is often translated as 'advocate' (a defender or encourager)*

By the 2nd century, Christians come to regard the *Paraclete* as the **Holy Spirit,** which is the power of God at work in the souls of believers, guiding and strengthening them and answering their prayers.

Implications

The idea of making a commitment to love and follow Jesus and receiving spiritual strength to do this and **Eternal Life** (p87) as a reward sounds like a simple recipe for a good religious life. But of course it's often not that simple.

The first Christians regarded a ceremony of baptism as essential to make this commitment to Jesus Christ and receive the Holy Spirit. Many of them experienced exciting SPIRITUAL GIFTS when they did this: prophesying, healing, speaking in tongues. However, over time, conflicts emerged. One of the main ones was what to do about believers who lapsed back into sinful ways after being baptized. Did this mean they were *no longer* living in Jesus' Name because they weren't following his commands? Or did being baptized mean that you were guaranteed Eternal Life *even if* you subsequently sinned?

Some churches ejected members who didn't live up to the high standards of Jesus' Name, whereas others offered multiple chances. Over time, the churches got organised about this. Confessions were introduced so that people could be forgiven for their sins and sins were ranked into venal ones (which could be forgiven) and mortal sins (which couldn't). Christianity developed very strict ethics about sexual behaviour but many of Jesus' warnings about money were taken less seriously.

Reformers have always tried to get back to the exciting offer of a life lived in Jesus' Name. Their churches emphasise religious experiences, being **'Born Again'** and the Gifts of the Spirit during worship; the Holy Spirit is something they experience personally. These days, these Christians refer to themselves as EVANGELICAL.

Other mainstream churches focus on less individualistic worship; the Holy Spirit is something they encounter more indirectly through the Sacraments of Eucharist and Confession.

There's a similar split between whether the Eternal Life the Gospel promises is something that believers will get after they die, or something they are supposed to receive in the here-and-now **C.H. Dodd** calls this second view REALISED ESCHATOLOGY and argues that Jesus taught that Eternal Life was a timeless experience to be enjoyed in the present. Some passages in the Fourth Gospel support this:

> *Whoever hears my word and believes him who sent me has eternal life and will not be judged but has crossed over from death to life* – **John 5: 24**

That sounds like Realised Eschatology; but then the next verse sounds like Future Eschatology:

> *a time is coming when all who are in their graves will hear his voice and come out* – **John 5: 28-29**

Dodd argues that only the first verse represents the *IPSISSIMA VERBA* (the actual words) of Jesus. Most Christians believe that the new Life in Christ is something that is **both** offered in the present **and** consummated in the future – but there's a tendency to focus on one rather than the other.

Is the purpose of John's Gospel to offer believers "Life in Jesus' Name"?

YES

The purpose is clearly stated in the **Prologue** and at the end of the Book of Glory. **Eternal Life i**s the main theme of the Fourth Gospel and all Jesus' **Discourses** and **Signs** illustrate the way to get it: not by following the **Law** but by **believing in Jesus** as the **Son of God**.

Jesus doesn't impose an impossible standard. For one thing, he offers the *Paraclete* or Comforter: his **Holy Spirit** which strengthens the faith of anyone with sincere intentions. Also, Eternal Life brings such a quality to living that it's worth exchanging for mere comfort and prosperity.

NO

There turns out to be a catch to this offer: to receive Eternal Life you have to live your life as Jesus lived his, which is to say, perfectly. Jesus' life led him to self-sacrifice and an ugly death. Even if people wanted to live this morally perfect life, most ordinary people can't measure up to it.

The history of the Church shows that living in Jesus' Name isn't as straightforward as it sounds, even with the Comforter helping out. Even if you can deal with backsliders, it's not clear whether Eternal Life refers to the Afterlife or just a better quality experience in *this* lifetime.

SPIRITUAL GOSPEL

Clement of Alexandria (150-215 CE) was a Christian convert who wrote about the origins of the Gospels. Clement argues that **Matthew** was the first Gospel but adds this comment on the Fourth Gospel:

> *But, last of all, John, aware that the physical facts had been set out in the Gospels, was encouraged by his disciples & divinely motivated by the Spirit, composed a spiritual Gospel* – **Clement of Alexandria**

What does Clement mean by calling John's Gospel "*a spiritual Gospel*"?

In what way is the Fourth Gospel a 'Spiritual Gospel'?

Clement uses the words **Flesh and Spirit** (p99) to contrast the other Gospels with **John**. The Synoptics describe Jesus in a fleshy way – in terms of the physical facts – but John goes for the deeper, spiritual meaning behind Jesus' words and actions. Other critics have pointed out that the Synoptics are DESCRIPTIVE but John is REFLECTIVE – or that the Synoptics record *the IPSISSIMA VERBA* (the true words) of Jesus, but John captures the *IPSISSIMA VOX* (the true voice, Jesus' real intentions).

The Protestant reformer **John Calvin** relates Johns Gospel to the Synoptics with this illuminating phrase:

> *This Gospel is the key which opens the door to the understanding of the other Gospels* – **John Calvin**

Martin Luther, the founder of the Protest Reformation, argues that, if some tyrant were to destroy all the books in the Bible, so long as one copy of the Gospel of John survived, "*Christianity would be saved*".

An example of this comes in the **Prologue** (p77) with the idea that Christ is the **pre-existent Word of God** (p81) who has been active all the way through the Old Testament and participated in the Creation of the World itself. None of the Synoptics comes close to such an exalted view of Jesus – and the author of John's Gospel presumably only developed this understanding over time.

The Fourth Gospel is written in fairly basic Greek. It's not clumsy like **Mark** but it has simple vocabulary and short, direct sentences. However, the everyday concepts in the Fourth Gospel like birth, light, bread and water take on multiple levels of meaning. This is summed up in a very popular quote describing the Gospel:

> *The Gospel of John is like a swimming pool: shallow enough that a child may wade and deep enough that an elephant can swim* – **Leon Morris**

Everyday things become **symbols** of spiritual realities beyond physical sight. Bread becomes a symbol of the spiritual nourishment given by believing in Jesus, who is the **"Bread of Life"** (p120). Water is the symbol of baptism by the Holy Spirit (**John 7:37-39**), to be given to believers when Jesus has been glorified.

> *In Topic 2 (The Person of Jesus) studied the "I Am" statements and the 7 Signs in John's Gospel: these are all good examples of the spiritual depth to the Gospel.*

The Fourth Gospel has a distinctive style that draws attention to this spiritual meaning. Jesus makes an claim that can be taken in more than one way. His words carry a spiritual meaning, but he is misunderstood by someone who understands him in a purely earthly way. Jesus then clarifies things. For example, the conversation with **Nicodemus (John 3:3-8)** uses a Greek word "*anothen*" that may mean "born from above" (Jesus' meaning) or simply "born again" (which is how Nicodemus understands it). Nicodemus simplistically asks how a man can be born a second time without climbing back into his mother's womb? Jesus corrects him:

> *No one can enter the kingdom of God unless they are born of water and the Spirit* **– John 3: 5**

Jesus adds that **flesh** (*sarx*) gives birth to flesh, but the **Spirit** (*pneuma*) gives birth to Spirit (p99). Very simple words are being used here (birth, water, spirit, flesh), but the meaning involves baptism with water into a **new eternal life in Jesus' Name** (p216).

Implications

The apparent simplicity of John's Gospel makes it the most popular Gospel in polls of church-goers. However, this simplicity of language disguises layer upon layer of symbols and codes and some deeply mysterious insights into the nature of God and faith. John's LANGUAGE may be simple but his MEANING is not.

This spiritual depth has allowed some readers to get quite carried away. In the 2nd century, the Johannine churches were split between Christians who took a conventional view of the meaning of the Gospel and those who read a completely different set of meanings into it. These were the **Gnostics**, who believed that a secret wisdom (in Greek, *gnosis*) was coded into the Fourth Gospel. The Gnostics concluded that spiritual realities were the only thing that mattered, that the physical world was evil and that Jesus had been a spirit-being who only *appeared* to be human

Raymond E. Brown calls these people "secessionists" (meaning 'splitters' who broke away from the church's teachings) and thinks that their beliefs were "*a plausible exaggeration... of certain features of the Fourth Gospel*".

In other words, they took the idea of being Born from the Spirit and receiving **Eternal Life** (p87) to an extreme conclusion. The New Testament contains 3 **epistles** (letters) supposedly written by 'John' that condemn these splitters and argue for the correct interpretation of the Fourth Gospel.

Most scholars don't think these letters were written by the same **John** who is supposed to have written the Fourth Gospel – and certainly not by the **Beloved Disciple** (p207). They are from the 2nd century and not even **John son of Zebedee** (p206) lived that long. But they are clearly from the same **Johannine Community** (p208) that created the Fourth Gospel and they are still wrestling with the same electrifying spiritual themes the Gospel raises.

These themes continue to excite and trouble Christian communities today. John's Gospel suggests a powerful inner transformation is needed for a Christian believer to understand spiritual realities. There are many people who claim to have experienced this transformation and they offer to teach the secrets to followers. This is how cults form. The mainstream churches have always guarded against cults and distrusted people claiming to have secret spiritual wisdom. However, sometimes they go too far and resist genuine spiritual insights and calls to reform corrupt practices. John's Gospel offers a vision of Christian living as more mysterious, exciting and transformative than just 'going to church' every Sunday, but Christians have not found it easy to put such ideas into practice.

Is the Fourth Gospel intended to be "a spiritual Gospel"?

YES	NO
The **Prologue** begins with a spiritual power from outside of time and space coming into our world. All the way through, Jesus insists that behind our ordinary objects and activities (eating, drinking, washing) are spiritual realities waiting to transform us. The Gospel encourages us to see the world with new eyes, which is what being 'Born Again' means.	These 'spiritual realities' are very vague: people seem to find whatever they want in John's Gospel. The Gnostic interpretation is just as valid as the Johannine Church's official interpretation. John's Gospel is best when it avoids these muddles and focuses on its key message of Christians loving one another. The spiritual symbolism is a distraction.
John's Gospel emphasises that there is more to the Christian life than good deeds and regular worship. It encourages Christians to seek transformative religious experiences and become united with God through Christ in a much deeper sense. The **Eternal Life** offered by John's Gospel is a transformed way of living in the world today.	The Synoptic Gospels also call for people to live their lives in a transformed way, although they call it 'repentance' rather than being Born Again. **C.H. Dodd** claims that Realised Eschatology is present in Luke's Parables just as much as John's Signs. John's Gospel differs in style from the Synoptics but not in its main message about believing in Christ.

THE FULFILLMENT OF SCRIPTURE

Matthew's Gospel uses **proof-texts** (p33) to link Jesus to prophecies about the **Messiah** (p12, 210) in the Old Testament, but **John's Gospel** is just as concerned about fulfilling Old Testament prophecies, even though it isn't quite so explicit about it.

How does Jesus fulfill the Scriptures in the Fourth Gospel?

The Fourth Gospel presents Jesus Christ as the **Messiah** that the Old Testament predicted hundreds of years previously. **Isaiah 53** features the **Suffering Servant** (p20) who is tortured by the very people he tries to help. The Fourth Gospel refers to this at the beginning:

> *He came to that which was his own, but his own did not receive him* – **John 1: 11**

Isaiah 9:6 describes the Messiah as ruling over an eternal and everlasting kingdom. The Fourth Gospel presents Jesus as divine and existing eternally. All of Jesus' **"I Am" statements** (p119) imply this, but when he declares "*Before Abraham was born, I am*", Jesus makes it explicit that he is the eternal **Son of God** (p112, 213).

Isaiah 53: 4–6 explains that this **Suffering Servant** would die in the place of his people. In the Fourth Gospel, the High Priest Caiaphas urges the death penalty for Jesus saying that *"one man dies for the people"* (**John 11: 50**) which fulfils the prophecy.

The Fourth Gospel crafts the story of the Crucifixion to show many prophecies being fulfilled, such as:

> *a pack of villains encircles me; they pierce my hands and my feet* – **Psalm 22: 16**

This is fulfilled when Jesus is crucified between two outlaws:

> *they crucified him, and with him two others – one on each side and Jesus in the middle* – **John 19: 18**

While he is dying, Jesus' clothes are divided up between his executioners; finding the cloth to be seamless, the soldiers throw dice to see who gets it:

> *They divide my clothes among them and cast lots for my garment* – **Psalm 22: 18**

After Jesus dies, a soldier checks he is dead by stabbing him in the ribs with a spear while Jesus' mother watches on:

> *They will look on me, the one they have pierced, and they will mourn for him as one mourns for an only child* – **Zechariah 2: 10**

However, unlike the other executed victims, Jesus' bones are not broken. This fulfils the instruction in **Exodus 12: 46** for preparing the **Paschal Lamb** (the animal sacrificed at Passover), that none of the bones should be broken.

Implications

Redaction Critics point out that the **Johannine Community** (p208) experienced a lot of conflict with the Jewish Synagogues over whether or not Jesus was the Messiah. As a result, the Fourth Gospel has been carefully crafted to support the Johannine Community's position. Some Critics might suggest that the Gospel-writer has added details that weren't historical just to get a 'match' with an Old Testament prophecy.

> *However, if we apply the **Criterion of Multiple Attestation**, then the dividing up of Jesus' clothes is also described in **Matthew 27: 35**, so this may be a historical detail*

The fulfillment of prophecy is important because it supports the argument that the entirety of the Old Testament and the Law was both inspired *by* Jesus (as the **Logos**, p81) and is also *about* Jesus. Everything that happens in the Old Testament, from Moses meeting God in the burning bush through to King David's unhappy family life and the Babylonian Exile, it's all supposed to prepare the Jews to recognise the **Christ** (p210) when he appears. The irony is that they don't.

It's important in another sense, because it shows that God is in control of history. It often appears to humans that God is not in control and that the power of evil – the Darkness – rules the world. The Fourth Gospel begins by proclaiming that the **Darkness** can never overcome the **Light** (p90) and demonstrates this by showing how every detail of Jesus' suffering fits into a plan laid down by God in the Scriptures hundreds of years before.

Is the purpose of the Fourth Gospel to show how Jesus fulfils Scripture?

YES

In the **Prologue**, the Gospel refers to the **Suffering Servant** and the Crucifixion scene contains multiple references to the Psalms, the Prophets and the Paschal Lamb. This shows that Jesus is the source and also the subject matter of the Scriptures.

The way that Scriptures are fulfilled despite (or even because of) the plots of evil men shows that God is completely in control of history. Even when the evildoers think they have the righteous man at their mercy, they are only acting out a script created by God centuries before.

NO

Redaction Criticism would say that the whole of the Fourth Gospel has been crafted precisely to provide 'ammunition' for the arguments between the **Johannine Community** and the Jewish Synagogues that have rejected them. We can't be sure these details are historical.

This has troubling implications for **freewill** and **God's goodness**. If God created these prophecies, does it mean that people like Judas, Pilate and Caiaphas have no freewill? And why would a good God choose a plan that involves so much unnecessary suffering?

A GOSPEL TO CONVERT JEWS & GENTILES

Who was the intended audience of the Fourth Gospel: who was it written *for*? There are two main answers:

- it is aimed at **Jewish readers**, trying to persuade them that Jesus is the **Messiah** (p12)
- it is aimed at **Gentiles** (non-Jews), trying to persuade them that Christ's offer of **Eternal Life** (p87) is for them too.

Christianity began as a messianic sect within Judaism and could have stayed that way. However, it became a MISSIONARY RELIGION, because Christians set out to convert other people to their faith.

The Gospels present this as a commandment from the Risen Christ, which is known as the **'Great Commission'** in Matthew's Gospel (**Matthew 28: 19**). A version of this appears in the **Fourth Gospel** at the end of the Book of Glory:

As the Father has sent me, so I send you – **John 20: 21**

> *You might remember the **Sign of Healing the Blind Man**, which involved going to a pool called Siloam ('sent'). The idea of being 'sent' by God is a theme in John's Gospel and it always ends in the **Word of God** being proclaimed.*

Christians call trying to persuade others to convert to their faith EVANGELISM and the four Gospel-writers are often referred to as the EVANGELISTS because their writings are intended to persuade non-believers that Jesus is **Christ** (p210) and the **Son of God** (p213).

Argument: Converting Jews

On first reading, the Fourth Gospel is aimed at converting Jewish readers to Christianity. The Gospel starts with an imitation of the **Book of Genesis** – its opening words are *"in the beginning..."* which are the same words that begin Genesis. In fact, the Book of Genesis is named *BERESHIT* in Hebrew, which simply means "In the Beginning".

The first person to become a Disciple of Jesus is Andrew who tells his brother Peter that, *"We have found the Messiah"* (**John 1: 41**). The Gospel here uses the Aramaic word *Messian* rather than the Greek word *Christos*, which emphasises its Jewish credentials.

More than this, the whole of the Fourth Gospel is taken up with debates between Jesus and Jewish leaders: first of all **Nicodemus**, then the **Pharisees** (p64) and priests and finally the High Priest **Caiaphas**. In these discussions, Jesus corrects the Jews' beliefs about God and the **Jewish Law** (p102). The Gospel-writer refers to many specific places in Jerusalem and often knows about Jewish feasts and traditions. Jesus' actions often correspond to Jewish festivals, such as Jesus' **"I Am the Light of the World"** Discourse (p123) occurring during the Feast of Tabernacles, when the Temple was lit up. A lot of the conflict in the Gospel is over how to keep the Sabbath regulations (for example, in the **Sign of the Healing of the Blind Man**, p155).

However...

The Fourth Gospel doesn't read like something that would be very persuasive to a Jewish reader. Jesus' enemies are referred to as "*the Jews*" even by the Disciples themselves and Jesus refers to "*your Law*" as if he isn't a Jew either. More than that, the Jews are called *children of the Devil* (**John 8: 44**) and presented as murderers and hypocrites.

> *It's possible these insults are only meant for the leaders of the Jews, not ordinary Jewish believers, but it's still a strange way to try to persuade someone*

There's also the problem of the 'high Christology' in the Gospel that would be offensive to many Jews. Jesus links himself with God when he says, "*before Abraham was, I am*" (**John 8: 58**) and this is a blasphemous idea for Jews. Possibly even more disgusting to a Jewish reader would be Jesus saying:

> *Whoever eats my flesh and drinks my blood remains in me, and I in them* – **John 6: 56**

Jesus is referring to the **EUCHARIST** ceremony where Christians share bread and wine, but a Jewish reader would probably not know that. They *would* know that eating anything with blood in it is completely forbidden in Judaism, so this statement would sound shocking to them.

> *In short, it's hard to imagine a worse Gospel for trying to convert Jews to Christianity – **Matthew** would work much better.*

Argument: Converting Gentiles

An alternative argument is that the Fourth Gospel is aimed at a Gentile audience, persuading them to give up their pagan ways and convert to Christianity. There was certainly an audience for this sort of message in the 1st and 2nd centuries CE; many Roman pagans attended Synagogues to learn more about God, but were put off becoming Jews because of the extensive Laws (and of course, circumcision for men). They were referred to as *metuentes* ('God-fearers').

The Fourth Gospel would have an appeal for this audience. It presents Jesus in **Hellenic** (p48) terms, using concepts from Greek philosophy like the **Logos** (p81). It also uses universal symbolism of **light and darkness** (p90), **flesh and spirit** (p99), bread, water and birth. Many of these Gentiles were **DUALISTS** who would have been interested in these symbols of two worlds: a physical world we can see and a heavenly world we cannot see. The concept of **Jesus as the Son of God** (p112) would not have been offensive to pagans.

Jesus also rejects many of the details of the Jewish Law, which would have appealed to Gentiles since this was off-putting for them in Judaism. Instead, Jesus offers spiritual re-birth and **Eternal Life** (p87) without complicated rituals or surgical operations – a very attractive idea.

However...

Gentiles don't feature much in the Fourth Gospel. **Matthew's Gospel** goes out of its way to present many Gentiles as recognising Christ whereas the Jews don't (e.g. the **Magi visit Jesus after he is born**, p34). **Luke's Gospel** presents Jesus as offering a universal message to all people, Jewish and Gentile alike. But in the Fourth Gospel, Jesus spends most of his time arguing with Jewish leaders. He *does* visit the Samaritans and convert them – but to pagan Gentiles, the Samaritans would have looked like just another type of Jew. The specific details about Jerusalem and Jewish festivals would have been off-putting (or incomprehensible) to a Gentile reader.

Argument: Converting Crypto-Christians & followers of John the Baptist

Raymond E. Brown offers a different solution: an audience of "*crypto-Christians*".

'*Crypto-*' means 'secret'. These people were Jews in the local Synagogues who were secret Christians (or at least, who believed Jesus was the **Messiah** but kept quiet about it).

Brown argues that, when the **Johannine Community** (p208) was expelled from the Synagogues after 90 CE, they left behind many friends and family members who secretly shared their faith but who didn't have the courage to stand up for their beliefs and take the consequences. These people kept quiet when the Christians were expelled, but they were sympathetic to Christianity and just needed a 'push' to 'come out' as believers in Christ.

The Fourth Gospel seems to refer to these crypto-Christians when it says:

> *They would not openly acknowledge their faith for fear they would be put out of the synagogue* – **John 12: 42**

> *The crypto-Christians perhaps agreed with criticisms of the Jewish Law, would have known that the Eucharist didn't really involve blood-drinking but just needed persuading that Jesus was the **Son of God**.*

Brown also speculates that a Jewish sect following **John the Baptist** was still in existence in the late 1st century CE. These Baptizers would perhaps have been hostile to the Pharisees too, but not willing to admit that Jesus of Nazareth was greater than John the Baptist. The Fourth Gospel tries to win them over by presenting John in a positive way, but making it clear that Jesus, not John, is the true **Light** (p90) from God.

Can we work out the intended audience of the Fourth Gospel?

YES	NO
The Fourth Gospel contains such specific details about Jewish festivals and laws as well as a precision about Judean geography, it must surely have been written for a Jewish audience who would understand these references.	The Gospel is too hostile to Jews to be for a Jewish audience unconvinced by the claim the Jesus is the Christ. However, it's too Jewish-focused to be aimed at Gentiles, who would not pick up on these references or care about the arguments over Sabbath rules, Moses or Abraham.
The Fourth Gospel doesn't make a serious attempt to win over hostile Jewish readers and doesn't show much interest in Gentiles (other than Samaritans). Brown's argument that the Gospel was aimed at an audience of 'crypto-Christians' fits the best.	Since we don't know for sure who wrote the Gospel, or where, or when, any attempt to work out its audience is futile. The Gospel addresses itself to one audience: YOU, the current reader, who is invited to believe in **Jesus as the Son of God** and receive **Life in His Name**.

TOPIC 3 KEY SCHOLARS

Raymond E Brown

Topic: 3.2 Purpose & Authorship of the Fourth Gospel

Raymond E Brown (1928-1998) is an American Roman Catholic priest and Bible scholar whose work features in other topics in this course too: **1.1 (Prophecy regarding the Messiah), 2.2 (Titles of Jesus)** and **2.3 (Miracles & Signs)**.

Brown carries on the work on John's Gospel started by **C.H. Dodd**. In *The Gospel & the Epistles of John: A Concise Commentary* (1988), Brown goes through John's Gospel passage-by-passage, exploring the terminology and the symbolism. Brown follows Dodd's concept of 'realised eschatology' – he thinks Jesus' acts and words reveal timeless truths about life and God rather than predicting things that are going to happen after death or at the end of time.

In *The Community of the Beloved Disciple* (1979), Brown explores the **Johannine Community** and how its situation influences the way John's Gospel presents Jesus. The subtitle of the book is *The Life, Loves and Hates of an Individual Church in New Testament Times*. Notice the word "Hates": Brown focuses on the deep rift between the Johannine Christians and the Jewish Synagogues that expelled them in the 80s and 90s CE.

Brown didn't discover the idea of the Johannine Community. **J. Louis Martyn** was the first to develop this concept, but Brown references Martyn in his book and builds on his scholarship.

Brown argues that the Johannine Christians experienced a deep trauma when they were expelled from the Jewish religion. Not only did they lose friends and family, but they were exposed to danger. Now that they were no longer Jews, they were expected by the Roman authorities to join in pagan sacrifices. Those that refused were arrested and even executed. Brown suspects that the Jewish leaders sometimes informed on these Christians. This explains the 'Hate' towards "*the Jews*" and what he calls "*the deep sense of 'us' against 'them'*" in John's Gospel.

Brown also suggests that the entirety of John's Gospel tells a coded story of the Johannine Community's experiences and the development of their faith. Brown thinks the Johannine Community was founded by Jewish followers of John the Baptist who came to believe Jesus was the Messiah. They came under pressure from the Jewish leaders for their beliefs and developed a higher Christology when they were joined by Samaritan converts.

Eventually, they were expelled from the Synagogue in the 80s or early 90s CE. Brown believes they wrote the Fourth Gospel to appeal to "*crypto-Christians*" in the Jewish community who concealed their faith in Jesus.

Brown believes that the Beloved Disciple was a real person: not John son of Zebedee nor a member of Jesus' Twelve Disciples, but an actual follower of Jesus who preserved some eyewitness memories of Jesus and some distinctive beliefs about him. The Fourth Gospel was written in its final form after this Beloved Disciple died.

C.H. Dodd

Topic: 3.1 Purpose & authorship of the Fourth Gospel

Charles Harold Dodd (1884-1973) is a Welsh Protestant Bible scholar whose work features in other topics in this course too: **2.1 (Prologue in John), 2.2 (Titles of Jesus in the Synoptics and selected 'I Am' sayings in John), 2.3 (Miracles and Signs)**.

Dodd is a very influential figure in Bible scholarship. His work argues against the conclusions drawn by **Albert Schweitzer** and **Rudolph Bultmann**. Both of these scholars tried to analyse the Bible to uncover the historical Jesus by stripping away the supernatural elements. They concluded that Jesus was a rather murky historical figure whose political and religious ambitions were pretty remote from modern life. Dodd argues against this, saying that we can reconstruct details about Jesus' teachings and these are still relevant to people in the modern world.

Dodd wrote two books relevant to this part of the course. *The Interpretation of the Fourth Gospel* (1953) goes through all John's key concepts and analyses them in terms of their link to the Old Testament or Hellenic philosophy. It's a dense read because Dodd is the sort of scholar who writes 'Logos' as $\lambda o \gamma o \sigma$ and expects you to know your Greek alphabet well enough to understand it.

Historical Tradition in the Fourth Gospel (1963) is a little more accessible. Dodd argues that the author of John's Gospel is a '*historian*' and not a '*chronicler*'. In other words, the author of the Fourth Gospel is interested in the *meaning* of historical events and freely edits and alters stories and puts speeches into characters' mouths to draw out this meaning. However, Dodd *does* think there are historical details in the Gospel and that they can be reconstructed by scholars.

Dodd's main contribution is the idea of REALISED ESCHATOLOGY. 'Eschatology' is philosophy about the 'End Times' (from the Greek, *Eschaton*) such as death, Judgement Day and the Afterlife. A typical Jewish eschatology among the Pharisees in the 1st century was that at some point in the future, God would send his Messiah to begin the Messianic Age where God would rule the world, abolishing sin and suffering.

According to Dodd, Jesus taught a 'realised eschatology', that these End Times were ***already happening***. This means that Bible passages Heaven, Hell, Judgement Day etc should be interpreted symbolically as religious experiences Christians have in the present (e.g. Hell is the loneliness of being selfish; Heaven is the experience of God and love in your life right now). According to this view, Jesus was trying to make his listeners open their hearts to God and each other – he wasn't telling them about things that would happen in the future or after death.

Dodd's views are popular with Liberal Christians, because they involve focusing on the spiritual meaning of the Bible rather than predictions about the end of the world, the threat of damnation in Hell or a focus on going to Heaven after you die. His views are unpopular with Conservative Christians who prefer to take the supernatural elements in the Bible more literally and have a 'futurist eschatology' (Judgement Day is a literal event coming in the future).

GLOSSARY OF TERMS

Abraham: Ancestor of the Jewish race and founder of Judaism (lived perhaps 2000 BCE)

Apocalypticism: Belief in the coming end of the world

Assyrian Empire: huge empire in the Middle East that lasted from pre-history through to 7th century BCE; responsible for destruction of the Jewish kingdom of **Israel**; replaced by the **Babylonian Empire**

Atoning Death: A death that makes up for sins

Babylonian Empire: empire in the Middle East that replaced the **Assyrian Empire**; responsible for the destruction of the Jewish kingdom of **Judah** and the **Babylonian Exile**; replaced by the Persian Empire

Babylonian Exile: Lasting from 597 BCE to 539 BCE, the **Jews** of **Judea** were taken into exile in Babylonia (modern Iraq) after their kingdom was destroyed

Beloved Disciple: Figure who appears from chapter 13 of John's Gospel; may represent the author of John's Gospel, who was an eyewitness to Jesus' ministry

Bethany: Village just outside Jerusalem where Mary and Martha live; scene for 7th Sign (raising Lazarus from the dead)

Bethlehem: Small village 5 miles south of **Jerusalem**; birth place of **David** and of the **Messiah** according to the **prophecy** of Micah

Cana: Village in the Galilee hills; scene for first 2 Signs (water into wine, healing the official's son)

Christology: Theory about the status of Christ, from an **exalted** human (low Christology) to an **incarnated** divine being (high Christology)

Conservatism: Trend opposed to **liberalism** and trying to conserve Biblical truths; see **traditionalism**

Crypto-Christians: Jewish Christians who concealed their faith to avoid expulsion from the **Synagogues** after 90 CE

David: Greatest king of a united **Israel** who reigned around 1000 BCE; the descendants of David ruled **Judah** until the **Babylonian Exile**; the **Messiah** is descended from David

Discourse: An extended speech or sermon; in John's Gospel, Jesus delivers these instead of **Parables**

Enlightenment: Period from mid 17th to late 18th century when European scholars pioneered a new scientific outlook

Eschatology: Beliefs about the end of the world and the afterlife

Essenes: Jewish sect that retreated to the desert to await the **Messiah** and opposed the cult of the Jerusalem Temple run by the **Sadducees**

Eternal Life: Spiritually transformed life, either after death or in the present

Eucharist: Christian act of worship involving shared bread and wine representing Jesus' body and blood

Exaltation: Promotion of a human to a divine rank

Exorcism: Driving out demons or spirits that possess a person; a type of **miracle** in the **Synoptic Gospels**

Flesh: Not just the physical body, but the whole worldly way of living opposed to spiritual things

Form Criticism: Interpretation of the Bible based on its origins as *pericopae* circulating among the first Christian communities

Fourth Gospel: Another term for John's Gospel

Futurist: Interpreting a **prophecy** so that it refers to events in the future or at the end of the world

Galilee: Region to the north of **Judea** consisting of wooded hills and farmland surrounding Lake Galilee; an agricultural society with a mix of **Jews** and **Gentiles**

Genealogy: Family tree showing someone's ancestors

Gentile: Someone who isn't **Jewish** by birth

Grace: God's free gift or favour to humanity

Hellenism: The Greek culture of the Roman Empire, especially its pagan religion, philosophy and art

Herod: King of a wider Judea from 37 BCE to 4 BCE; infamous for his massacres and murders but also his grand building projects; known as Herod "the Great"

I Am: The sacred Name of God in Hebrew, revealed to **Moses** by God and claimed by Jesus in 7 Discourses

Incarnation: Arrival of a divine being in physical form

Isaiah: Prophet who lived in **Jerusalem** around 700 BCE at the time of the fall of the Kingdom of **Israel**; also Book of the Old Testament written by him

Israel: the united kingdom ruled by **David** around 1000 BCE; also the name of the northern kingdom after the break-up of David's kingdom that lasted until the **Assyrians** invaded in 722 BCE; can also refer to the entire **Jewish** nation collectively because Israel was the name of their ancestor

Jerusalem: Capital city of **David**, later the capital of the Kingdom of **Judah**; home to the **Temple** and centre of Jewish culture

Jew: A person who follows the Jewish religion and is born into a Jewish family descended from the Old Testament children of **Israel**

Jewish Revolt: Rebellion against Rome 67-73 CE, resulting in the destruction of the Temple in 70 CE

Johannine Community: Community of Jewish and Samaritan Christians who were expelled from the Synagogues, perhaps in Antioch c. 90 CE; composed John's Gospel

John the Baptist: Figure mentioned in all the Gospels who preceded Jesus and baptized many followers but was executed by Herod Antipas

Judah: Southern kingdom with **Jerusalem** as its capital and ruled by the line of **David** that endured until the **Babylonian Exile**

Judea: Kingdom of **Herod** (including **Galilee**); after his death a smaller province (not including Galilee) ruled by a Roman governor

Kerygma: Greek for 'preaching'; the original Christian message of Jesus and his Apostles

Law: The religious rules of Judaism passed from God to Moses and written in the Torah; **Pharisees** believed in applying these rules to every aspect of life

Liberal Christianity: Christian trend opposed to **conservatism**, rejecting tradition and freely interpreting the Bible to new circumstances

Logia: Sayings of Jesus passed on by his followers as part of the **oral tradition** (singular: *logion*)

Logos: The Word of God; a divine force or being that represents God in the universe and in the Old Testament

Markan Priority: Theory that Mark is the earliest Gospel and was copied by Matthew and Luke

Messiah: The Anointed One; predicted saviour or king in Judaism (*Christos* in Greek)

Messianic Secret: Theory of Wilhelm Wrede that Jesus never claimed to be the **Messiah** and that Mark's Gospel treats his Messiah-ship as a secret

Miracle: A divine act that breaks the laws of nature

Modernism: Trend opposed to **traditionalism** that redefines Christian teachings for the modern world

Moses: Greatest prophet and lawgiver in Judaism; received the **Law** from God (lived perhaps 1400 BCE)

Nicodemus: Senior **Pharisee** who secretly visits Jesus to learn from him; later defends Jesus at his trial and helps to bury Jesus' body

Oral Tradition: Accounts of Jesus memorized and passed on by word-of-mouth before the Gospels came to be written

Parable: Story told by Jesus, usually with peasant characters but containing a spiritual message; there are several in the **Synoptic Gospels**, especially Luke

Pericope: In **Form Criticism**, a textual unit that was original a memory of Jesus passed on by word of mouth before the Gospels were written (plural *pericopae*)

Pharisees: Jewish sect concerned with obeying the Law in every aspect of life; represented as in conflict with the first Christians

Preterist: Interpreting a **prophecy** so that it refers to events occurring in the lifetime of the prophet

Prologue: The introduction to a Gospel

Proof Text: The use of an Old Testament **prophecy** to link with an event in Jesus' life and prove that he is the **Messiah**

Prophecy: A statement (often in the form of poetry) that reveals the will of God to humans

Proto-Gospel: Theoretical early Gospel which is now lost but was the basis for the Synoptic Gospels

Publican: A **Jew** who collaborates with the Roman Empire by helping the Romans collect taxes from other Jews

Q-Source: Theoretical source for material common to Matthew and Luke that is not shared by Mark; from German *Quelle* ('source')

Redaction Criticism: Interpretation of the Bible based on the idea of a redactor editing earlier material to address issues going on in the church in his time

Sabbath: The 7th day of the week (Saturday); Jewish Sabbath regulations forbid many types of work

Sadducees: Jewish sect that ran the Jerusalem Temple and collaborated with the Romans

Sign: Word used in John's Gospel for a miracle, to draw attention to its hidden meaning

Sitz im Leben: 'Life Situation'; the context in which the **pericopae** were first composed, according to **Form Criticism**

Son of Man: Title Jesus adopted for himself based on prophecies in the Old Testament; indicates a special servant of God but also a cosmic judge who appears at the end of the world

Son of God: Title Jesus' followers gave to him to reflect their belief in his divinity; also a title claimed by the Roman Emperor

Source Criticism: Interpretation of the Bible based on the different sources each Gospel is composed of

Suffering Servant: A character who appears in the Book of **Isaiah** who serves God loyally but is tortured by his enemies; may represent either the **Jewish** nation or Jesus

Synagogue: Local prayer house and centre of Jewish worship after the **Jewish Revolt**

Synoptic Gospel: Matthew, Mark and Luke; from the Greek 'seen together' because of the shared content and structure of these Gospels

Synoptic Gospel: Matthew, Mark and Luke; from the Greek 'seen together' because of the shared content and structure of these Gospels

Synoptic Problem: The problem of explaining the similarities and differences between the **Synoptic Gospels**

Temple: Central place of Jewish worship in **Jerusalem**; originally built by **David**'s son Solomon around 950 BCE but destroyed by the Babylonians in 597 BCE; the Second Temple was built after the **Babylonian Exile** and expanded by **Herod** but destroyed by the Romans in 70 CE

Traditionalism: Christian trend opposed to **modernism** that resists redefining Christian teachings for the modern world

Zealots: Jewish sect that believed in armed revolt against the Roman occupation

LOOKING BACK OVER YEAR 1 AND AS...

If you are studying for the AS exam, you have reached the end of the New Testament Studies course. When revising this course, it is helpful to 'work backwards'.

Start off by considering what the Gospels *are*: are they eyewitness accounts of Jesus' ministry? or are they stories written decades later, by people who never met Jesus in life and perhaps never really understood him? This latter view is very popular with scholars, but there is also a lot of evidence for eyewitness material in the Gospels (such as the substantial agreements between the Gospel accounts, the presence of hard-readings and embarrassing details, the use of Aramaic phrases and Jewish traditions and locations).

Once you understand **Raymond E. Brown**'s ideas about the **Johannine Community**, you can go back over the **Prologue**, **"I Am" statements** and **Signs** in the Fourth Gospel. Do these passages seem like later additions to Jesus' life story or are they events and arguments that actually took place in Jesus' lifetime? Reflect on the consequences of either interpretation: if the Fourth Gospel records Jesus' actual words, does that support Christian teachings on the Eucharist or later Christian anti-Semitism? if it doesn't record them, are Christian beliefs discredited?

You can then consider the Synoptic Gospels. If the theory of **Markan Priority** is correct, does that lend support to **William Wrede**'s claims about the **Messianic Secret** in Mark? Did Jesus really claim to be the **Christ/Messiah**, the **Son of God** or the **Son of David** in his lifetime or were these titles given to him later, by subsequent Christians who had exaggerated his importance?

You should conclude by looking at the 1st century context. Was Jesus a traditional Jew, opposed to Hellenism and the Roman occupation and devoted to worship in the Temple? Or was he a Hellenized Jew, with a positive view of the Romans and a critical view of Jewish traditions and Temple worship? Given that the Gospels were written in Greek decades later, in the Roman Empire, after the Jewish Revolt had been crushed, can we trust the Gospels to give an accurate picture of what Jesus really thought?

Going back to the idea of oral tradition and redaction, what are we to make of Jesus' disputes with the Pharisees? We know that Pharisees took over leadership of the Jewish community after the destruction of the Temple in 70 CE and we know that the early Christians fell out with the Pharisees because of Christian claims about Jesus – but did Jesus also fall out with the Pharisees during his ministry or are these disputes the inventions of later Christians?

You should finish by reflecting on Christology: did Christianity start with a 'low' Christological view of Jesus as a prophet which then got exaggerated into a 'high' Christology of Jesus as God? or did Jesus' followers recognise him to be divine right from the start?

LOOKING AHEAD TO YEAR 2...

If you are studying for the A-Level exam, you have covered half of the content at this point (but only about a quarter of the Anthology – there's a LOT more of that to cover).

Topic 4 builds on the concepts in Topic 3: how did the Gospels come to be written and how should they be interpreted today?

The biggest problem the Gospels pose for modern believers is the presence of supernatural events: not just miracles, but angels and demons, voices speaking from Heaven, prophecy predicting the future and an afterlife of eternal heaven or hell. Some scientifically-minded people in the 21st century find ideas like these hard to take seriously, and they feel that the New Testament's ethical teachings about love and forgiveness are spoiled by these magical and superstitious beliefs. (In fact, this isn't a new view at all: these criticisms were leveled at Christians in the 2nd century CE and were restated very forcefully during the 18th century Enlightenment in Europe).

One response by believers is to argue that some (or most) of the material in the New Testament should be interpreted **non-literally**. Prominent Bible critics like **Rudolph Bultmann** argue that the Bible needs to be DE-MYTHOLOGIZED so that modern readers can get something out of it.

EXAMPLE	LITERAL	NON-LITERAL	DE-MYTHOLOGIZED
Miracle (e.g. Feeding the 5000)	Jesus really did multiply loaves and fishes supernaturally	The miracle symbolises the Eucharist or Jesus' teachings	Miracle shows us the power of what we can accomplish by sharing
Afterlife (e.g. Hell)	You are tortured for eternity for your sins	Your conscience will punish you with guilt	Hell represents an inauthentic life of anxiety and fear
Jesus' Resurrection	Jesus physically rose from the dead	What Jesus represented survived after his death	An authentic life takes away the fear of death

Topic 5 and **Topic 6** will apply these ideas to Jesus' death and **Resurrection** and the discovery of his **empty tomb** on Easter morning. Did this fantastic miracle really occur or should it too be interpreted non-literally or de-mythologized? Did Jesus' followers start off believing he had returned to Earth as a spirit and then, much later on, start thinking he had risen physically from death? Or was it the other way round, with a belief in physical Resurrection gradually changing into a more spiritual sort of vision? Or was the whole thing a hoax staged by his over-keen disciples or other more mysterious conspirators?

Topic 5 will introduce you to one of the more perplexing features of Jesus' teaching: the arrival of the **Kingdom of God** on Earth. This is often taken to be a belief in the Apocalypse (the end of the world) and many early Christians believed that the world would end when Jesus returned from Heaven (an event known as *Parousia*). Did Jesus also believe this? Or did he believe that the Kingdom of God was a spiritual kingdom in people's souls? Or a Heavenly reward after death?

Jesus' ideas about the Kingdom and his ethical teachings are presented in the form of **Parables** throughout the Synoptic Gospels (but especially in **Luke**). These Parables need to be analysed in detail and different interpretations considered.

AS LEVEL/A-LEVEL YEAR 1 IN THE EXAM

AS-Level Paper 3 (New Testament)

Section A

1   Explore the key ideas about the Suffering Servant. (8 marks)

"Explore" questions award marks for AO1 (knowledge & understanding). You don't need to evaluate any of these ideas – just describe them. This question is pretty specific but it could be phrased more broadly, such as "explore the key ideas about prophecy".

2   Assess the significance of the "I Am" statements in the Fourth Gospel for understanding the identity of Jesus. (9 marks)

"Assess the significance" questions award some marks for AO1 (3 marks in this question) but more for AO2 (evaluation – 6 marks in this question). You need to describe a bit about the content of this topic (such as "I Am the Good Shepherd"), but more about the debates concerning how it should be interpreted (historical or later addition? claim to be God or just to teaching authority? link to the Johannine Community's conflicts with Judaism).

3   Assess the significance of theories about the authorship of the Fourth Gospel. (9 marks)

"Assess the significance" questions award some marks for AO1 (3 marks in this question) but more for AO2 (evaluation – 6 marks in this question). You need to describe a bit about the content of this topic (such as the Beloved Disciple) but more about the debates concerning this (is the Fourth Gospel an eyewitness account? is it the work of a Johannine Community?)

Section B

4   (a) Explore **two** key ideas of Form Criticism. (8 marks)

Another "explore" question that only awards marks for AO1 (knowledge & understanding), so all that is required is description. If you only describe one key idea (such as pericopae), then you cannot attain higher than Level 2 (5/8).

(b) Analyse the view that the Gospels do not record the historical words and actions of Jesus. (20 marks)

This "Analyse" question awards some marks for AO1 (5 marks in this question), but mostly for AO2 (15 marks in this question). You need to describe a bit about the content (such as the idea of oral tradition), but more about how whether the Gospels have been redacted by later editors who 'put words into Jesus' mouth' to reflect their own concerns..

Total = 54 marks

A-Level Paper 3 (New Testament)

Section A

1   Explore the key ideas about the Suffering Servant. (8 marks)

> *"Explore" questions award marks for AO1 (knowledge & understanding). You don't need to evaluate any of these ideas – just describe them. This question is pretty specific but it could be phrased more broadly, such as "explore the key ideas about prophecy".*

2   Assess the significance of the Prologue in John's Gospel. (12 marks)

> *"Assess" questions award some marks for AO1 (4 marks in this question) but more for AO2 (evaluation - 8 marks in this question). You need to describe a bit about the content of this topic (such as the idea of the Word becoming Flesh), but more about the debates concerning how it should be interpreted (symbolic or literal? Jewish or Hellenic? high or low Christology?).*

Section B

Read the following passage before answering the questions.

The Good Shepherd and His Sheep

10 "Very truly I tell you Pharisees, anyone who does not enter the sheep pen by the gate, but climbs in by some other way, is a thief and a robber. [2] The one who enters by the gate is the shepherd of the sheep. [3] The gatekeeper opens the gate for him, and the sheep listen to his voice. He calls his own sheep by name and leads them out. [4] When he has brought out all his own, he goes on ahead of them, and his sheep follow him because they know his voice. [5] But they will never follow a stranger; in fact, they will run away from him because they do not recognize a stranger's voice." [6] Jesus used this figure of speech, but the Pharisees did not understand what he was telling them.

[7] Therefore Jesus said again, "Very truly I tell you, I am the gate for the sheep. [8] All who have come before me are thieves and robbers, but the sheep have not listened to them. [9] I am the gate; whoever enters through me will be saved. They will come in and go out, and find pasture. [10] The thief comes only to steal and kill and destroy; I have come that they may have life, and have it to the full.

[11] "I am the good shepherd. The good shepherd lays down his life for the sheep. [12] The hired hand is not the shepherd and does not own the sheep. So when he sees the wolf coming, he abandons the sheep and runs away. Then the wolf attacks the flock and scatters it. [13] The man runs away because he is a hired hand and cares nothing for the sheep.

Quote from New International Translation, John 10: 1-13

3   (a) Clarify the ideas about how Jesus' identity is revealed in this passage. *You must refer to the passage in your response.* (10 marks)

"Clarify" questions only award marks for AO1 (knowledge & understanding), so all that is required is description. There is no need to evaluate whether Jesus really made these claims – just explain about the symbolism of shepherds and sheep, who the 'hired hands' are, what the gate and the pastures refer to and what 'laying down his life' predicts.

(b) Analyse the idea that Jesus never clamed to be God. (20 marks)

This "Analyse" question awards some marks for AO1 (5 marks in this question), but mostly for AO2 (15 marks in this question). You need to describe a bit about the content (such as Jesus' "I Am" claims)), but more about whether this is a claim to be divine or not (does Jesus say these things in the Synoptic Gospels? what else does he do that suggests he is divine? what counts against John's Gospel being a record of what Jesus really said or did?).

Section C

4   "We cannot know who wrote any of the Gospels."

Evaluate this view. In your response to this question, you must include how developments in New Testament Studies have been influenced by one of the following:

- Philosophy of Religion
- Religion and Ethics
- the study of a religion (except Christianity)

(30 marks)

This "Evaluate" question awards some marks for AO1 (5 marks in this question), but mostly for AO2 (25 marks in this question). You need to describe a bit about the content (such as the authorship of John's Gospel), but more about whether these ideas are persuasive (are the Gospels eyewitness accounts or redactions of oral traditions?). In order to attain beyond the top of level 4 (i.e. score 25+) you must link to another area of the course (such as religious language, divine command theory or the authorship of other religious scriptures).

Total = 90 marks

In these examples, all the questions are drawn from Topic 1-3. A real AS exam would draw from Topics 1-3 but a real A-Level exam would also draw from Topics 4-6 (Year 2 material).

ABOUT THE AUTHOR

Jonathan Rowe is a teacher of Religious Studies, Psychology and Sociology at Spalding Grammar School and he creates and maintains **www.philosophydungeon.weebly.com** and the **www.psychologywizard.net** site for Edexcel A-Level Psychology. He has worked as an examiner for various Exam Boards but is not affiliated with Edexcel. This series of books grew out of the resources he created for his students. Jonathan also writes novels and creates resources for his hobby of fantasy wargaming. He likes warm beer and smooth jazz.

Printed in Great Britain
by Amazon

59172547R00134